Immortals

Football people and the evolution of Australian Rules

Immortals

Football people and the evolution of Australian Rules

LIONEL FROST | FOREWORD BY RON BARASSI

WILEY
John Wiley & Sons Australia, Ltd

First published 2005 by
John Wiley & Sons Australia, Ltd
33 Park Road, Milton, Qld 4064

Offices also in Sydney and Melbourne

Typeset in 11.5/14 pt Dante MT

National Library of Australia
Cataloguing-in-publication data:

Frost, Lionel Edwin.
Immortals: football people and the evolution of Australian Rules.

Includes index.
ISBN 1 74031 104 3.

1. Football players — Australia — Biography. 2. Australian football — History. I. Title.

796.3360922

Cover photos: Newspix (top right),
Getty Images/Jonathan Wood (bottom right)

Printed in China by
Printplus Limited

10 9 8 7 6 5 4 3 2 1

Contents

Foreword by Ron Barassi *vii*

Preface *ix*

Acknowledgements *xiv*

Part 1 **The game takes shape** **1**

1 Henry Harrison (1836–1929) 7

2 Albert Thurgood (1874–1927) 25

3 Phil Matson (1884–1928) 41

Part 2 **Theme parks for football fans** **59**

4 Harry Collier (1907–1994) and Albert Collier (1909–1988) 67

5 Brighton Diggins (1906–1971) 89

6 Bob Quinn (1915–) 109

Part 3 **Modern football** **125**

7 Len Smith (1912–1967) and Norm Smith (1915–1973) 131

8 John Kennedy (1928–) 173

9 Jack Oatey (1920–1994) 197

Part 4 **Nationwide** **227**

10 Barry Round (1950–) 235

11 Tim Watson (1961–) 249

12 Jason Akermanis (1977–) 271

References *295*

Index *305*

Foreword

What a pleasure it is to read about footy people doing something positive for the sport they love. *Immortals*, Lionel Frost's collection (and selection) is a first-rate look into the history of some of Australian Rules football's movers, shakers, creators and stars. The book moves across the nation, as befits the modern game's efforts to become more than a quaint winter recreation played in the southern regions of a faraway country called Australia.

I have no doubt that any sport which has seduced the masses has evolutionary patterns. Sport imitates life and our national winter pastime is no exception. It would be strange if this wasn't so. After all, in the end footballers are human, as are their comrades in arms — the spectators — and the game's watchdog, the media.

Having known a number of Lionel's *Immortals* personally, I can tell you that he has done them proud. To read about the great Norm Smith (my only senior coach and the man also selected as coach of the AFL team of the century) and his brother Len Smith (in my opinion the father of modern football and a man I worked with for nine years) gave me particular pleasure. I also enjoyed reading about the lives and careers of John Kennedy, Tim Watson, Barry Round, Jack Oatey and the others.

I loved the quotation from Richard Twopeny, who said that although he played soccer and rugby, he felt that our game was by far the most skilful and the best to play and watch. My sentiments exactly, but that bloke knew more than me because he played over 250 games of the other codes of football!

Our game is enriched by books like this. Enjoy the read.

Ron Barassi 31

Ron Barassi

Preface

Australian Rules football is followed passionately in cities, suburbs, and country towns in most parts of Australia. Communal support of local clubs has built a tradition of fierce loyalty among football fans that has been handed down from one generation to the next. When a match is being played, a football ground is not normally a place where much appreciation or goodwill is extended to opponents or umpires. The 'one-eyed' supporter is usually admired by other members of his or her club, while the player who sees an opponent as a natural enemy is regarded as 'good in the trenches' and a valuable team mate. People who love watching football are single-minded about wanting to see their team win, at the expense of others.

Every so often, however, events demonstrate that there is something about the game that transcends this parochialism. During the 2003 AFL season, the passing of Bob Rose, an honest, brave and unselfish man, brought a deep sense of loss that was felt not only by Collingwood fans, but also by football fans in general and by the wider community. As Martin Flanagan wrote in an article titled 'The meaning of football' (*The Age*, 20 February 2004), the night that Bali bombing victim Jason McCartney returned to football, 'the game was a mirror in which people around the country looked and saw an image that consoled them at a time of national grief. Jason McCartney's behaviour at the time of the blast embodied certain selfless qualities we like to think of as Australian and which many people fear are being lost'. Immediately after the game, McCartney announced that he had played his last game of football and, as he left the field, the Richmond supporters present — a group widely regarded as among the most fanatical of football fans — responded with warm applause. When people who are involved with football respond with dignity and courage to events that are beyond their control, as Rose and McCartney did, they remind us that, as people who love football, and as Australians, we are kindred spirits. As Flanagan concludes:

> By the traditional measures of television, cinema, books, music, theatre, Australian culture is in retreat, but I believe passionately that people still want Australian stories with Australian

> characters, values and humour. Australian football provided them, and that's why I think a lot of people in this part of the world talk footy a lot of the time.

As Australian football enters the twenty-first century, an indigenous sport, played at the elite level in only one country and operating in the face of the increasing power of global competitors such as soccer, there is a pressing need for information about those who were involved in the game in the past. Though the game was first played nearly 150 years ago on the parklands of Melbourne, it has gone through a process of evolution that continues today. For all the profound changes that have taken place in the past twenty years or so in the way that Australian football is organised, played, and presented — the national competition, the improved grounds, the level of television coverage, the crackdown on violence and racial vilification, and the wages paid to players — the sport has remained one in which it is still possible for an individual to make a telling contribution. The game is, and always has been, played by men who usually began kicking a footy as kids and then progressed to organised games of increasing standard. How far players go in the game depends not only on their level of talent and dedication, but also on a range of factors that are beyond their control, such as regulations about which clubs players can transfer to and the stability and dynamism of the club they join. National and even global conditions, such as wars, depressions and periods of inflation also affect the circumstances under which football competitions operate. Through it all, players and coaches from several clubs and states have been able to adapt to these conditions and enrich the game in the process. This will continue into the future. If fans of today can develop empathy for the players and coaches of the past, they will be better able to understand the pressures faced by today's players and coaches. This empathy will provide meaning to the changes that unfold as football evolves.

Although Australian Rules is often referred to as 'the people's game', on account of its broad popularity and appeal, most writings on the history of football pay insufficient attention to individual people, and the stories they tell often lack a human face. The context in which club histories are generally written — with a focus on events that happen on the field, or the broad issues that affect the way a club is organised — do not allow much scope for deep insight into the lives of key individuals. With few exceptions, football biographies and autobiographies fail to place their subject in the historical context needed to assess the contribution they made to the development of the game. Some authors adopt a cavalier approach when writing about the lives and careers of footballers, repeating errors that were originally made by journalists. Once such errors appear in print, they are often regarded by later researchers as fact.

This book is a set of biographies that illustrate the role played by individuals in the evolution of Australian Rules football. They show how people responded to what others in the game were doing and how they adapted to the wider social, economic and political setting in which they lived. These stories of persistence, ingenuity, accomplishment and, at times, failure are examples of the process that established the characteristics of the Australian game and carried it forward from a local, amateur pastime to the national industry that we know today.

This is not an attempt at a comprehensive history, but rather a view of the development of our game as it unfolded through the eyes of some of its key participants. My selection is not meant to imply that these are necessarily the most important figures in football history. Their lasting influence on the way that football was played or the degree to which their careers are representative of what it was like to be involved with football in changing times makes them *Immortals*; but they are not *The* Immortals. Each of these people had a significant football career which deserves to be described with accuracy and respect, and placed it in its appropriate context. In writings about football, and other sports, the line between fact and legend is often blurred but, as Stephen Jay Gould wrote about baseball's Mickey Mantle (in the collection of essays titled *Triumph and Tragedy in Mudville*), 'the rounded man is so much more interesting than the cardboard legend'.

To provide a context for the characteristics and relevant facts about these lives, the book divides the history of Australian Rules into four periods. In the first of these stages, the game evolves from a somewhat chaotic, amateur sport to organised competitions. The second stage occupies the period between the two World Wars, when clubs drew most of their support from the local communities they represented. In the third stage, from the end of World War II until the mid-1970s, clubs were engaged in competition to attract new fans in an era of gradually rising costs. The fourth stage, from the mid-1970s to the present, sees the emergence of the game as a national industry.

Like many baby boomers who grew up in Melbourne, I have been watching footy for close to 40 years. It is impossible to convey how important football was to me when I was growing up and, over the years, countless 'football people' have, without knowing it, inspired and encouraged me and others with their words and actions. To have met some of these people personally and talked with them about their careers has been a wonderful experience. I am therefore indebted to Jason Akermanis, John Kennedy, Bob Quinn, Barry Round and Tim Watson. Norma Harmes, Robert Oatey, Pam Paull, Peter Smith and Lynnette Thornber shared valuable information with me about their fathers, as did the late Beth Brighton about her husband, Brighton Diggins. Ron Barassi supported the project wholeheartedly and it was most generous of him to write the Foreword.

Others who assisted me, by talking football, commenting on draft chapters, providing research material, or simply offering support and encouragement, were Rod Austin, Paul Bagshaw, Kevin Bartlett, Rhett Bartlett, Alan Bell, Barry Bourke, Ben Buckley, Tony Burgan, Peter Burgoyne, Troy Busch, Keith Chessell, Tony de Bolfo, Colin Dent, Graeme Dunstan, Lynda Carroll, Brian Cunningham, Dave Edwards, Charles Fahey, Judy Francis, Warwick Frost, Len Fitzgerald, Brendon Gale, Malcolm Greenslade, Tommy Hafey, John Halbert, Wayne Harmes, Sarah Harvey, Rob Hess, Col Hutchinson, Daryl Hicks, Ken Hunter, Wayne Jackson, Bruce Jarrett, Allan Jeans, Dulcie Kennedy, Col Kinnear, Liam Lenten, Sean Lenten, John Longmire, John Lysikatos, David McKay, Geof Motley, Peter Motley, Kim Mouritz, Dave Nadel, 'Sandy' Nelson, John Nicholls, Chris Pavlou, John Paynter, Sam Perisanidis, Brian Phillips, David Prentice, Morris Reid, Michael Salvagno, Michael Schneider, Bob Skilton, Bob Stewart,

Richard Stremski, Patricia Swallow, Alan Thornber, Rodney Trower, Dean Wallis, Stephen Williamson and Stuart Wilson. I am indebted to Michael Williamson for the excellent interviews he recorded with several important figures in football history, and to the AFL for allowing me access to these. Thank you all.

Thanks also to Lesley Beaumont and the team at John Wiley & Sons for their support, to Julie Stanton for her skilful and sympathetic editing, and to Lucy Russell and Dan Logovik for their patience.

I'm grateful to my Dad, John Frost, and my late mother, Gwen Frost, for taking me to the football and then having the good judgement to let me go on my own when I was not yet a teenager. Mark, Robert and Monica spent many happy days with me at the football when they were growing up. They are adults now, but we still love our footy and each other. I'm also proud that Matthew and Emma think of me as a friend.

Finally, all my love to Jenny Coates, whose skills as a historian and good taste has improved every page of this book.

Acknowledgements

The publisher and author would also like to thank the following copyright holders.

• pp. 10 (last quote), 12 (last two quotes): A. Mancini & G.M. Hibbins (eds) 1987, *Running with the ball: football's foster father*, Lynedoch, Melbourne • pp. 29 (first quote), 71 (second and third quotes), 76 (third and sixth quotes), 81 (first quote), 83 (last quote), 85 (first quote in second para), 87 (first quote): Richard Stremski 1986, *Kill for Collingwood*, Allen & Unwin, Sydney • p. 31 (first quote), 36 (second quote in last para), 39 (last quote), 257 (first quote): Michael Maplestone 1994, *Flying higher: history of the Essendon Football Club 1872–1974*, Essendon Football Club, Melbourne • p. 63 (second para): Martin Flanagan/*The Age* • pp. 67 (2 quotes), 70 (first quote), 73 (last quote), 74 (second quote), 74–5 (conversation), 75 (first quote in fourth para), 81 (last quote in first para), 82, 83, 85 (first quote in second para), 98–9: © Dr Richard Stremski • p. 71 (first quote), p. 131 (second quote), 134 (second and third quotes in third para) p. 166 (second para), p. 177 (last quote), p. 180 (second quote), 182 (last 2 quotes in first para): AFL Films, Australian Football League • p. 77 (first quote): Peter Smith (for the late Norm Smith) • pp. 77–8: The Warne-Smith family/*The Argus*, 16 June 1933 • p. 89 (first para): Lynette Thornber • pp. 109, 112 (last two quotes), 116 (first quote): Pam Paull • p. 113 (last quote): Port Adelaide Magpies Football Club Inc. • p. 143: Ron Barassi • p. 161 (second quote), 168 (last quote): Norm Smith/*The Age* • p. 170 (third quote), 171 (first and second quotes): Geoff Kingston/*The Advertiser* (Adelaide) • p. 174 (first quote), 175 (first quote), 177 (first quote in second para), 182 (second para), 183 (first para), 186 (3 quotes in second para), 193 (last quote), 196: Harry Gordon 1990, *The hard way: the story of the Hawthorn Football Club*, Townsend Publishing, Sydney • p. 198 (first quote), 199 (last quote in first para, first quote in second para), 208 (last para), 221 (first quote in second para): Fos Williams and Michelangelo Rucci 1999, *Dynasty: a legend, a family and the Port Adelaide Football Club*, Peacock Publications, Adelaide • p. 201 (two quotes), 202 (two quotes), 205 (4 quotes in second para), 223 (last quote), 224 (first 2 quotes), 225 (second quote): Sturt Football Club • p. 249 (first quote), 250 (first quote), 251 (last quote in first para), 253 (first quote in second para), 258 (last 2 quotes in second para), 265 (first quote): Simon Matthews (ed.) 2002, *Champions of Essendon*, Hardie Grant Books, Melbourne • p. 254: Tim Watson/*The Age* • p. 255 (second and third quotes in second para), 263 (first quote): Tim Watson/*The Bomber* • p. 290 (2 quotes in first para), 291 (last 2 quotes in third para), 292 (first quote): Jason Akermanis/*The Courier-Mail*.

Every effort has been made to trace the ownership of copyright material. Information that will enable the publisher to rectify any error or omission in subsequent reprints and editions will be welcome. In such cases, please contact the Permissions Section of John Wiley & Sons Australia, who will arrange payment of the usual fee.

Part 1

The game takes shape

Henry Harrison (1836–1929)

Albert Thurgood (1874–1927)

Phil Matson (1884–1928)

ALL OF THE WORLD'S major varieties of football were codified and developed in the second half of the nineteenth century by middle-class sports enthusiasts who wanted to play winter games that would keep them fit and healthy. Although societies in many parts of the world had played ball games for centuries and distinctive styles of football were played in each of England's major public schools, by the late 1850s, no single variety of football was sufficiently well established to be the natural game of choice whenever young men got together to kick a ball.

The game that H.C.A. ('Colden') Harrison and others established, which eventually became known as Australian Rules, had several unique features but, like all football codes, it started as a game played by gentlemen according to amateur principles; enjoyment of the game and playing it in a fair, disciplined way was seen as more important than winning. Harrison was one of football's pioneers. He played the game with distinction and, as captain of the Melbourne Football Club, helped to draft important modifications to its rules.

The Australian gold rushes brought together a large group of immigrant and Australian-born men in a single city — Melbourne — that enjoyed a mild winter climate and plenty of open parkland. Lying on the main sailing routes from Europe and being close to major Victorian fields and the Murray–Darling river system, Melbourne was the natural gateway to the Australian goldfields. Close to 300 000 people migrated from Britain and Ireland to Australia between 1852 and 1860, as did tens of thousands of Europeans, Americans and Chinese, most of them seeking fortune and business opportunities in Melbourne's hinterland. The provincial cities and towns built to service the goldfields, and the farming and pastoral regions linked by railways, attracted people who had spent time in Melbourne and brought with them an enthusiasm for 'Melbourne Rules', as the game was then called. Football thrived in country communities where, as Paul Daffey writes, watching and playing the game was 'a weekly tonic against loneliness and isolation'. In the 1870s and 1880s, men from football clubs in Adelaide, Hobart, Brisbane, Sydney, Launceston, the Riverina and Perth formed associations that agreed to play under Victorian Rules. In Melbourne, games attracted crowds of several thousand from the early 1860s, and the formation of the Victorian Football

Association in 1877 increased spectator interest further by setting up regular fixtures and a league ladder.

The early football games were played on open parklands and the crowds that gathered to watch them were a blend of professional and working people, and of men and women. While football matches in England were overwhelmingly a male working-class preserve, crowds in Australia were, as the English journalist John Stanley James ('The Vagabond') observed, 'truly democratic ... [T]he mixture all around the ground was as heterogeneous as might be'. Crowds of up to 12 000 watched football games in Melbourne during the 1870s, while the biggest crowd at the English FA Cup final in that decade was only 5000. A mass market for watching football was fuelled by Australia's growing population, and the jobs and high wages that its economy created. Clubs founded to allow their members to play football were now increasingly controlled by growing numbers of non-playing members.

The crowds that watched football, and bought membership tickets to have a say in how their club was run, brought about significant changes in how the game was organised and played. The only way that clubs could control the large crowds at their games and prevent them from encroaching onto the field was to move to enclosed cricket grounds with proper fencing. The move from oblong-shaped playing fields, marked out by ropes or flags, to larger cricket ovals allowed clubs to collect gate money from spectators. Some clubs used this money to compensate players for the time they took off work to attend training. Football clubs came to represent a source of civic pride to their communities, and fans generally supported their teams by walking to a local home ground or catching a train or tram to a rival suburb or town. Support for clubs was tribal and territorial, and the introduction of the 'electorate system' of recruiting zones by the South Australian National Football League in 1897 — a system that was later copied by the Victorian Football League and other leagues — reinforced the differences between communities. An *Adelaide Chronicle* writer noted in 1903 that 'whereas in years gone by the clubs were a mere name, ... owing to the fact that players were recruited from the various localities indiscriminately, now the clubs are district entities, and particularly so to the rising generation'. Competition between clubs encouraged captains to organise training and develop systems of position and team play. The establishment of the VFL in 1897 heightened the rivalries between Melbourne clubs by raising the standard of matches, and, within a few years, clubs were starting to appoint coaches to develop the fitness and discipline of their teams. The development of tactics by coaches to exploit the weaknesses of other teams and curb opposing stars also became a feature of the game in South Australia and Western Australia. For club members, games existed for no other purpose except to be won. The player who remained a gentleman at all times on the field and did not expect some sort of financial compensation for his efforts was rapidly becoming exceptional.

Inevitably, these changes and the rapid pace with which they unfolded brought problems. Players could easily fall out with their clubs over the issue of match payments. Even a star player like Albert Thurgood, who could, and did, win games and premierships off his own boot, remained at loggerheads for much of his career with the clubs he played for over his entitlement to financial rewards. Some footballers resented coaches telling them how to play, and how to live their lives, and only a few coaches could instil discipline and develop patterns of team play while still retaining the loyalty of their players. One was Phil Matson, a South Australian who made a living playing for Boulder City in Kalgoorlie and for Sturt, and then playing and coaching in Western Australia and country Victoria.

Gambling on football was widespread and some players were bribed to 'play dead' and deliberately lose matches. Any player whose performance was affected by injury (players at the time could not be replaced during matches) or poor form fell under suspicion of corruption, and such accusations were levelled at both Thurgood and Matson during their careers.

Matches were often marred by violent play as players used physical pressure and intimidation to unsettle their opponents. Although Irish immigrants to Australia were dispersed widely throughout cities and did not cluster in ghettoes, as they did in English and American cities, sectarian tensions persisted and some football clubs were controlled by committees that allowed sectarian biases to influence the recruitment of players and officials. Many of these problems were still in evidence in the second half of the twentieth century.

Although, by World War I, the VFL had cornered the biggest market of football fans in Australia — the inner suburbs of Melbourne — clubs in other competitions were still able to recruit actively. The standard of play in most suburban and country games was sufficient to retain the interest of local supporters and maintain a steady revenue; this meant that the game's major competition did not force its rival leagues out of business. The VFA could hold its own in the Melbourne market as a competition of high standard because its clubs were able to pay the wages of a few big name recruits and develop talent in their local areas. In Adelaide and Perth, clubs depended on officials and local supporters who ran businesses, or had business contacts, to arrange jobs for prospective recruits, especially those who were unskilled and had families to support. In boom towns like Kalgoorlie, where the discovery of gold attracted young men from all over Australia, player payments were used by football clubs to build up their teams, even though this was still illegal at the time. A player of high skill, such as Matson, could ply his trade in Adelaide or in Western Australia, either in Perth or in the strong goldfields league. 'Few clubs are free from paid footballers,' complained the editor of the *Kalgoorlie Miner* in 1906. 'Season after season, clubs ... send in their balance sheets to the association with entries such as chewing gum, eucalyptus, petty cash, board and lodgings and other items with exorbitant sums opposite each and which are no doubt placed there as a mantle to mislead the association and substitute for none other than wages to footballers.'

In 1908, fifty years after members of the Melbourne Football Club wrote the first rules, the Australasian Football Council commemorated the jubilee of Australian Rules football by holding an interstate carnival in Melbourne. Predictably, Victoria won the tournament, but teams from every other state competed, as did New Zealand, and the matches were both a celebration and a demonstration of the extent to which football talent and enthusiasm for the game had diffused around Australasia. South Australia won the carnival in 1911 and Western Australia in 1921. The leagues outside the VFL operated in restricted geographical areas and built up coaching structures that developed a critical mass of talented players.

1

Henry Harrison
(1836–1929)

A number of us, principally cricketers, got together, and began to play. It was a rather go-as-you-please affair at first, but a set of rules was gradually evolved, which experience taught us to be the best.

H.C.A. Harrison

Henry Colden Antill Harrison, commonly known as 'Colden', was still at school in Melbourne in 1851 when gold was discovered in Victoria's Great Dividing Range. His father joined the gold rush immediately and headed to Ballarat with his two teenage sons. Later, they moved on to Castlemaine in search of gold, and then to Bendigo.

Born in 1836 on a homestead at Picton, New South Wales, Colden was descended on his mother's side from emancipated convicts. Jane Howe was aged 14 when she married John Harrison, a former ship's captain who was twice her age. When Colden was aged around one, his father decided to try his hand at squatting, and the family spent three months travelling overland with sheep and cattle to the Port Phillip district. They eventually took up land on the Plenty River, not far from Melbourne, but the run was too small to be profitable; after a failed attempt to drove his stock through thick bush in search of suitable grazing land in Gippsland, and a spell living in Melbourne, John Harrison found land in the Wimmera, close to where the town of St Arnaud would be located. By 1850, Colden was a boarder at the Melbourne Diocesan Grammar School, and his father, who had not been able to do much physical work after accidentally shooting himself in the arm, moved the rest of the family to Melbourne.

In his autobiography, *The Story of an Athlete*, published in 1923, Colden Harrison made no mention of his mother's convict ancestry or the two years his father spent in prison in Uruguay after attempting to run a blockade against British ships. Captain Harrison was a radical republican who was so heavily involved with political activities on the diggings that he neglected his two sons. Colden had a miserable time — one of his strongest memories was being unable to sleep because of fleas in his blankets — and in the second half of 1853 the lonely and underfed boy hitched a ride back to Melbourne with a family friend.

Every bit as quiet and methodical as his father was hot-tempered and accident-prone, Colden joined the Customs Department after leaving school at the end of 1853. A tide officer based at Williamstown, Colden's job was to board the ships that had arrived in the colony and assess the value of their cargoes and the import duties payable. There was plenty of work for him: Harrison had returned to a Melbourne that was growing faster than any city in the world. The peak of the Californian gold rushes had passed and Melbourne had become the principal magnet for the fortune seekers of the world. When the gold rush started, Melbourne was a thriving frontier town with a population of 29 000; by late 1852, an extra 15 000 people per month were arriving on immigrant ships. It was a rough, raw place, physically immature and ill equipped to cope with such population growth. New arrivals had to sleep on floors and tables in boarding houses, pubs and cottages close to the wharves in the western part of the city or in tents on the south side of the Yarra. The city grid, drawn up by surveyor Robert Hoddle in 1837, had wide main streets but they were unpaved, undrained and unlit. People ate and drank in cheap restaurants and taverns and, because there was no sewerage or piped water, they washed in public baths and bathhouses.

Melbourne's boomtown chaos made it a seedbed of sporting activity. Before the gold rush, football games were played in Melbourne on public holidays. These games were probably based on the folk football that had been played for centuries in the streets of British towns and villages. The way these games were played varied from place to place and were based on customs rather than written rules. At Melbourne's holiday sports gatherings, people could come forward and try to climb a greasy pole or take part in a wheelbarrow race. At other times, the Irish sport of hurling was played, and the town's Scots formed a shinty club (both games are broadly similar to hockey). In gold-rush Melbourne, crowds of people looking for something to do with their leisure time found it on the streets. As historian Graeme Davison writes, the streets of the 'wild' west end of the city were the scene of 'knuckle fights, drunken melees and impromptu horse races'.

This culture of spontaneous, boisterous games and pastimes was already fading, however. It belonged to a pre-industrial world, in which the workday started and ended with the rising and setting of the sun, and frequent holidays gave people ample leisure time. In Britain, the birthplace of a new industrial world, workers lived increasingly in towns where public space was at a premium, and the working day was regulated by factory whistles and time clocks. The rising middle class of merchants, factory owners, clerks and professional people, that the Industrial Revolution created, disapproved of riotous sports because they saw such activities as occasions for drunkenness or violence that would affect the efficiency of workers. At England's public schools, a culture of violence, both on and off the playing field, was taken for granted until Thomas Arnold, headmaster of Rugby School from 1828 to 1842, began to organise games in a formal way. Arnold himself was no lover of games but saw cricket and football as activities that enhanced discipline and, in turn, the scholarly performance of boys. In the early 1850s, this attitude was embraced by other headmasters, especially at the new public schools established in response to the rising demand for institutions to educate the sons of the rising middle class and prepare them for careers in commerce and the professions. The middle classes were at the forefront of a revolution in British society in which the old values of brutality and intemperance were supplanted by 'muscular Christianity', a set of ideas that emphasised the importance of physical exercise as a means of developing values of morality and patriotism.

It was inevitable that British migrants would transfer these ideas to Australia, as middle-class Britons who could afford the long journey were the major source of Australia's population growth. The gold rush accelerated the process by depositing masses of migrants in a short period at one main location — Melbourne. As historian Geoffrey Serle wrote, 'this cross-section of the British Isles — with only the aristocracy, the paupers and the aged seriously under-represented — ... regarded themselves as part of Britain still ... [and] took an immense pride in their creation of "another England"'. Melbourne's mild climate and abundance of open parkland helped to popularise established sports imported from Britain, such as horseracing and cricket: a crowd of 59 000 attended a horseracing meeting at Flemington in 1859 and, on New Year's Day in 1861, 25 000 people turned up at the Melbourne Cricket Ground for a match against a touring eleven from England.

Sport in Melbourne was a cult that appealed not only to immigrants who had been to school in Britain, but also to young Australian-born men, such as Colden Harrison, who were sympathetic to British values and the increasingly important part that sport played in them. Colden grew up to be a conservative man, 'somewhat unbending and puritanical, upright and honourable', as historian Ian Turner described him, who tended to show a reverence for things British. Australia, Harrison wrote in his autobiography, was a land that he was proud of, which 'should in time produce a truly fine race, worthy, in every way, of the stock from which it has sprung'. After Colden was transferred to the customs house in Melbourne in 1858, he took up cricket and athletics — he was Victoria's amateur athletics champion for nine years, defeating all challengers over 100 and 440 yards, and over hurdles and steeples. The very embodiment of muscular Christianity, Harrison never smoked or drank as a young man, and spent his adult life devoted to physical activity and self-discipline.

There were several young men in Melbourne who, like Harrison, wanted something to do with their leisure time during winter. The novel *Tom Brown's School Days*, published in 1857 and set in Rugby School, was a bestseller in Melbourne and helped to stimulate interest in playing football. At the time, however, football was still a game played mostly by British schoolboys, with rules that varied greatly from school to school. At Eton and Harrow, the ancient schools of the aristocracy, and at Cambridge University, play was congested and the ball could not be handled and was moved with short 'dribbling' kicks along the ground. At Rugby, boys learned to play a more free-flowing type of game in which they were allowed to pick up the ball and run with it; this game was also popular at the new public schools. When the headmasters of Melbourne's schools began to organise football matches for their boys, and when the young men of Melbourne began to think of playing football as a way of filling their winter leisure time, no single code of football was sufficiently well established to be transferred from England. Three Melbourne private schools played football games in 1858 — Melbourne Grammar, Scotch College and St Kilda Grammar — but their headmasters were from different backgrounds in England, Scotland and the Channel Islands and they could not agree on which rules to use in games against each other. When an MCC member named Jerry Bryant, who owned a hotel next to the Richmond Paddock (Yarra Park), advertised that he would provide a football for anyone who wanted to turn up for a game, the result was a scratch match in which just about everyone seemed to play by their own rules. One of the participants in Melbourne's early football games, an English migrant named William Hammersley, recalled that, 'after a severe fight in the old Richmond Paddock when blood had been drawn freely, and a leg broken, it occurred to some of us that if we had rules to play under it would be better'.

The peoples' game

Colden Harrison's grandmother, Sarah Harding, arrived in Australia on a convict ship in 1799 with her husband Edward Wills, who was transported for highway robbery. The Wills prospered in Sydney as storekeepers and traders, and raised three children, one of whom, Horatio Wills, became a wealthy squatter. After Edward died, Sarah married another former convict, George Howe, who became the colony's government printer. The couple's only child was Jane Howe, Colden Harrison's mother. Horatio Wills's oldest son, Thomas, was born in Parramatta in 1835 and spent much of his early childhood near Ararat in western Victoria, where he played with the local Aboriginals and learned their language. When he was aged 14, Tom was sent to England to attend Rugby School where he played football and was captain of the cricket XI. Tom returned to Victoria in 1856, and the wily bowler and big-hitting batsman soon established himself as the colony's finest cricketer. On the field, Wills's technique was all instinct; off the field, he was somewhat disorganised and lethargic, as his one-year term as secretary of the Melbourne Cricket Club and his failed career as a solicitor showed. Tom and his half-cousin, Colden, were good friends and with Tom's encouragement Colden took up cricket and athletics. In *The Story of an Athlete*, Colden remembered Tom as 'the beau-ideal of an athlete'.

In 1858, Tom Wills wrote a letter to a weekly newspaper, *Bell's Life in Victoria*, suggesting that a football club be formed to help cricketers stay fit during the winter. Wills's letter encouraged some of his fellow cricket club members to form the Melbourne Football Club and, in the autumn of 1859, Wills was part of a subcommittee that drew up a set of rules. These were intended to formalise how matches would be played, in the hope of avoiding the inevitable disputes between players if matches continued to be played in an impromptu way. In his memoirs, Harrison credits his half-cousin with single-handedly creating the game of Australian Rules. 'When T.W. Wills arrived from England, full of enthusiasm for all kinds of sport, he suggested that we make a start with it,' Harrison wrote. 'He very sensibly advised us not to take up Rugby although that had been his own game because he considered it as then played unsuitable for grown men, engaged in making a livelihood, but to work out a game of our own.' Martin Flanagan, whose novel *The Call* is based on the life of Wills, writes that if Australian Rules 'had a white father ... he was a reckless young dandy capable of dismissing the suggestion of an English school game with the merest shake of his curly brown head, saying, No, we'll have a game of our own'. Flanagan contends that when Wills was growing up he probably watched Aboriginals playing *marn grook* — a game of keepings off played with a ball made of possum skin stuffed with charcoal that several white people reported seeing — and that this planted in Wills's mind the idea that football could be played in different ways and using a variety of skills. Flanagan's Wills is a 'sporting visionary' with a 'cranky, contradictory' temperament, that enabled him to reject an English game, and an ability to get others to agree with his way of thinking, that stemmed from his popularity as the colony's leading cricketer. Wills had left Victoria by early 1861, travelling with his father to Queensland to take up a new pastoral run about 400 kilometres west of Rockhampton. The northern Queensland frontier was then the site of a guerrilla war between Aboriginals, white settlers and police; one day when Tom was away from the camp, heading to Brisbane to buy supplies, a group of Aboriginals attacked and killed 19 people, including Tom's father. Wills's mental health probably began to deteriorate as a result of this tragedy and, after he returned to Victoria to play cricket and football, he became an alcoholic. He committed suicide at the age of 44. His grave was neglected and fell into disrepair but, when it was later restored by the Melbourne Cricket Club, they added a gold inscription including the words 'Founder of Football'.

To attribute this much to Wills implies that he was able to exert a dominant influence over the subcommittee of the Melbourne Football Club and steer it away from rugby towards a game that was uniquely Australian. Wills probably chaired this subcommittee; his name is at the head of the list of committeemen on the handwritten copy of the rules which was rediscovered in 1980 in a tin storage trunk at the MCG. However, other members appear to have had a greater influence on those rules. Seven men were appointed to the subcommittee but only four of them attended the formal meeting and one, Thomas Smith, later wrote that he, Wills and Hammersley decided on the rules beforehand while walking across the Richmond

Paddock. Hammersley and the fourth member of the subcommittee, James Thompson, were Cambridge graduates who favoured the kicking game, and the new Melbourne rules clearly established kicking the ball, rather than running with it, as the primary focus of the game. The subcommittee considered the rules of Rugby School football, which had been written in 1845, but then largely rejected them. There were some minor concessions to rugby — players were allowed to handle the ball by catching it (and could take a free kick if they called out 'mark') or picking it up before it had bounced twice — but the ball could not be thrown 'under any circumstances', 'hacking' (the kicking of an opponent's legs) was banned, and the goals had no crossbar that the ball had to be kicked over. This was not the sort of football that Wills had envisaged — as Hammersley recalled, 'Tom Wills suggested the Rugby rules but nobody understood them except himself' — but like most others in Melbourne who favoured rugby, Wills accepted and played the new game. Melbourne's footballers did not split into two camps — one wanting to run with the ball and the other to kick it — as their counterparts in England would do when the Football Association was established in 1863.

This remarkably simple set of rules was the work of a group of practical men who wanted to create a game that combined the best features and eliminated the worst of the various forms of football played at the time. Wills's contribution was to encourage the formation of a club that would play a type of football that appealed to a wide range of people. Wills's own preference was for rugby, and he could have sabotaged the creation of an Australian game by insisting that a rugby club be formed. The early start of the Australian game owed much to Wills's energy and vision, and gave it an advantage over the other codes, which were not yet fully established. The Australian game emphasised kicking, but used a rugby ball, which bounced unpredictably, rather than the round ball of soccer and Gaelic football, the other kicking games. The omission of an offside rule, which probably reflected the subcommittee's desire to keep things simple, established that kicking the ball forward to where players would contest for it was the main feature that differentiated the game from other football codes. By the time rugby, soccer and Gaelic football had been codified in Britain, the Australian game was Melbourne's most popular winter sport and it would have been difficult to graft elements of other games onto it without altering its unique nature.

Some writers place Harrison as a member of this subcommittee — some even suggest that Harrison was instructed by the Melbourne Football Club to draw up its rules — but this is incorrect. At the time, Harrison was not a member of the Melbourne Football Club and, as Gillian Hibbins points out, had he helped to shape the rules he would have said so in his autobiography, 'for he was not a man to shun the limelight'. Harrison's main contribution to the development of Australian Rules was as a player and captain. After transferring in his work from Williamstown to the city, he joined the Richmond Cricket Club and played for and captained a football club from Richmond (not to be confused with the Richmond Football Club, founded in 1885, that eventually joined the VFL). After Wills moved to his family's pastoral run near Geelong, Harrison took over from Wills as captain of the Melbourne Football Club in 1861. In 1862, Harrison was transferred by the Customs Department to Geelong where he succeeded Wills as captain of the Geelong Football Club. Harrison returned to Melbourne in 1863 and was again appointed as captain, a position he held until his retirement as a player in 1871. He was obviously a fine footballer, who could drop-kick a goal from 50 metres, and was voted 'champion of the colony' by a panel of journalists in five seasons. The ease with which Harrison moved from club to club reflected the free-and-easy way that matches were arranged by club secretaries and captains at the time. This attitude was in evidence in a match in 1861, when Melbourne was so far in front of Geelong that it sportingly allowed Harrison to play for the other side in the second half to even things up a little.

As a captain, Harrison held considerable sway over the way a match was played because, under the original rules, it was not compulsory for clubs to appoint an umpire and the two captains were usually the sole judges of what constituted fair play. Harrison was one of a group of players, who, as Geoffrey Blainey notes, were either born in Australia or were recent migrants who owed no loyalty to a particular code 'and tended to prefer a game that favoured their own personal skills'. At 5 foot $10\frac{1}{2}$ inches (179 cm) tall and weighing 12 stone 5 pounds (77 kg), Harrison was stronger than most players at the time and could use his strength and speed to win the ball in congested play. He loved to run with the ball and dodge other players and, although this was against the rules, Harrison never awarded a free kick against himself. The latitude that Harrison allowed in interpreting the rules was a reflection of his competitive nature, but as an amateur it was still important to him that matches were played fairly. He was part of a network of captains and leading players that developed to oversee the orderly conduct of matches. This included Hammersley and Thompson, who played for Melbourne, and Wills, who captained Geelong. Some of the captains at other clubs, such as Royal Park's Theodore Marshall and Carlton's Jack Conway, were former Melbourne players whom Harrison knew well. George O'Mullane, the captain of South Yarra, was a prominent cricketer. Harrison and Hammersley helped to form the Amateur Athletics Club, a body that fostered football by awarding a Challenge Cup. Years later, when Marshall spoke of the early days of football, he recalled with pride 'the class of men who established the sport and invested in it from its birth with the highest respectability'.

By the time Harrison had turned thirty, in 1866, he had emerged as the statesmen of this group of footballers. When representatives of the four leading clubs (Melbourne, South Yarra, Royal Park and Carlton) met that season to discuss and adopt a new set of rules, Harrison was asked to draft a set of rules before the meeting, and was elected to the chair. Harrison was an effective communicator and was flexible rather than dogmatic in his dealings with others. Significantly, one of the crucial rule changes that Harrison proposed required him to give ground on the issue of bouncing the ball. A few years earlier, most captains had got together before games and agreed that no-one could run with the ball without bouncing it every few yards — something that was difficult with an oval ball on rough parkland. Harrison refused to accept this until a match against Royal

Park in 1865, when Marshall instructed his fastest player to run as far as he could as soon as he got hold of the ball. When Harrison complained, the two captains agreed that, in future games between their clubs, players could run no more than ten yards without bouncing the ball. In writing the rules, Harrison probably sensed that the other club representatives would not approve of players being allowed to run ten yards without bouncing the ball, so his new rule pragmatically allowed players to pick up the ball and run with it, provided it was bounced 'every five or six yards'. Hacking and tripping were still outlawed, but players could now be bumped ('pushing with the hands or body is allowed when any player is in rapid motion') or tackled ('held') when they had the ball. Each team had to appoint an umpire before the game to adjudicate whether a goal had been scored or rules breached. The Amateur Athletics Club printed many copies of the 1866 rules which were available for purchase from Harrison for 11 shillings per thousand copies.

Other clubs liked Harrison's rules because they confirmed that the game was developing a particular style that was proving popular with spectators. In the early years of football, games had been slow and defensive and play often became bottled up in tight, rugby-style packs. The play of 'dodgers' like Harrison who could run with the ball and evade opponents brought welcome flair to the game. Those without the ball could now develop their own methods of tackling the dodgers and bringing them to ground. Players who could break away from a pack could then kick towards team-mates who, because there was no offside rule, were able to position themselves close to goal. The defining moment in a game would often be a run by a player bouncing the ball, or a physical contest for the ball between a forward and a defender. These physical contests were something that Harrison relished. After a game in 1870, when he was criticised for throwing an opponent to the ground and then stomping on him, Harrison wrote a letter to the *Australasian* stating that 'football is essentially a rough game all the world over, and it is not suitable for men-poodles or milksops'.

Although Melbourne's major sports — football, cricket and horseracing — were established by clubs that were founded by the city's elite, each was characterised by a high level of interest from general society. Football clubs were formed to allow their members the opportunity to play in matches, in return for payment of a subscription fee, but the matches were also a form of entertainment for a significant number of spectators. One game in 1859 was reported in the press as being 'attentively watched by upwards of two thousand spectators', and by the early 1870s, crowds of 10 000 regularly attended important games. The city was growing — its population increased from 140 000 in 1861 to 216 000 in 1871 — and with most people enjoying significant amounts of disposable income and leisure time, the demand for playing and watching football increased. Sixteen clubs played home matches on the rough parkland at Royal Park in the early 1870s and one of these, Carlton, had more than twice as many members as any other club. Although it was founded by members of the Carlton Cricket Club, Carlton was predominantly a club for working men, and 'the wildmen of Carlton', as one newspaper called them, established a rivalry with Melbourne that drew in crowds by the thousands. Melbourne won the Challenge Cup in 1868, 1870 and 1972; Carlton won the cup in 1871 and lost only one match from 1872 to 1874.

Crowds of that size were a major problem because none of the grounds on which football was played were enclosed: there were no fences to prevent people from watching the game, and therefore no way of charging an admission fee, and no way to keep spectators from encroaching onto the ground to get a better view. In the early 1870s, Melbourne's main football venues were Yarra Park, which stretched from the river to Wellington Parade, where Melbourne and several clubs from the Richmond area played, and Royal Park. Yarra Park had three enclosed cricket grounds — the MCG, the Richmond Cricket Ground (the Punt Road Oval) and the East Melbourne Cricket Ground — but, as at Royal Park, the footballers had to mark out, with flags and ropes, an oblong-shaped field on the rough parkland. Royal Park was 'covered with flinty stones' and play at Yarra Park was made difficult by the presence of several large red gums which sent out branches that interfered with play, and roots that players had to avoid. Harrison wrote to the Mayor of Melbourne in

1868 asking that the trees be removed, but his request was ignored. The following year, Harrison persuaded the Melbourne Cricket Club to allow a football game to be played on the MCG but, when he inspected the ground the next day, some solemn-faced members of the committee told him, 'Harrison! You have ruined our ground'. It was not until 1877 that the MCG was made available to football on a regular basis, and by that time several country towns were using their cricket grounds for football. As more and more clubs moved to oval grounds (of varying sizes), a further distinctive feature of Australian football was added.

At the end of the 1871 season, Harrison took his Melbourne team to play Carlton at a neutral venue at Albert Park Oval to decide which club would be awarded the Challenge Cup. Football matches then had no specified period of play and the first team that scored two goals won the game (if neither team had scored two goals by the time it was dark, the match was declared a draw). Teams did not change ends until after a goal was scored, so it was a considerable advantage to win the toss and kick with the wind first. Harrison lost the toss and, when he kicked off from the goal line that his team was defending, the howling wind blew the ball back over his head, about 20 yards behind the goal. At almost 35 years of age, Harrison was still feeling the effects of a game Melbourne had played a few weeks earlier in Ballarat, fielding a team of 14 against the locals' 20. Later in the day the wind died down, but by that time the Melbourne team had tired badly and Carlton scored the second goal it needed to win the game. After the match, the exhausted Harrison went home to bed. It took him a month to recover from the game, and he never played again.

Leagues of extraordinary gentlemen

Many of the young men who arrived in Australia in the 1870s and 1880s found the game that Harrison played to their liking. One was Richard Ernest Nowell Twopeny, who played Australian Rules football in Adelaide, where at that time the game was known as 'Victorian Rules'. In his book *Town Life in Australia* (1883), he wrote that 'after having played all three games, Rugby, Association [soccer] and

Victorian — the first several hundred times, the second a few dozen times, and the third a couple of score of times — I feel bound to say that the Victorian game is by far the most scientific, the most amusing both to players and onlookers, and altogether the best'. Press reports suggest that Twopeny was a robust competitor who tended to hold onto the ball and try to burst through packs, as befitted his rugby background, and was an excellent kick. He wore a pair of spectacles while playing, and it was reported that as captain of his club he could be heard 'leading and urging' his team 'on in stentorian tones'. Born in England in 1857, Twopeny spent much of his childhood in South Australia before returning to England to finish his schooling. By 1876, he had returned to Adelaide and was working as secretary to the owner of the *South Australian Register.* After 1878, he lived in several other Australian capital cities and spent time in New Zealand; he played football for only one season in Perth and may not have added to the 40-odd game total he referred to in his book.

Twopeny made a major contribution to the development of Australian Rules, however, through the part he played in the formalisation of the rules and organisation of the game in Adelaide and, indirectly, in Hobart, Launceston and Perth. The Australian game, as defined by the Melbourne or Victorian rules, had its followers in the other colonies, but confusion over the rules and lack of agreement between clubs about what rules would be used retarded the spread of the code. Football began in Adelaide in 1860 when the Adelaide Football Club was formed, but the rules developed there, which were eventually codified in 1873 and called 'Kensington Rules', were different from the Victorian rules in important ways. The ball had to pass over a crossbar and under a rope for a goal to be scored. In Melbourne, players who were tackled had to drop the ball immediately, but under Kensington rules they were allowed to hold onto the ball until the tackle forced it from their grasp. This gave the game in Adelaide a more physical edge, and by 1875 the tendency for 'scrummages' to develop took the game further towards rugby. Historian Bernard Whimpress writes that, at this time, football 'almost died out in the city itself'. In 1876 Adelaide's leading clubs made another set of rule changes which removed the distinctive goalposts and the restriction on the distance that players were allowed to run with the ball. The Victorian game was popular in New Zealand in the 1870s, especially on the South Island. Queensland had over 300 clubs in 1883 and the code enjoyed a strong core of support in Brisbane and Ipswich. But migrants from Britain, who tended to bring a preference for rugby with them, helped to push the Australian code in those colonies into the background. In 1874, rugby clubs in Sydney organised an association, the Southern Rugby Football Union, that restricted access by other codes to much of the city's limited area of parkland. In Tasmania, where there were strong commercial links to Melbourne, the game developed in a way that incorporated rugby rules. Rugby was at first the dominant code in Western Australia. By 1882, Perth had four clubs, each of which played rugby, but when a new club, ironically called 'Unions', was formed that year it decided to play under Victorian rules. The following year a club called 'Swans' was founded by two Western Australians who had played the Victorian game at school in Adelaide and decided to experiment with the Australian code in the Perth club.

It was difficult for any one code to establish an advantage over its rivals while the clubs themselves were responsible for the organisation of matches. Even when clubs could agree on which rules to play under, there were often disputes on the day over issues such as violent play or the encroachment of crowds. With matches being organised by club secretaries, it was next to impossible to run a league competition that would enable a trophy to be awarded to the most successful club. In April 1877, Twopeny took the initiative of arranging a meeting between representatives of Adelaide's football clubs to discuss the possibility of forming a football association. Thirteen clubs sent delegates to the meeting and it was agreed that they would meet again in a fortnight to establish an association and agree on a set of rules. Twopeny chaired the meetings, although he was aged only 19 and, as a *South Australian Chronicle* reporter noted, 'his experience of conducting public meetings appeared to be somewhat meagre'. The *Chronicle* reported that at the second meeting Twopeny produced the by-laws of 'the Sydney Football Association' —

presumably this was the Southern Rugby Football Union — and these were accepted as the template for the new association. There was then a debate over the rules and, although Twopeny 'spoke very warmly in favour of running with the ball, urging that it was a *sine qua non* of genuine football', the meeting voted to accept Victorian rules in their entirety as this would help to facilitate matches between teams from the two colonies, and elected Twopeny as the secretary of the South Australian Football Association.

The South Australian example set off similar developments in some of the other colonies. In the following month, Melbourne's five major clubs formed the Victorian Football Association. Two Geelong clubs joined the Association and, upon payment of a fee, provincial clubs were also permitted to send delegates. Colden Harrison was the inaugural vice-president of the VFA, but this was a figurehead title and he played no part in the management of the Association. Like its South Australian counterpart, the VFA was established to clarify and, if need be, amend the rules of the game, settle disputes between member clubs, and arrange fixtures, including those against teams from other colonies. In 1879, Hobart's major clubs formed the Tasmanian Football Association which adopted Victorian rules, except for the use of a crossbar which the ball had to be kicked over for a goal to be scored (this crossbar was used until 1883). Associations were formed in Queensland in 1879 and New South Wales in 1880. Clubs and competitions were established in the Riverina by the early 1880s. Matches between the north and south of the colony started after the Northern Tasmanian Football Association was founded in Launceston in 1882. By 1885, football in Perth had, as the *Western Australian* put it, degenerated 'into one continuous round of close scrummages, which are neither edifying to spectators nor exciting'. Seeking a more open, attractive game for their playing members and spectators, more clubs began playing under Victorian rules. Hugh Dixson, the secretary of a new club called 'Victorians', called a meeting of clubs to discuss forming an association. At the meeting, the 20-year-old Dixson, who had been to school at Melbourne's Scotch College and Adelaide's Prince Alfred College where Australian football was played, read out the rules of the SAFA and these were adopted by the new Western Australian Football Association.

The formation of leagues and associations marked a turning point in the development of the game. They established a framework which allowed future changes in the rules and organisation of the game — such as the introduction of handpassing, the abolition of the 'little mark', the inclusion of behinds in team scores and the introduction of the 'district' system of recruiting. As the *Western Australian* wrote after the establishment of the WAFA, 'it is quite apparent that the popularity, interest and success of the game in the colony depended upon some such arrangement being come to . . . Without such an institution it would be impossible to make satisfactory arrangements for a succession of interesting matches, or to preserve the high and manly tone becoming to this ancient sport, and save it from the licence of roughs and rowdies'.

The game's administration was now in other, younger hands, but Colden Harrison maintained a close interest in its progress. In 1864, he married Emily Wills, his half-cousin and sister of Tom Wills. They lived in suburban Kew and raised 11 children, but Colden never lost his love of football. He organised charity matches and while on long service leave he travelled to England and attempted to convert the rugby and soccer associations to the Australian game. After the VFL was formed, Harrison chaired its investigation committee which heard charges against reported players. In 1905, Harrison chaired the conference that established the Australasian Football Council and was elected as the body's first life member 'for special services rendered to Australian Football'. At the 1908 Carnival, Harrison was honoured as the 'father of the game', primarily because he was the last of football's pioneers who was still alive. A new grandstand built in 1908 at the MCG was named after him, and later the VFL's headquarters in East Melbourne was named Harrison House. He remained fit and active after his retirement from work — he loved gardening and fishing, and once rode a bicycle to Sydney to watch Australia play England in a test match — and lived to the age of 92.

In 1926, a journalist who saw Harrison at the MCG wrote:

> Every groundsman and official and member is a friend of his. He loves to loiter in the dressing-rooms, where there is the reek of training oil and perspiration. It is the smell of powder to a war horse. Before the game starts, he has some advice to give both sides. It is to tell them to play the game, and to remember that football is a game.

2

Albert Thurgood

(1874–1927)

> Thurgood, the invincible, played a lone hand that simply drove the spectators frantic with admiration. He played back, forward, and on the ball, everywhere with great credit — one of those special feats of which Thurgood, alone, seems capable.
>
> *The Argus*, 1894

On a cold, wet Melbourne Saturday in July 1893, a match was contested between the VFA's two top teams. Both Essendon and Melbourne had won all of their eight games that season; Essendon had been premiers in the past two seasons, while Melbourne had not won a trophy since the VFA had been formed in 1877. Despite the weather, a big crowd turned up, some arriving on special trains from Ballarat and Bendigo, and 'that it was not larger was only because there was not more room'. Melbourne gained an advantage when it won the toss; normally only one ball was used throughout a match so Melbourne was able to kick with the wind before the ball became waterlogged. In the first quarter, while Essendon fumbled the ball and hesitated, Melbourne handled it surely, kicked it quickly and ran up what appeared to be a match-winning lead of 4.7 to 0.0 (at the time, behinds were recorded but did not count in the final score). Melbourne maintained its lead in the second quarter by crowding around the ball to bottle up play. In the third quarter, Essendon's captain, Alick Dick, moved two of his players from the forward line into the ruck to restrict Melbourne's scoring. The tactic worked: Melbourne failed to score in the quarter, even though it was kicking with the wind. But Essendon still trailed by three goals (5.8 to 2.12) and, even though the Melbourne players were tiring, the muddy ground and heavy ball made further scoring difficult. During the last quarter, Dick moved a young forward named Albert Thurgood into the ruck.

After Thurgood died in 1927, the writer of his obituary in the *Leader* recalled that, in the 1893 game:

> Essendon appeared to be so hopelessly beaten by Melbourne, on the Melbourne Cricket Ground, that several of their supporters left the enclosure a few minutes before time in a disappointed frame of mind, and were staggered to learn upon reaching the city that in those few brief moments Essendon had kicked three goals and won the match. The player who changed the fortune of Essendon in that thrilling encounter was . . . Thurgood, who was placed in the ruck as a last resource and took command of the game. His fast dashes down from the centre towards the goal at the Richmond end of the arena, and his long, accurate kicks between the posts, completely flabbergasted the Melbourne backs, who appeared to be spellbound and unable to check the rapid movements of the champion, who was cheered to the echo as he returned immediately after his record feat through a throng of excited admirers to the dressing room.

In another tribute, written less than 24 hours after Thurgood's death, a writer in *The Argus* considered Thurgood's performance in the 1893 game as 'the greatest individual effort in the history of the game'. He remembered that Thurgood scored four goals 'in as many minutes . . . took complete control of the ruck, marked when and where he liked, and got the four goals necessary to win the game'. Contemporary reports tell a different story, however. The 1893 match referred to above was not played on the MCG, but on Essendon's home ground, the East Melbourne Cricket Ground.

Essendon did not score four goals in the last quarter to win the game; it scored three to draw it. Thurgood was not moved into the ruck in the last few minutes; he was moved just after the last quarter started, after Essendon's leading ruckman injured a leg. Although Thurgood's running and marking played a part in Essendon's comeback, he did not score four goals in four minutes; in fact, he scored only one of his team's five goals for the day and, in the report of 'Observer', *The Argus*'s football writer of 1893, Thurgood was not even listed among Essendon's best players.

The conflicting reports of this game are typical of the accounts of Thurgood's life and career in general, few of which are free of significant inaccuracies. Another obituary, by John Worrall in the *Australasian*, states incorrectly that Thurgood 'was of American parentage' (Thurgood's wife was born in Canada and presumably this was the source of Worrall's mistaken belief that Thurgood's parents were American). In his *History of Australian Rules Football* (1958), Cecil Mullen cited the 1927 *Argus* tribute, identifying it as an 'old-time newspaper report' and repeated Worrall's claim that Thurgood's parents were American. Mullen also claimed that Thurgood played 209 games for Essendon, 53 games for Fremantle and kicked a career total of 714 goals. It is difficult to imagine how those figures were arrived at as records show that Thurgood kicked only 272 goals and played around a hundred games for Essendon. Mullen's errors, which have been perpetuated in some modern histories, tell only the legend of Thurgood. The facts provide a different version of his life and career, one that Thurgood himself deserves to have told, and which provides illumination and understanding of the way that football in Melbourne developed during the 1890s and early 1900s.

Thurgood was, undoubtedly, a remarkable footballer, probably the best to play the game before World War I, with a singular ability to change the course of matches quickly with brilliant high marking and long, accurate kicking for goal. A big man for his time, standing six foot (183 cm) tall, Thurgood had a lean build in the early stages of his career but matured into a strong man. Nevertheless, he retained his natural athleticism and played the game with pace and endurance. He had no trouble kicking drop-kick goals from 55 metres out; his placekicks went even further, with some of them measured accurately (rather than estimated) by journalists at over 90 yards (about 82 metres). (Before World War I, the placekick was the usual way that players took a set shot for goal; the kick was still in common use in the 1930s.) In an era when six or seven goals was a good score for a team, Thurgood scored 183 goals in his first three seasons for Essendon, before he turned 21. Thurgood's career took a different direction in 1895 when he went to Western Australia in search of work. After returning to Melbourne in 1898, his career was marked by lengthy periods of absence that football writers have never been able to explain fully. From the time he was eligible to play again at the start of 1899 until his final game at the end of 1906, Essendon played 145 VFL matches; Thurgood appeared in only 46 of these. During those games, Thurgood played some brilliant football, especially during the 1901 finals series, but overall his career lacked the sustained lustre of those of the game's greatest figures. His career highlights, stunning as they were, were more like sparks struck from a stone than the lasting shine of a diamond.

Thurgood played at a time when increasing amounts of money were coming into the game, from gate money and the support of members and patrons. As the star player of the day, the situation ought to have been to his considerable financial advantage. But there was much tension between the clubs that were prepared to pay players, and the game's administrators who had been brought up to believe in the ideal of amateur sport. Because payment of players was forbidden under VFA (and later VFL) rules, some clubs found ways of compensating players surreptitiously by paying them training expenses or finding them jobs in which they were expected to do little or no work. If clubs were prepared to pay players, they still wanted to keep their wages bills as low as possible. In these circumstances, it was difficult for those, who at first were prepared to play for nothing, to negotiate better terms as their careers progressed. Thurgood's lengthy periods of absence from Essendon teams, which accounted for the equivalent of close to nine seasons, were for the most part the outcome of his failure to reach agreement with his club over pay.

Albert Thurgood's career represents a crucial link between two eras in football history. When Thurgood started playing for

Essendon, team play was virtually non-existent and players generally adopted a 'go-as-you-please' attitude towards the game. This was in keeping with the amateur philosophy that participation in sport itself, while behaving in a 'gentlemanly' way, was far more important than winning. As Richard Stremski writes, 'games were so slow at the turn of the century that players were known "to sit down and have a rest" while the ball was at the other end of the ground, knowing that it would not be back in their area very quickly'. This slow movement of play helped weaker teams to restrict the scoring of stronger ones, and many games degenerated into tests of the brawn of players and the patience of spectators. Players like Thurgood, who could seize control of a game and exert an impact on its outcome, were rare. As Mullen wrote, Thurgood 'brought art and culture into the game and introduced a new type of fast big man into the field with his beautiful high marking, brilliant running, clever ground play and uncanny goal sense'. By the time Thurgood had finished playing, opposition teams had developed systems of team play which were instilled into them by coaches who demanded high standards of fitness and discipline. The winning teams were now those that 'played as one man', as *The Argus*'s football writer put it. They did not rely on star players to win matches for them, and they were able to use tactics that made things difficult for the opposition's key players. Football was transformed in a short time into a game that was quicker and more open, the results of which were more difficult to predict. However, issues relating to the payment of players, and the possibility of them being bribed, remained unresolved.

The mysterious stranger

Albert's father, John Thurgood, was a carpenter and builder who was born in London in 1839 and migrated to Australia with his two brothers in 1865. He married another Londoner, 16-year-old Amelia Buckland, in Melbourne in 1869. Shortly after their only child, Albert John Thurgood, was born in Hotham (North Melbourne) in January 1874, the Thurgoods moved back to London. John established a business as a master carpenter, employing six men and two apprentices. In April 1881, the British census recorded them living in a house in

Newington, in south London, with Amelia's sister Jemima, her husband John Waugh and their six children. By that time John Thurgood had become seriously ill with endemic syphilis, and the Thurgood and Waugh families were preparing to migrate to Australia, presumably to move John Thurgood to a warmer, drier climate. In September, soon after arriving in Melbourne, John Thurgood died, at the age of 42. Amelia was aged only 28 when she became a widow and she re-married in 1884. She moved to a house in Champion Street, Brighton and Albert was enrolled at Brighton Grammar, a small private school established only two years earlier. Albert excelled at sports and was an impressive athlete and cricketer. After leaving school, he retained an interest in athletics, competing in the final of the one mile at the Victorian championships of 1893 and in the final of the shot-put the following year. He also played football at school, so well that several VFA clubs attempted to sign him. St Kilda, the club closest to where he lived, even named him in its team for a match in 1891 in the hope that he would join them. Instead he decided to try out at Essendon.

Essendon Football Club was formed in 1872 and, unlike most football clubs at the time, was not started by or affiliated with a local cricket club. The founders of the Essendon club were local business-people, many of whom had horseracing, pastoral and agricultural interests. Essendon played its first matches in a paddock in Ascot Vale, behind the house owned by the club's first president, Robert McCracken. After becoming a founding member of the VFA, the club moved to a bigger ground at Flemington Hill, but by 1882 it was apparent that it would need a larger venue. The club applied to the Essendon Council for permission to use the Essendon Recreation Reserve, even though the Essendon area itself was still predominantly rural in character. On the casting vote of the mayor, the council refused to allow the football club to play on the reserve so Essendon accepted an offer from the East Melbourne Cricket Club to play on its ground, which could hold crowds of over 30 000 and was a convenient training and playing venue for players who had jobs in the city. Like their near neighbours Melbourne, Essendon did not recruit players from a specific geographical area, but from middle-class areas all over the metropolitan area. As Essendon club historian Michael

Maplestone writes, 'composed almost entirely for some seasons of Public School boys, university men and the sons of Collins Street professional men, Flinders Lane and Flinders Street warehousemen, or Bourke Street retailers, Essendon now wore the "school tie"'. Even the club's nickname, the 'Same Olds', after a song their supporters used to sing during matches, had genteel connotations. At such a club, Albert Thurgood blended in rather than stood out.

Though he had played only schoolboy football, Thurgood was selected in the reigning premiership team for the first game of 1892. There was no fanfare about his selection; the *Leader* simply commented that 'Essendon have secured a prize in Brighton junior Thurgood'. Playing in a key forward position — press reports do not reveal whether this was full-forward or centre half-forward — Thurgood's achievements in his early matches were modest. The *Leader*'s football writer noted disapprovingly that Thurgood tended to 'take liberties' by kicking for goal from difficult angles or distances and ignoring team-mates who were in better positions. As the season progressed, however, Thurgood developed greater judgement about when to pass the ball and when to kick for goal himself. By the end of his first season, Thurgood had set a VFA record by scoring 56 goals, and the *Leader* was unstinting in its praise:

> Thurgood's achievement was in every way phenomenal, and especially remarkable for a young player in his first season of senior football. He not only exhibited great coolness and excellent judgement, but, unaffected by any desire for personal distinction, passed the ball to another player whenever any benefit to his side was to be obtained by so doing.

To the football public, in one season Thurgood had gone from being a virtually unknown public schoolboy to the biggest name in the game. It would be 57 years before a first-year player — another Essendon forward, John Coleman — made a similar immediate impact on Victorian football.

Thurgood followed up by scoring 64 goals in 1893. In the second last match of that season, he kicked nine of his team's ten goals with a ball that was so badly out of shape that he had to run in to goal and tap the ball through from close range; in the following game he kicked 12 of Essendon's 14 goals. 'His play has been even better than last season,' wrote the *Leader*'s football reporter, 'and he is without doubt the most brilliant and reliable goal kicker that Victoria has yet produced'. In 1894, Thurgood scored 63 goals, and a panel of football journalists voted him Champion of the Colony for the second consecutive year. With Thurgood in its ranks, Essendon was dubbed 'the invincibles' by the press and won its fourth successive premiership in 1894. The club lost only three games during those four seasons.

Little is known about Thurgood's personality and temperament. The press rarely reflected upon these issues, and Thurgood himself made few public statements. The *Leader* once wrote of his 'not unjustifiable self-confidence', but press reports overall paint a picture of a popular footballer whose modesty, unselfishness and even temper were much admired throughout the football world. As the *Leader* once commented, 'if a majority of football players were of similar stamp the great winter pastime would soon defy hostile criticism'. In 1902 he was suspended for three games for striking two St Kilda players but, aside from this blemish, his conduct both on and off the field was beyond reproach.

Show me the money

Essendon dominated the VFA competition during a period when complaints about the payment of players were made with increasing frequency. To many observers, this was no coincidence. During the 1880s, when the economy of 'Marvellous Melbourne' was booming and an increasing number of clubs moved to grounds that were enclosed, more money came into the game. Essendon was one of the major beneficiaries of this: after moving to the East Melbourne Cricket Ground, the club began making substantial profits, which increased from £16 in 1884 to £343 in 1890. Essendon was first accused of making payments to players in 1886, in the form of reimbursement of expenses and the payment of signing-on fees to players from country Victoria and other colonies. Because new recruits were free to join any VFA club they wished, professionalism was seen as something that gave an unfair advantage to the richest and most powerful clubs. The issue polarised the football community; those who believed that players deserved some compensation for the wages they lost while training were at odds with those who held the view that 'football was intended to be a recreation, not a business'. The officials of middle-class clubs, such as Essendon, made the strongest statements in support of amateurism and were critical of those who had 'allowed the game to sink from the level of a noble pastime to that of a trade'. Essendon had many players who were studying for, or had obtained, professional qualifications, and such men usually had independent sources of income, or jobs outside of football. Nevertheless, Essendon's administration was not prepared to conform to the amateur ideal literally, so was willing to bend the rules prohibiting payment of players to accommodate some players who needed extra cash to pay their bills and assistance in finding a job. This became known in 1892 when the VFA's permit committee denied an Essendon player, W. Webb, clearance to Richmond. Webb wrote to the VFA and claimed that an Essendon delegate, who was a member of the permit committee, had paid him for several years. Essendon asked for an independent inquiry over the Webb case but, by the time this was held, Webb had left Australia and gone to South Africa. The inquiry exonerated the club but did find that Webb had been employed by the club's treasurer and probably received secret payments from Essendon supporters.

Did the Essendon Football Club pay Thurgood during these years? When Thurgood joined Essendon, other clubs wanted to know what had made him join that club rather than his 'local' club, St Kilda. Essendon officials were adamant that they had never approached Thurgood at any time and that he had joined the club because some of his former schoolmates were playing there. It is certainly plausible that a young man like Thurgood, straight out of school, would have jumped at the chance to try out at a club like Essendon, without asking for any money to do so. Perhaps the strongest evidence that Thurgood received little or no financial compensation during his first three seasons at Essendon was his decision to move to Perth at the end of 1894. With Melbourne's economy in the grip of depression, and Perth's booming, several Victorian footballers of note made the move west. Essendon lost Thurgood and two other important players, William 'Poss' Watson, who had represented Victoria, and a promising young player, Mat Wilson. Thurgood probably left because he had not learnt a trade or obtained any professional qualifications, which would have made it difficult for him to find work in Melbourne. A few years earlier, Essendon had been able to retain Webb by finding him a job and paying some of his expenses but, with the economy now depressed, the club was probably unable to find supporters who could afford to take on Thurgood, Watson or Wilson as employees. Thurgood appears to have left Melbourne under his own initiative and without any Western Australian club making a prior offer to him. These were not the actions of someone who was making much, if any, money out of playing in Melbourne.

Even though the clubs in the WAFA first began collecting gate money in 1895, the local businesspeople provided the jobs and cash that clubs needed to attract and retain players. Given Thurgood's middle-class background, it is unlikely that he had any intention of moving on to Kalgoorlie and working at gold mining. In his study of football in Fremantle during this period, Clement Macintyre writes that Thurgood 'arrived in the west in 1895 and was immediately the subject of considerable speculation as to which club he would join'. Thurgood eventually signed with the Fremantle Football Club, where Watson had been appointed captain, and where players received payments of around £30 per season. This was not a lot of money — an unskilled labourer in Melbourne might expect to earn about £2 in a full week of work — and the club probably found a job for Thurgood to help him pay his bills during the off-season. Thurgood dominated the Perth competition and scored 15 goals in one game. But, given the enormous discrepancy between Thurgood's talent and that of the average Western Australian footballer, it is surprising that he kicked only 53 goals in 1895 and a total of 74 goals in the next two seasons. Football in Perth was not the challenge that it was in Melbourne, and Thurgood only had to go through the motions to keep his employer, the Fremantle Football Club, satisfied. It is hard to see how the time that Thurgood spent as a football mercenary, in a competition that was of a lower standard than he was used to, did much to develop his skills and enthusiasm for the game. When

Thurgood returned to Victoria in 1898, Alick Dick was of the view that Thurgood was now 'slower, heavier and less keen'.

Thurgood was aged 24 when he returned to Melbourne, and was a very different character from the wide-eyed boy, straight out of school, who was prepared to play football just for fun. In 1897, Fremantle had missed winning the WAFA premiership, for only the third time in the 13 seasons of the competition's existence. As Macintyre reports, the club had fallen out with its patrons and 'several key players had left after being told they were now responsible for meeting their own personal expenses' (a bankrupt Fremantle Football Club collapsed in 1900 and the WAFA admitted South Fremantle in its place). Thurgood returned to Melbourne, but under VFL rules he had to serve a 12-week residential qualification period before he was eligible to play. Mullen claimed incorrectly that at the start of the 1899 season Thurgood had still not received permission from the League to play, and that he was only allowed to take the field during the middle of the season after an outcry and campaign in the press. Thurgood was in fact eligible to play in the opening round of the season, and *The Argus* reported that 'Essendon had hoped to have their old forward, Thurgood, in the field again, but he was absent, and some of the Melbourne fellows think he will strip for them against Collingwood next Saturday'. Thurgood's failure to turn up to play, and the rumour that he might seek to join another club, point to him being in dispute with Essendon over his pay. He was married by now, to 20-year-old Ida Thomas, and most likely could not afford to play for nothing. Two weeks later, it was apparent that negotiations were still ongoing; *The Argus* reported that 'Thurgood has not appeared yet, but Essendon hope to have him against Melbourne'. Thurgood did line up two weeks later in the match against Melbourne, and *The Argus* reported that:

> There was jubilation in the Essendon camp when it was known that Thurgood, the erstwhile champion, would once more lend aid to the Red and Black, and when the big fellow came out he received a tremendous ovation. He has not altered in appearance since he last played, and the barrackers were prepared to cheer him all day.

Albert's game was rusty, and he scored only one goal. One of his two placekick shots for goal grubbed along the ground. He was again absent for the following game. No reason for this was given to the press, and he did not play again that season. He was again missing when the 1900 season started but, when Essendon played Collingwood in round 3, *The Argus* simply reported that he was 'back in harness'. After barely touching the ball in the first half, 'he got his dangerous right foot to work, and kicked six goals with placekicks, drop kicks, punts, and snaps in his old form'. The press reported that 'Thurgood failed to appear' the following Saturday, although five weeks later he returned to the side, with his differences with Essendon apparently settled, and he became a regular for the rest of the season.

There is no way of knowing what brought this protracted period of haggling between club and player to an end. Either side may have backed down, or they could have met halfway. It is, however, possible to make a case as to why Essendon might have changed its mind about whether it would be worth paying Thurgood and risk facing heavy penalties, such as loss of premiership points or even expulsion from the competition for breaching League rules.

In Thurgood's first spell at Essendon, the club won three flags in three years; the 1894 premiership was the club's fourth in succession. So pronounced was the domination of Essendon and its star player over the rest of the competition that, towards the end of the 1894 season, the *Leader*'s football writer was of the view that 'the long continued success of Essendon has to a great extent robbed the premier matches of interest'. *The Argus*'s view was that 'if Thurgood continues to show the form of recent years, it would seem that Essendon will have to allow opponents an extra player in order to try to make a game of it'. There were reports that at some of Essendon's games the umpire was at least subconsciously biased towards the underdog: in one Essendon game in 1893, the *Leader* observed that the umpire 'was particularly severe ... giving no fewer than 28 [free] kicks against them, while St Kilda were debited with but five'. When Thurgood left Victoria in 1895, it would have been reasonable to assume that his absence would not have been fatal to Essendon's chances of success.

While Thurgood was in Perth, the VFA's strongest clubs, after years of wrangling with the weaker clubs over issues relating to the standard and popularity of the game, broke away and formed the Victorian Football League. The depression of the 1890s had cut crowds at football games generally, and this had put most clubs in an awkward financial position. Although Essendon slipped down the ladder in 1895 and 1896, the gap in standard between the VFA's strongest four or five clubs and the rest of the competition remained wide and the outcome of many matches was either predictable or irrelevant to the premiership race. The delegates of the weaker clubs usually voted as a bloc to protect their own interests, which meant that issues relating to the crowding of play, violence on the field, and the poor behaviour of some crowds, were not acted upon. Throughout the 1896 season, there was ever-increasing talk in the press about the need for the VFA to restructure itself by reducing the number of teams (through club mergers) or splitting the competition into two divisions. The new League was the outcome of a long period of dissatisfaction among the strongest clubs over the economic implications of the way the game was organised.

Play in the new competition was faster, more open and more even than before. The VFL introduced several rule changes designed to increase the attractiveness of the game to spectators: a kick had to travel ten yards (9.1 metres) before a mark could be claimed; numbers in a team were reduced from 20 to 18; behinds became part of the score, with six points being awarded for a goal; and a finals system was used to decide the premiership. Most clubs responded to their members' demands for success by developing systems of teamwork and tactics to counter the strengths of the opposition. Essendon had been good enough to win the first VFL premiership in 1897, but Fitzroy won the following two flags, and another two in 1904–05. As the pride of a large suburb, Fitzroy was a prosperous, well-administered club and established firmly as the team to beat. The Maroons' hated rival, their neighbours Collingwood, developed a system of 'machine-like passing', as *The Argus* put it, which brought it premierships in 1902–03. In such a competition, Essendon needed Albert Thurgood in its team to have a better chance of competing with Fitzroy and Collingwood. The success of the Maroons and the Magpies may have caused the Essendon administration to revise upward its estimation of Thurgood's worth to the team.

Thurgood started playing regularly again for Essendon in the ninth round of the 1900 season. He still scored 26 goals that season, enough to make him the VFL's leading goalkicker. Injury kept him out of the side for the first four games of 1901, and he did not play for five weeks after his mother died of cancer during the middle of the season. When Albert returned there were only three rounds to play before the finals series. He scored five goals against South Melbourne, and five goals against Geelong two weeks later. By now, his form was white-hot. In the semifinal, he scored five of Essendon's six goals; three of them after marking more than 45 metres out from goal. Another came after he kicked for goal from more than 65 metres out and, as the ball fell short, he ran to the goalmouth scramble and kicked a goal off the ground. In the same game he played in defence during the last quarter when his team kicked into the wind and hung on to a one-point lead. *The Argus* reported that 'Thurgood's influence on the game cannot be over-estimated, for, in addition to his five goals, he did a power of work and marked magnificently'. Although the windy conditions on grand final day did not suit him, Thurgood still played a brilliant game, kicking three of Essendon's six goals. As the *Leader* put it, Collingwood had no answer to Thurgood's 'high marking, running and passing'. One of his goals, with a placekick into the wind, was later measured at 93 yards (85 metres). The press voted Champion of the Colony, for the third time.

As great a triumph as the 1901 finals series was for Albert Thurgood and Essendon, in retrospect it serves to illustrate what the club, and football fans in general, had missed out on seeing during Thurgood's periods of absence from the game in his early to mid-twenties when he would have been at his peak. He was still aged only 27, potentially with several years of good football left in him. Instead, the 1901 grand final was Thurgood's last great moment as a footballer. Twelve months later, Essendon cut him from its list of players.

Thurgood missed only four games in 1902, due to suspension. Essendon made the grand final but Collingwood was able to turn the tables on them, containing Thurgood by playing a centreman on him who could keep pace with him, with a tall defender close by to punch the ball away. Thurgood still got plenty of the ball, but kicked badly. His one goal from five scoring shots was enough to fuel rumours that he had been bribed by Collingwood supporters to 'play dead'. Essendon conducted an internal investigation, which found no evidence of wrongdoing on Thurgood's part, but nevertheless removed him from its squad. Thurgood took such pride in his integrity that earlier in the season, when he appeared before Colden Harrison and the VFL investigation committee to answer charges of striking, *The Age* reported that Thurgood 'declared that if his reputation after eleven years' association with the sport was not a sufficient answer to a charge of foul play, football was no game for him'. Essendon's decision to ostracise him must have been a bitter pill, and Albert did not pull on a football boot for the next three seasons. In 1905, Thurgood applied unsuccessfully for a clearance to Collingwood. At the start of 1906, he expressed a desire to play again for Essendon, but the committee wrote to tell him that he was not required as a player. This prompted Thurgood to write an open letter to the club members in which he argued that, as he had been exonerated by the club of bribery allegations in 1902 (he offered to donate £50 to charity if anyone could provide proof of any corruption on his part), 'it is, therefore, very obvious that personal animosity only must be the cause' of the committee's refusal to play him. The most likely cause of this was lingering bitterness over Thurgood's continuing demands for match payments and his performance in the 1902 grand final. The club president, Dr Wilfred Kent Hughes, was a strong supporter of the amateur ideal and once told a meeting of university students that 'the man who sold his services to any particular club would also sell his club when sufficient inducement was offered to him'. In his letter, Thurgood claimed that Kent Hughes had 'threatened the trainers with instant dismissal should they render me any assistance in my training; consequently, though a member of the Club, I am compelled to employ a private trainer'.

Thurgood's letter brought an immediate response from the players; a letter of protest, signed by 17 players, was sent to the committee and this resulted in Thurgood being reinstated. Essendon made the finals that year but was defeated comfortably in the semifinal. Thurgood kicked the first goal of the game with a running shot but, in doing so, injured his ankle so badly that he had to leave the ground (at the time, injured players could not be replaced). It was his last game of football.

Football in Melbourne was entering a boom period when Thurgood retired, and most clubs no longer expected players to play as amateurs. After Thurgood retired as a player, he had only a limited involvement in the game. He remained a patron of Essendon, and organised and played in a past players' football carnival for charity in the early 1920s. But his interests mostly lay elsewhere. He was an avid golfer, and Worrall recalled that 'in the early days of the Yarra Yarra Golf Club at Rosanna he worked like a navvy in grubbing and dynamiting trees, and [had] more to do in the formation of the course than any other man'. He became a bookmaker, and bought a house named 'Greyholm' close to Caulfield Racecourse, where he lived with Ida and his daughters, Marjorie and Gwen. Albert later turned to owning horses, and in one season, 1924–25, his horses won five races and he collected £630 in prize money (the Commonwealth basic wage at that time was £4 2s. per week).

One Sunday afternoon in May 1927, Thurgood was driving west along Toorak Road with Ida, Gwen and a friend of Gwen's. They were heading out of the city to pick mushrooms. As they crossed Kooyong Road, a car driven by a university student, with two passengers, and travelling at a speed that witnesses estimated as between 35 and 45 miles per hour (56 and 72 kilometres per hour), entered the uncontrolled intersection and smashed into the left-hand side of Thurgood's Cadillac. Both of the cars flipped over and all of the occupants were injured. Albert died on his way to hospital. He was aged 53. The student was charged with manslaughter, and was represented by a young barrister, R.G. Menzies. A jury found the student not guilty after the judge directed that the evidence about the speed of the two cars was too unreliable to be considered.

3

Phil Matson
(1884–1928)

He has a wonderful record as a footballer and as an instructor of footballers.

Richmond Guardian, 1926

It is ironic that Phil Matson, the man who Western Australians came to describe as 'the prince of coaches', and one of the first coaches to insist on hard training and the development of a disciplined system of team play, was himself a natural, intuitive footballer. As one observer put it, Matson was 'a natural, born player. He was a champion mentally, too. Never did he expend unnecessary energy. In his day he played in almost every position, and was a trump wherever played'. Another writer recalled that 'he could handle the ball with a sureness that was remarkable, his high marking was phenomenal, he was a good kick over long and short distances alike, and although he played the game with unrestrained vigour, his methods were never questioned'. Although, like Thurgood, Matson 'could in his heyday win a match on his own', he had also learnt from bitter experience as a player that success also depended on an even, disciplined contribution from players working as a team. His highly competitive nature saw him develop a method of play that would win games and a system of training drills to teach it to his players. Though Matson lived his own life in a footloose and intemperate way, like all great coaches, he could communicate with his players and insist on high standards without alienating them. As a motivator and tactician, Matson was ahead of his time. Richmond appointed him as coach in 1926 but, in mysterious circumstances, he was denied a permit by the VFL. At the time of his death after a motor accident in 1928, Matson was aged only 43 and increasing numbers of Western Australians were crossing to the VFL. Had Matson lived longer it seems likely that he would have eventually been given the opportunity to test his skills in Victoria. His coaching record in Western Australia, where he won eight premierships in 12 seasons, is suggestive of the more prominent place in football history that he might have achieved.

Of all the people featured in this book, Matson's footsteps are the most difficult to follow. He played and coached in an era when press coverage of football — especially in Western Australia — was not extensive and his thoughts about football were rarely recorded. A typical journeyman footballer who depended on football and football contacts to make a living, Matson never put down deep roots anywhere and moved around a great deal in search of work and football offers. He came from a humble background, had little formal education and learned no trade. He worked at various times as a miner, a railway navvy, a storeman, a tram driver, a farmer, a fisherman, a brewery salesman and a trotting bookmaker, and ran two-up schools in hotels and an illegal gaming house. Matson lived in Western Australia in four separate spells, moving back and forth between Kalgoorlie, Bunbury and various suburbs of Perth, with two of these spells being broken by periods of playing in Adelaide and coaching in Victoria. In his travels, however, Matson left several clues about his life as a professional footballer because of the phenomenally high level of success he enjoyed. Matson played with and/or coached nine clubs and had a major impact on virtually all of them, being premiers or runners-up in 16 of 21 completed seasons of football.

Hired gun

Phil's parents, Emma Duffield and George Matson, moved from their native Fremantle to Port Adelaide shortly after they were married. When their first child was born, in Alberton in 1875, Emma was aged 21. She gave birth to 12 children, three of whom died as infants. The Matsons' sixth child, Phillip, was born in Exeter in 1884. Although George Matson was a skilled bootmaker, he and Emma would have found it difficult to make ends meet with such a large family. The South Australian economy, which had been buoyant when the Matsons arrived, was in a depressed state by the early 1880s and jobs in Adelaide were hard to come by. The Matsons kept an orchard and a vegetable garden that helped to put food on the table and, when Phil was around 10 years of age, he was sent to sell fruit from a basket on the wharf at Port Adelaide. Phil also carried memories of a summer diet made up predominantly of bread and tomatoes. He was aged only 14 when he went to Kalgoorlie and found work mining, but returned home broke after he lost his savings in a two-up game on a steamer from Albany to Port Adelaide.

Phil Matson was still a teenager when he went to Perth in 1902. He was of above average height for that era, standing just over 5 foot 10½ inches (179 cm), but his working-class diet had given him a lean, almost frail build. He was, however, a gifted natural athlete. At first, swimming was the only sport that interested him. He took it up competitively and soon held state titles in events ranging in distance from 100 yards to 5 miles. His best event was the 220 yard breaststroke: an event at which he won the Australasian championship three times — in 1905, 1907 and 1908 — and twice held the world record. Turning professional in 1909, for a stake of £20, deprived him of the chance to compete at the 1912 Olympics at Stockholm.

Matson appears not to have played football competitively until 1903, when the owner of the Claremont swimming baths asked him to fill in for the Claremont seconds, who were a man short. Phil played with his trouser legs rolled up and, as 'Groper', a writer for the *Sporting Globe* later recalled, he 'slogged through with muscle and vim the only features of his game'. He also played one game for West Perth that season. In 1904 Matson moved to Bunbury and played in two premierships in two seasons with South Bunbury. He was back in Kalgoorlie in 1906, lining up for Boulder City. It is not known whether Matson shifted from town to town in search of work of his own accord and joined a local football club upon arrival, or whether clubs approached him first and offered him financial inducements to join them. Given the amount of money that was circulating in goldfields football, and the vigorous debate about professionalism in the goldfields press at the time, it seems likely that Matson received some sort of financial compensation for playing for Boulder City, although the fact that he retained his amateur status as a swimmer until 1909 might suggest otherwise.

The Goldfields Football Association, as it was then known, was a strong, tough competition. After gold was discovered in the Kalgoorlie–Boulder–Coolgardie region in the early 1890s, a flood of new arrivals, most of them male and many of them from Victoria and South Australia, encouraged the foundation of football clubs. As Les Everett explains in *Gravel Rash: 100 Years of Goldfields Football*, many teams came into and went out of existence quickly, while the arrangements for playing matches were loose and unstructured. The peak of the region's gold production had been reached by the 1900s, but deep reefs of gold remained and created continuing work for miners and workers in other industries, especially construction. With a stable population of around 15 000, Kalgoorlie-Boulder now supported a well-organised football competition that continued to attract quality players. Perhaps the best was Hugh Gavin, who had captained Essendon and been named Champion of the Colony by the Melbourne press in 1902 before accepting a coaching job in Boulder. Alec Robinson, who played with Matson at Boulder City, was another former Essendon player who, as Everett writes, 'was strong and robust, yet clever and perfectly fair'. William 'Nipper' Truscott, who came to the goldfields from New South Wales where he had played rugby, developed into an outstanding centreman and went on to have a stellar career at East Fremantle. The competition also had its share of rough players; before 1909, all of the matches in this semiarid region were played on ovals with gravel rather than grassed surfaces. The standard of the goldfields competition was probably comparable to that of the Perth-based WAFL, and both leagues were represented equally in the Western Australian squad for the 1908 Carnival.

Though young and inexperienced, Matson was anything but out of his depth in such company. The *Kalgoorlie Miner* judged him to be the best player on the ground in his first game for Boulder City. Four weeks later Boulder City took on Boulder Stars, which was led by Hugh Gavin. Gavin had dominated play at centre half-back until Matson, who had been playing in the ruck, was moved on to him in the third quarter. As the *Kalgoorlie Miner* put it, the result was 'a magnificent trial of strength and skill between two champions'. In Matson, 'Gavin had met his match at last'. Boulder City were minor premiers in 1906 but lost the grand final. They made amends by winning premierships in 1907–08–09, with Matson playing in two of these. Matson also impressed at the 1908 Carnival. As one football writer recalled, 'in those days there were no numbers or programmes to help one distinguish the players, but five minutes after the game against the West had commenced everyone knew that the big fair-haired champion in the green and gold was Matson'.

Any doubts about Matson's status as a professional footballer disappeared when he signed a two-year contract to play with Sturt in 1909–10. He was one of a group of recruits who made up what became known as 'Dempsey's Immigrants'. John Dempsey was a wealthy Sturt supporter who owned a tobacco shop in Unley Road. Dempsey had a network of contacts from his service in the Boer War and former career as chief inspector of the Adelaide Tramways Trust; as a result of this, Sturt was able to recruit half a dozen interstate stars while they were playing at the 1908 Carnival in Melbourne. Like the other 'Immigrants', Matson received a job, accommodation and match payment through Dempsey or his contacts. Matson himself would later tell football writers that he played the best football of his career at Sturt. Relishing the soft grounds of Adelaide, Matson, playing at centre half-back, flew so high for his marks that he earned the nickname 'Aeroplane'. As Sturt historian John Lysikatos writes, Matson 'was a brilliant reader of the game who hardly made a mistake and knew when to spoil or take a mark.

In his two years at Sturt, Matson beat every centre half-forward in Adelaide and did not play a bad game'. In 1910 he was runner-up in the Magarey Medal to Port's 'Shine' Hosking and he was best afield for South Australia against the VFA at North Melbourne. An *Argus* reporter praised his 'bold defence' throughout that game and noted that 'his work at half-back was magnificent'.

Sturt was at that time the only league club based in Adelaide's fast-growing southern suburbs, and the possibility that it might be building a team capable of winning its first premiership drew lockout crowds of up to 12 000 to Unley Oval. The club had not won a game in 1908, but came fifth in 1909 and finished on top of the ladder after the home-and-away rounds of 1910. That was an impressive rate of improvement but, given the talent in Sturt's ranks, the club's failure to win a premiership during these years was a major disappointment. In Bert Renfrey, a tactician who later masterminded South Australia's win in the 1911 Carnival through the use of a 'loose man' on the forward line, the Double Blues had an outstanding captain-coach. A footballer who, like Matson, had moved from state to state in search of work, Renfrey began his League career in his hometown of Adelaide, then moved to Broken Hill, Boulder City (before Matson was there) and St Kilda. His team of stars included Harold 'Vic' Cumberland, a champion ruckman who had played in Tasmania, Western Australia and New Zealand, and had joined Sturt after quitting St Kilda following a dispute with its committee. Cumberland's ruck partner was Francis 'Diver' Dunne, an athletic Western Australian who did most of the heavy work, providing Cumberland with space to use his marking and passing skills. Another Western Australian, Frank Golding, and a local recruit, Herbert Limb, were the key forwards. Matson and Renfrey anchored the defence.

Sturt defeated Port Adelaide in the final home-and-away round of 1910 to secure the minor premiership but, when the two teams met again in the final, Port turned the tables. Sturt was trailing by five points with less than a minute to play when Golding marked and took a placekick shot for goal. The ball hit the goalpost. The grand final was an anticlimax; Port was too consistent and determined on the day for a Sturt team that tended to play as individuals. For

Vic Richardson, who grew up in Unley and went on to have a great football and cricket career, 'the team never seemed to mould into a combination, and Australian Rules Football is above all a team game. Few of these champions ever hit top form at the same time'. Years later, Tasman Gay, writing in *The Western Mail*, remembered that 'Phil Matson once told me that the 1910 Sturt team, known as "The Immigrants", was the best team he ever saw, although they lacked system'.

Sturt's failure in the 1910 finals, and the reasons for it, probably had a lasting influence on Matson's thinking about football. In later years, the evenness, teamwork and aggression associated with the teams coached by Matson contrasted sharply with the brilliant but individualistic nature of the team he played with at Sturt. Matson was himself an instinctive player, but his competitive nature made him a firm believer in the benefits of organised team practice. After the 1914 Carnival in Sydney, in which Matson captained Western Australia, he complained that the team had been given insufficient time to practice and prepare for the games. 'We should have won that series,' he later told a reporter. 'We had a wonderful side and their combination was amazing. The trouble was that we arrived on the Tuesday and had to play the next day. We had 24 men, one trainer and no towels or oil.' Poor planning and preparation hampered none of the teams that Matson coached. Though he kept himself in superb condition through a routine of skipping and kicking a football in his backyard, Matson took nothing for granted with his teams and trained them hard.

Matson's meticulousness as a coach was in stark contrast to the spontaneous way that he led his personal life. He married his cousin, Ethel Pope, who was the daughter of his mother's sister, in Boulder in 1907. In the following year the first of his two sons, Glen, was born. As a young athlete, he had rarely touched alcohol but, by the time he returned to Perth from Adelaide, he had developed a fondness for beer and the bonhomie of fellow drinkers. The owner of the Subiaco Hotel paid Phil a retainer to sit in the bar to attract and talk to the customers. 'Matson was a mixer and a democrat if ever there was one', was how one journalist remembered him. Matson said what was on his mind, but was also a good listener when it was the turn of others to speak. With his way of dealing with people, he could make friends easily, attract punters to his two-up schools and inspire the loyalty of team-mates. But there was a shadowy side to Matson's sunny personality. Despite his football connections, Matson found it difficult to hold down a steady job. The family moved house frequently. They lived in North Fremantle while Phil played for the local club during the 1911 season; after Phil transferred to play with Subiaco the following season, they lived in the Shenton Park area, west of Subiaco, before moving to a house close to Subiaco Oval. By the time World War I had started, the family had moved to the beach at Crawley on Swan River and Phil had become a fisherman. At that time the Crawley area was, as historian Ken Spillman notes, 'an assemblage of canvas and hessian tents and other temporary structures erected by those desirous of a rate-free existence'. It was not unusual for young, working-class people to live in tents in Perth, as the city was experiencing rapid population growth and was short of housing. While most of the families who lived this way saw it as a means of cutting costs until they could buy their own land and build their own houses, Phil Matson needed to live cheaply because money was constantly slipping through his fingers. As Lyall Hunt writes in his entry for Matson in the *Australian Dictionary of Biography*, 'heavy gambling made him alternately flush and broke'. The family later moved to a house in Nedlands, near the University of Western Australia, but in the early 1920s Phil and Ethel separated and Ethel took her two sons to live with her parents in Kalgoorlie. Phil and Ethel never divorced and, at the time of his death, Phil was living with a woman named Kate Owens.

The Matson system

Matson joined Subiaco, which had finished last in 1911, just as Sturt had done the year before he arrived there. Subiaco was another club on the rise: its large supporter base drawn from Perth's growing western suburbs, the spacious Subiaco Oval, which the club had moved to in 1908 and was developed with the help of a sympathetic local council, and the largesse of local patrons, gave the club the funds for a major recruiting drive. Committeeman (and later club president) John Scaddan, who was premier of Western Australia from 1911 to 1916, spearheaded this, assembling a team drawn from far and wide. Full-back Sid Snow was a local product, but the other key defender, W.H. 'Horrie' Bant, had played for West Perth, St Kilda and Essendon. Rover Billy Orr had played for Perth and was a Western Australian representative at the 1908 Carnival. Centreman William 'Digger' Thomas, vice-captain Ernie Nelson and rover H. Weston were from the Goldfields League. Star forward Herbert Limb had played with Matson at Sturt. Captain-coach Joe Scaddan, John's younger brother, was from Bendigo, as was ruckman Tom Cain. Joe Scaddan was recruited from Collingwood where he had played every game in 1910, his only season in the VFL. As Ken Spillman writes in *Diehards*, his history of the Subiaco Football Club, the recruitment of Matson, who would play at centre half-forward, was 'the icing on the cake'.

Subiaco finished on top of the ladder in 1912 which meant that, if it lost the final or the semifinal, it would have the right to challenge the winner of the final in a 'grand final'. After they lost the final to East Fremantle, the WAFL scheduled the challenge match to be held at Fremantle Oval, and Matson's view was that the local crowd had intimidated his players and the umpires. Years later, Dolph Heinrichs recalled in his history of East Fremantle Football Club that 'years afterwards Phil told me that ... he had seldom left Fremantle Oval a winner. In his own inimitable way and with a delightful vocabulary, Phil expressed the opinion that the barrackers frightened the umpires at critical stages'. The defeat was a humiliating one, 13.19 to 2.4, but Subiaco was able to reverse the result in the grand final. At a neutral venue (Perth Oval) and with Limb returning after injury and kicking four of the team's five goals, Subiaco won its first premiership, 5.8 to 4.5. Matson played a fine game, as he had done the previous week, and Scaddan moved him into defence during the last quarter when Subiaco was kicking into the wind and defending a narrow lead.

Matson took over the coaching job in 1913, when Joe Scaddan stepped aside because of family commitments, and soon displayed the blend of organisation and flair which marked his coaching career.

In an era when many players took a free-and-easy attitude towards attendance at training, Matson devised a series of drills that the players enjoyed. These drills perfected a method of play-on football in which the ball was passed to team-mates who were in space, rather than kicked to a pack. Marking and kicking skills were taught and practised. The result was that in matches Subiaco 'played like a machine', as a writer in the *Western Australian* put it. 'There was no selfish individual play, each man looked only to the success of his team, and it was a treat to witness the carefully mapped-out system of passing.' As a Victorian football writer later noted after watching a Matson-coached team play, 'they kept the ball going all the time, with quick zig-zag passing often perplexing their opponents, who were frequently yards away from the men they were supposed to be watching'. Matson demanded that his team play as he did — with aggression at the ball. In the article 'Is Matson Australia's greatest coach?', a *Sporting Globe* writer observed that:

> The man who lags behind, and is a little fainthearted, is no good to Phil. He likes his players to get into the fray with deadly earnest. They must not hang out, and must bump harder than they are bumped.

Matson was not afraid to make changes in his positional placement of players in an attempt to exploit the weaknesses of opponents. For example, Limb was often moved from full-forward to roving and Orr, who in the later stages of his career was slowed down by a knee injury, went to full-forward. In that era the tactic was novel and considered adventurous, but in modern football the strategy of creating mis-matches has become a commonplace aspect of coaching.

Few, if any, observers expected Subiaco to lose the flag in 1913, even after a shock loss to Perth in the semifinal. Again exercising the right of challenge, the Maroons won a close grand final. Perth was trailing by only 12 points at three-quarter-time, and kicked with the wind in the last quarter, but Matson moved himself into defence and Subiaco held on to win 6.7 to 4.7. For the *Western Suburban News*, the three factors that contributed most to the win — 'combination, condition, and generalship' — could all be attributed to Matson's coaching.

Subiaco Football Club deserved this period of success. The administration and the coaches it appointed to develop the team were bold, natural leaders. The club recruited effectively and cared about the welfare of its players. It developed a close bond with an appreciative local community, which saw membership rise from 220 in 1912 to 758 in 1914. Like all highly successful clubs, Subiaco raised the standard of the competition in which it played by forcing the rivals that attempted to keep up with it to develop more efficient methods of coaching and recruiting.

Subiaco blundered, however, in making two administrative decisions that ensured that it did not become the dominant Western Australian club of the post-war period. Each of these blunders impacted on the career of Phil Matson.

First, at the start of the 1914 season, officials from the club had arranged to meet South Melbourne star Jack Scobie at Subiaco railway station to discuss the terms under which he would join the Maroons. Scobie had travelled west by sea to play with Subiaco but was intercepted at Fremantle railway station by East Fremantle officials, who offered him a job as an accountant with a local firm. Not bothering to meet Scobie when he got off the boat was an error of complacency uncharacteristic of Subiaco's recruiting. It was, of course, a double blow to the club because Scobie's talents were not only unavailable to Subiaco, but could also be used by a rival club to counter its existing strengths, and it was East Fremantle, and not Subiaco, that won the flag that season. East Fremantle used Scobie to play on Matson and the former Victorian tended to have the better of these duels. Fast, strong and skilful, Scobie was, in Heinrichs's opinion, the 'most fully equipped and most accomplished player' to wear the East Fremantle guernsey before World War II; Matson's best football was behind him. During the 1915 season, Matson's fitness was reduced by influenza and by 1918 it was, as Heinrichs put it, 'wonderful that he was able to play at all for his heart had shifted round a few inches from its normal position and this made him somewhat easier to check than in his heyday as a player'. Lyall Hunt notes that Matson was rejected for military service on medical grounds.

Second, Matson was replaced as Subiaco coach in 1915 by former South Fremantle coach Jack Leckie, and as captain by South Australian Wally Steele. Matson appears to have taken the setback well and later coached Western Australia to victory in the 1921 Carnival. The club's decision to appoint Leckie, a fine leader and tactician, appeared to have been vindicated when Subiaco won the 1915 flag. When Leckie left to coach West Perth at the end of 1916, however, Subiaco's decision to appoint Steele rather than Matson as coach was hard to fathom. Steele certainly had the credentials to coach successfully; so, of course, did Matson. It was a judgement call by the Subiaco committee as to who would be the better man to coach the team in the future. With Matson's playing career nearing its end, and given his continuing ambition to coach, the appointment of Steele made it almost inevitable that he would leave Subiaco. For most of the 1920s, that decision came back to haunt the Subiaco Football Club, especially at finals time.

At the start of the 1918 season, Matson was offered the coaching job at East Perth. Before being admitted to the WAFA in 1906, East Perth (known as 'Young Easts' to distinguish them from 'Old Easts', East Fremantle) was known as Union Football Club and was founded by workers from the Union Soap and Excelsior Confectionery factories in the local area. Its status as a working-class club was confirmed in subsequent years as the suburb of East Perth was built up and areas that were low-lying or close to railway lines or open drains became the sites of factories and low-cost housing. The club drew supporters and players from local industries, such as the Perth gasworks and East Perth power station, while a local cinema, owned by the club president and managed by the club secretary, gave work to players who needed it. Coaching at East Perth probably suited Matson for several reasons. He had at least one friend there already — 'Digger' Thomas had transferred to the club a few years earlier. Matson was now working as a trotting bookmaker and Perth Oval, East Perth's home ground, was close to the trotting track at the WACA ground where floodlit meetings had been held since 1914. The suburb had several hotels and was within walking distance of central Perth, where Matson ran a gaming house.

The East Perth committee supported Matson fully, and recruited several players from other Perth clubs that the new coach had identified as necessary additions to the squad. Experienced ruckman Hector Groom and versatile defender Reg ('Nashy') Brentnall transferred from South Fremantle. A further coup was the recruitment of the best full-forward then playing in Western Australia, Hugh 'Bonny' Campbell, who won a clearance from South Fremantle in 1924 only after he had stood out of football for a year. One of the most accurate kicks for goal ever to have played the game, Campbell was the League's leading goalkicker in 1924, 1926 and 1927. 'The Royals' had brilliance on every line: 'Digger' Thomas won the Sandover Medal in 1923, as did ruckman George 'Staunch' Owens two years later. The Western Australian squad for 1924 included eight representatives from East Perth. But a Matson-coached team was always greater than the sum of its parts, and his East Perth team also had the level of discipline and team orientation needed to stand up to physical pressure and lift its game when matches, and premierships, were in the balance.

East Perth finished the home-and-away rounds as minor premiers in every season from 1918 to 1924. That was just as well because, in six of those seven seasons, they lost a semifinal or final and needed to exercise the right of challenge that they had earned. It is difficult to tell whether the team, and perhaps its coach, grew complacent in situations where a second chance was available, or simply whether the level of competition in the WAFL was high. East Fremantle was too strong in the 1918 grand final, but Matson's team made up for that by defeating 'Old Easts' in the next three grand finals. These were tight, low-scoring games (East Perth scored fewer than 10 goals in all but one of its grand finals in this era) and Matson's on-field presence and goal-scoring ability were invaluable. Matson took the field infrequently during his East Perth career, playing only 35 games in six seasons, but he still played in three premiership teams. His last game of football, the 1923 grand final in which East Perth won its fifth consecutive premiership, took place less than a month before his 39th birthday.

It is not known how much money Matson made from coaching East Perth during these years. His successor in 1928 was paid £4 per week, which was around the same as the basic wage. Matson almost certainly received at least as much, and probably more given the likelihood that he was paid bonuses for each premiership. Also, his celebrity status in Perth would have boosted his gambling and bookmaking businesses. There were dark rumours after the 1919 grand final that Tom Cain, a former Subiaco team-mate of Matson's who was then playing for East Fremantle, had been paid to 'play dead' during the game. Some supporters were also convinced that Matson, as both opposition coach and a betting man, had been involved in the conspiracy, but no evidence was produced to support this gossip. It seems unlikely that football made Phil Matson a rich man, and so it is not surprising that in 1925 he 'slipped away', as the Perth *Daily News* put it, 'to a lucrative coaching job at Castlemaine, Victoria'.

The offer to coach Castlemaine came from its club president, Chris Bant, and was presumably arranged by his brother, Horrie Bant, who was Matson's friend and former team-mate at Subiaco. Chris Bant ran a hotel in Castlemaine, at which Matson may have received free accommodation in addition to his remuneration. Castlemaine had just left a local football association and was competing for the first time in the strong Bendigo Football League. Matson's new team had no star players, just young local talent. Only one of Matson's Castlemaine players, full-back Roy Parkin, was later invited to try out for a VFL team (Parkin played one game for Richmond). As the Castlemaine committee wrote to Matson at the end of the season, 'when we consider the difficulties you had to encounter — coming as a stranger amongst us, and with a raw and inexperienced team to take in hand, we cannot but think that the transformation you effected was a marvellous one'. After the team overcame a half-time deficit to defeat South Bendigo in one home-and-away game, the *Castlemaine Mail* commented that the result 'only goes to show that Castlemaine can adapt themselves to the tactics of Phil Matson, and if their main objective is to carry out his advice it will take something good to beat them'. A week later the *Mail* wrote approvingly of 'Matson's system working beautifully'.

Matson took Castlemaine a long way in one season and, although the team fell short of victory on grand final day, its efforts reflected well on the ability of their coach as an educator and motivator. *The Argus*'s report of the grand final noted that, early on in the game, Castlemaine 'lost Barassi due to a broken collarbone'. This was Carlo Barassi, then aged 21, an elder brother of Ron Barassi Sr whose grandfather had arrived in the Castlemaine area from Italy in 1854. Castlemaine trailed South Bendigo at half-time and, as *The Argus* noted, 'playing with 17 men, and others weakened by injury, Castlemaine were applauded by the spectators for their courageous efforts in the third and final quarters'. South Bendigo was too strong; with captain-coach, Arthur Hando, a former South Melbourne player, dominating the match, they won by 14 points.

Matson's year at Castlemaine only enhanced his coaching reputation, and developed in him an ambition 'to finish my football career by coaching a Victorian League team'. Matson was considering an offer to coach Burnie in Tasmania when he was offered the coaching job at Richmond. The Tigers had slipped badly since winning back-to-back flags in 1921 and 1922. However, with the election of a reform group in 1924, Percy Page became secretary and the club added new blood to the playing list. The club was aware for some time during the 1925 season that a new coach would be required the following year: Dan Minogue, who had been captain-coach since 1920, became injured and announced that he would be leaving the club. Mel Morris was acting captain-coach while Minogue was unavailable but the Tigers clearly regarded Matson as the best person to oversee the rebuilding of the team. As the *Richmond Guardian* told the local fans, 'he has a wonderful record as a footballer and as an instructor of footballers'.

In *Tigerland*, the official history of Richmond Football Club, Brian Hansen writes that 'there had been much argument about the coaching position and West Australian P. Matson had originally been appointed and then ousted by Morris. Matson returned to Perth where he coached his team to the premiership'. In fact, as Lyall Hunt writes, the VFL refused Matson a permit to coach Richmond. The decision was made three weeks before the opening round and threw the Tigers' preparation for the season into chaos. The League's permit committee refused to give any reason for its decision when questioned by Page, and the League stated that 'it would listen to no complaints'. Matson returned to Perth a few days later, after being offered his old job at East Perth, and duly coached the Royals to the 1926 and 1927 flags. Richmond did appoint Morris as coach, but he lasted only one season. Morris's replacement, Frank 'Checker' Hughes, a former Tiger rover who had been coaching in Tasmania, would take Richmond into the finals in each of the next six seasons.

Lyall Hunt writes that the VFL's decision to exclude Matson from participating in its competition stemmed from complaints he had made as Western Australian coach to Victorian officials about rough play during the 1924 Carnival. The matches were certainly tough and *The Argus* reported that, in the decider between Western Australia and Victoria, 'men reeled from the packs, for the clashes were hard, incessant and bitter'. The Western Australians were not entirely innocent, however, as it was an important part of Matson's coaching style to make sure that 'every man who went out onto the ground knew he would have to play his hardest from start to finish'. Matson accepted that this was a normal part of football, and if he did complain about the Victorian tactics he did not do so publicly. He congratulated the Victorians in the rooms after the game.

There are more plausible explanations for the VFL's attitude to Matson's permit application. Relations between the VFL and interstate leagues were strained at the time over issues such as the rights of touring Perth and Adelaide clubs to play matches against VFL clubs, and attempts by the interstate leagues to make it more difficult for their players to move to the VFL. On the eve of the 1924 Carnival, the enmity flared up when the Perth Football Club, with the endorsement of the WAFL, played a match in Melbourne against the VFA, in defiance of the VFL. *The Argus* reported that the WAFL was considering breaking away from the Australasian Football Council and forming a new football body with the VFA, which might in the future include the SANFL. 'Old Boy', the paper's football writer, commented that the VFL 'is drifting like a ship without a rudder, and delegates, feeling blindly for a way out of the difficulties, have become sensitive to criticism, and resentful of anything that may be said, or written, which does not come under the heading of flattery or praise'. Such delegates may have excluded Matson simply because he was not a Victorian. Alternatively, they may have disapproved of Matson's gambling — he had been accused, without evidence, of being involved in fixing a game — his drinking, or his living with a woman who was not his wife.

Matson's legacy

In the early evening of 11 June 1928, Horrie Bant was driving a truck along Hampden Road towards Subiaco, where he owned a furniture shop. Phil Matson was travelling with him. Bant lost control of the truck at a slight bend in the road, not far from Matson's Nedlands house. The truck ran off the edge of the road, through some scrub, and crashed sideways into a telegraph pole. The impact threw both of them out of the truck and, while Bant landed safely, Matson's head struck the telegraph pole. Matson lay unconscious in hospital for two days before he passed away. According to a report in Perth's *The Mirror*, just after Matson was brought to the hospital 'a well-known Perth sporting man' told the chief surgeon 'you're on a thousand pounds, doctor, if you can save Phil'.

Matson's career might have gone in so many different directions that it seems pointless to speculate as to what he could have achieved had he lived longer. Relations between the VFL and WAFL became more cordial after the former introduced rules that prohibited Victorian clubs from paying signing-on fees and required interstate players to live in Melbourne for three months before becoming eligible to play in the VFL. These rules gave interstate clubs a better chance of retaining their stars by finding jobs for them. A Sandgroper, Johnny Leonard, received a permit to coach in the VFL in 1932; another Western Australian, Brighton Diggins, coached a VFL premiership team in 1938. It seems likely that had Matson wished to have another try at coaching in the game's biggest league he would have received an opportunity to do so. If that had been the case, it would be hard to imagine Matson's ideas not being copied in such a competitive environment and having a major impact on the way the game was played. Alternatively, Matson might have been content to remain in Perth and, in doing so, influence the thinking of a new generation of football protégés and rivals. It is equally possible that he might have tired of the routine of coaching and concentrated on his gambling interests. He might literally have 'gone fishing'. One thing is certain, however. As *The Mirror* put it, when Phil Matson died, Western Australia 'lost not only a great player, but the greatest football brain that it has ever possessed'.

Part 2

Theme parks for football fans

Harry Collier (1907–1994)
and Albert Collier (1909–1988)

Brighton Diggins (1906–1971)

Bob Quinn (1915–)

Much of football's heritage comes from people who grew up in inner city neighborhoods, suburbs and country towns where there was not a lot to do. In one such place, the Katanning district, an area of sheep and wheat country roughly halfway along the Great Southern Railway line between Perth and Albany, three Aboriginal brothers, Maley, Eric and Bill Hayward learned to play Australian Rules during the 1920s by kicking a ball with bare feet through forks in trees. It was a cheap form of entertainment that honed their skills and, after taking up the game competitively, the boys were unfazed by the rough ovals they had to play on and the 40 kilometres they sometimes had to walk to get to matches. When Maley Hayward joined Claremont, he was the first Aboriginal to play in the WAFL and one of the few in the first half of the twentieth century who left the isolated missions, sheep stations and country towns, where most Aboriginals lived, to play football in a capital city. Hayward needed the permission of Western Australia's Chief Protector of Natives to move to Perth. While he may have suffered discrimination and felt out of place there, his experience as a boy who learned to kick a ball in a paddock and then went straight into a junior team was in many ways not very different from that of most other footballers of his era. This was how Harry and Albert Collier, Brighton Diggins and Bob Quinn took up the game; they all learned to play in streets and paddocks and worked their way into the league teams that represented the working-class districts where they grew up, and went on to become immortals in their clubs' histories.

Most clubs could raise the funds to pay a coach, often one with VFL experience, to lead the local boys and teach them how to play. Some country football clubs played on immaculate ovals with excellent facilities, such as that at Maryborough, Victoria, which was laid out in the period of prosperity following the gold rush. Others, however, played in rough paddocks, with tin sheds for clubrooms. Regardless of the setting, football clubs were an important part of the social life of country towns. A survey of Victorian country towns in the 1940s found that 'sport is by far the most common form of organized recreation, and, for most people, is the main theme of life over the weekend, if not during the week also. [Football] creates what is perhaps the strongest common interest running through the town and its district'. One country girl wrote in the 1920s of the 'list of pleasures' of life in a rural community; she added, to activities such as tennis and country dances, 'the Saturday afternoons when we drive off to watch our district football and cricket players, and get just as excited over their prowess as our city friend watching her latest "movie hero"'.

The four capital city strongholds of the game were Melbourne, Adelaide, Perth and Hobart. Between the censuses of 1921 and 1947, their combined populations rose from 640 000 to just under two million. The increased numbers were made up almost entirely of people who had been born in one of these cities or who had moved there from another part of Australia; only a few thousand were migrants who had been born overseas. These cities were therefore full of people who had been born in Australia, of mostly English and Irish ancestry, and had grown up in an environment in which Australian Rules football was the dominant game. Although new suburbs were created, the old inner suburbs and port districts which were home to most league clubs continued to increase in population. Here, support for local football teams was a family and community tradition that was 'in the blood' of most people. In Sydney and Brisbane, cricket was just as popular as in the southern and western states but, in winter, rugby was growing rapidly and at the expense of the Australian game. These were the two fastest growing capital cities in Australia and they attracted greater numbers of overseas migrants, many of whom brought a preference for rugby with them. The period saw the emergence of a division between the parts of Australia that preferred to play Australian Rules and those that preferred rugby. In the 1970s, historian Ian Turner wrote that 'Australia is divided by a deep cultural rift known as the Barassi Line'. Named after Australian Rules' most famous player, the line marks the points at which Barassi's game ceases to exert a dominant influence on the lives of ordinary people. Turner's Barassi Line 'runs between Canberra, Broken Hill, Birdsville and Maringrida [Arnhem Land] and it divides Australia between Rugby and Rules'.

By modern standards, the houses of ordinary Australians during the interwar years lacked space, privacy and amenities. The capital cities offered welcome jobs and security, but one day would have seemed pretty much like any other. The routine nature of factory work, the predominantly Anglo-Celtic culture, and the limited variety of food and drink, was largely unchanging and without surprises. However, on a football ground — Australian Rules or rugby — a spectator could watch a thousand games without any two of them being exactly the same. In Melbourne, Adelaide and Perth, football competitions thrived and fans in these cities could become immersed totally in a world of football. Nearly all the grounds in each city were within walking distance or accessible by train and tram. Supporters could stay in touch with their team's progress by going to watch training on Tuesday and Thursday nights and by talking about the game to others in pubs and at work. There were few cars to clutter up the streets and kids played unsupervised.

Like many footballers, Bob Quinn and the Collier brothers lived and worked locally; they could be spotted in the street and were happy to stop for a chat. In Richmond in the late 1920s, coach Frank 'Checker' Hughes ran a pet shop in Bridge Road and full-back Vic Thorp ran a greengrocery in Church Street. In the 1940s, Essendon's Bill Hutchison ran a local petrol station, while Dick Reynolds had a grocery and dairy round, and later a newsagency. To be a league footballer, as Fitzroy's Allan 'Butch' Gale put it, 'meant you were a god in your street'. For dedicated football fans, these cities were like theme parks — places where opportunities for enjoyment and entertainment were concentrated and accessible, yet also diverse and seemingly endless.

While this was a golden era for football, the two world wars and the Great Depression in between them meant that football clubs were unable to cash in on the game's enormous popularity. The wars sent some clubs and leagues into recess and took the lives and health of many players. Bob Quinn volunteered to go to war when he was at his footballing peak, and when he returned he carried physical and emotional scars. The Depression reduced gate takings at a time when clubs could only retain players by paying them or finding jobs for them. Albert Collier went to play in Tasmania after Collingwood was unable to find work for him. New grandstands were built at most major grounds, sometimes by local councils to provide work for the unemployed, but these stands were generally modest in size. The stand with the most impressive amenities and architectural style was the Sir Edwin T. Smith Pavilion at Norwood Oval, but it seated only a few thousand. Most club grounds were managed by local councils or cricket clubs that were happy to collect revenue from football but were unwilling to pay for improvements to facilities for spectators. The Melbourne Cricket Ground could hold crowds of close to 100 000, but only one team played its home matches there and the VFL received no compensation for the Melbourne Cricket Club members who got in free to games, including the finals. Fans were generally prepared to stand in the open and put up with only basic sanitation facilities, so clubs concentrated on increasing the size of the banks of terracing at their grounds to squeeze in as many paying customers as possible. The admission prices set by leagues were low — in the VFL the standard admission charge (which was sixpence until the mid-1920s, when it was increased to ninepence) was roughly equivalent to the price of a bottle of beer or a loaf of bread — and normally within the reach of most supporters, but during the Depression many fans cut back their spending. In 1930, the VFL introduced a series of regulations covering player payments, known as the Coulter Law, which were designed to assist clubs that were struggling financially. Most clubs could not afford to pay the maximum wage of £3 per week but, although clubs were not allowed to offer direct financial inducements to prospective recruits, those which could organise jobs for players had a powerful advantage in the competition for interstate recruits. In states outside Victoria, players received little or no income from football and those who needed a job found it hard to ignore the offers made by VFL clubs. Port Adelaide found a job for Bob Quinn, but Brighton Diggins had to leave Perth and move to Melbourne to secure his financial future.

Football was a rough game during the 1920s, and several matches in Melbourne were marred by brawling players kicking each other. If anything, the game became even more vicious during the 1930s. The conventional explanation for this is that players who were without jobs during the Depression and depended on match payments to feed and shelter their families were desperate to be on a winning side, and so increase their chances of being picked the following week. Certainly there were players in the VFL who were prepared to do anything to unsettle their opponents, but this was also the case in the VFA, where players were paid virtually nothing. The WAFL was another almost amateur league, but as East Fremantle's historian writes, football in Perth during the Depression 'was infested with a foulness and viciousness it had not known previously and has not known since'. Some of the players who took part in the infamous 'Bloodbath' grand final of 1945, between Carlton and South Melbourne, were convinced that betting on the game was the main cause of the violence — players and club officials made bets among themselves and there were accusations that some players were promised bonuses by professional gamblers if their team won. The spitefulness of many games during the interwar years was a consequence of players knowing that they had a good chance of getting away with roughing up the opposition if it was done in packs or behind play, and that they could expect to be on the receiving end of such treatment themselves.

In 1925, the Australasian Football Council introduced a rule under which a free kick was paid against the team that last touched the ball before it went out of bounds. The rule, which remained in force until 1939, was intended to prevent packs from forming around the boundary line, where violent incidents had taken place in several games, but its main effect was to encourage teams to play through the centre of the ground. Teams that could move the ball quickly and direct their play to key forwards had a major advantage. Before the rule change, ten goals was considered a good score; after the change, a team usually had to kick 100 points to have a chance of winning. It was the era of great goalkickers such as Collingwood's Gordon Coventry and South Melbourne's Bob Pratt; Ken Farmer, who kicked 1419 goals in 224 games for North Adelaide; and East Fremantle's George Doig, who kicked 1083 goals in nine seasons. No club made better use of the rule than Collingwood, and its smooth teamwork and emphasis on discipline and team spirit — players, and even the coach, were paid equally — set standards that every other club attempted to match.

4

Harry Collier
(1907–1994)

and

Albert Collier
(1909–1988)

We were more of a family than a football club.

Harry Collier

You were part of Collingwood, in your own way, you thought.

Albert Collier

It was never a pretty place. Even before the arrival of white settlers, the area of dead flat land between the higher ground and the Yarra River drained badly, with its clay soil, rocks, creek and areas of marshy ground. After the land was made available for sale in 1838, its new owners were not bound by the building regulations of the Melbourne Corporation and could subdivide it and run streets through it as they saw fit. Building lots were narrow, with frontages typically about five metres, and in some cases a mere four metres. Streets tended to be narrow alleys and there was a shortage of parkland. When Melbourne was unsewered, open drains carried stormwater and seepage from cesspools from other suburbs across the flat land to the river. After the gold rushes, the area's population grew because of the arrival of people who had tried their luck at the diggings. The area's proximity to the centre of Melbourne and its low house prices and rents made it a convenient, affordable suburb for working-class people. By the 1860s, the suburb had begun to develop factories of its own, such as breweries, and noxious industries, such as slaughterhouses, woolwashers, tanneries, and soap and candle works, that relied on the Yarra for the disposal of their waste products. By the end of the 1880s, the population of the municipality had reached 35 000, where it remained until after World War II. This was Collingwood, the suburb that the architectural writer Robin Boyd commented was 'born with a wooden spoon in its mouth'.

Although significant numbers of Collingwood residents lived in poverty — especially those in households with large families or with only one breadwinner — and the quality of the urban environment left much to be desired, the area did have some redeeming features. There was a sense of community among the people who lived and worked there. As historian Bernard Barrett writes, 'families stayed in Collingwood for generations, often by choice as much as necessity ... Throughout Australia today there are people who will fiercely defend Collingwood as a place where they enjoyed life'. There was a high level of civic pride throughout the municipality, and one of the outcomes of this was the purchase by the Collingwood City Council in 1878 of Dight's Paddock, one of Collingwood's few remaining areas of open space, for use as a recreation reserve. The lack of parkland in the area meant that Collingwood had lagged behind most of Melbourne's other suburbs in the development of sporting clubs, but junior cricket and football clubs soon began playing on the council's new reserve, which was named Victoria Park. In Collingwood, there was wide support for the idea that the establishment of a well-organised sporting club would raise the status of the area. Neighbouring Fitzroy had a senior team in the VFA and the formation of a football club in Collingwood was an outcome of the intense rivalry between the two suburbs. When the club was formed in 1892, it applied successfully to join the VFA.

Harry and Albert Collier grew up in Collingwood and played for the local VFL team in the period between the two world wars when the suburb formed the epicentre of Australian Rules football. In the

20 seasons from 1917 to 1936, Collingwood won eight flags, four of them in 1927–28–29–30; in two great periods, they contested six consecutive grand finals from 1925 to 1930, and five from 1935 to 1939. Before World War I, Collingwood had won three premierships, with its team play being built around the stab kick — a short, sharp drop kick that allowed players to pass the ball quickly over short distances — which some Collingwood players had invented while on an end-of-season trip to Tasmania. By the late 1920s, the stab kick was in common use at clubs throughout Australia, but Collingwood was again pioneering, using the handball as an important part of its teamwork. Aptly known as 'The Machine', because its players saw themselves as interconnected components rather than individual performers, Collingwood combined precise teamwork with the application of constant pressure to its opponents. Norm Smith followed the team as a young man and recalled that 'in other clubs you would call it enthusiasm; at Collingwood it is fanaticism'. For the other VFL clubs, Collingwood was more than just the team to beat; it set standards of camaraderie and individual commitment to the team cause that they all aspired to reach. After home matches, the players themselves would clean up the training rooms for the dances they held there every Saturday night. On the weekend, players would get together for a drink. New players received a friendly welcome and players mixed well regardless of their age, background or religion. The players knew the sound of each others' voices and this showed in their teamwork out on the ground. At other League clubs, as well as VFA, country and interstate clubs, countless footballers learned how to play under the coaching of ex-Collingwood players. It is significant that the only teams to beat Collingwood in grand finals between 1927 and 1939 — Geelong (1937), Carlton (1938) and Melbourne (1939) — had coaches who could develop a Collingwood-like team spirit and stressed the importance of a team contribution rather individual brilliance.

Collingwood also enjoyed a high degree of stability in its administration, with the club being effectively run by a small group of men. Apart from a group of great players — some of whom, such as the

Collier brothers, the Coventry brothers, Jack Regan and Marcus Whelan rank with the legendary figures that the game has produced — three men are linked in the popular imagination with the Collingwood of this era.

First, James 'Jock' McHale, who played 261 games and was coach from 1912 to 1949, guided Collingwood's on-field fortunes for virtually the entire first half of the twentieth century. McHale expected every man to play his opponent shoulder-to-shoulder and keep him to as few kicks as possible. Players were forbidden to leave their men unmarked and McHale enforced this so strictly that, when wingman Bruce Andrew once ran downfield, bouncing the ball, he was dropped the following week, even though he kicked a goal. When Collingwood players had the ball, they used hand signals to let teammates know what side of the player they would pass to. McHale was an innovator and a tactician. His ruck division included only one tall player to contest hit-outs, with the second ruckman being a shorter, faster player, who played in a way that would later be called ruck-roving. In the 1929 grand final, he used his star full-forward, Gordon Coventry, as a decoy, creating space for forward pocket 'Tubby' Edmonds to kick five goals. McHale also had a wonderful knack of knowing how much work needed to be done to bring the team to the peak of fitness, and his half-time speeches were inspirational. McHale never made a speech to the team before a match — this was usually done by the club president — but at half-time the coach would point out what the team needed to do in a way 'that you could feel getting inside you', as one player put it.

There was a lighter side to Jock; when no official drinking venues were open, he used to take some players to the Carlton Brewery, where he worked as a foreman, to sample some of the beer. He rarely swore, and he greeted players with a broad smile and a handshake after a victory. At the same time, he was a disciplinarian. Bruce Andrew remembered that 'we were terrified of him. His word was law'. When Collingwood lost he reacted badly and made no attempt to hide his disappointment. Jock probably mellowed a little over the years. Len Fitzgerald recalled that he was 'a nice old bloke'. Bob Rose, who started playing when McHale's coaching career was coming to an end, remembered that 'he instilled in me and all the players that great love and team spirit and respect for each other and the club'.

Second, Ern Copeland, secretary from 1894 to 1924, dominated the administration. Such is the stature of the Collingwood Football Club that the name given to its best and fairest award — the Copeland Trophy — remains the only club award that is widely known by name among the football public. Copeland imposed his stamp on the club early on by insisting on high standards of discipline among the players. Unlike his counterparts at many other clubs, Copeland did not offer surreptitious payments to star players and potential recruits and, when professionalism became legal in 1911, Collingwood started a policy of paying all players equally. Equal pay for everyone, including the coach, reflected the view that no individual was more important than the team. Frank Wraith, who was secretary from 1930 to 1950, is less well known, but he continued to apply the Copeland philosophy during the most successful era in Collingwood's history. The club maintained that to pay one player more than another 'would lead to personal jealousies and discontent and would inevitably destroy that fine team spirit'. Under Wraith's tenure the club looked after players by helping them to find jobs and by establishing the game's first provident fund, which paid players a lump sum upon retirement based on the number of games played.

Third, John Wren was associated with the club from 1895 until his death in 1953. A product of the Collingwood area who became a millionaire through his betting shop and wide range of other business interests, Wren was a patron of the club and an important political contact. Contrary to popular belief, the Collingwood Football Club was not bankrolled or run by Wren. As Richard Stremski writes, Wren's lengthy involvement with the club has spawned a number of myths. 'Although he became a benefactor of the club after World War I in terms of political clout, favours, outings and rewards to players for outstanding efforts, his direct financial support to either the Club or the team has been wrongly perceived or exaggerated.'

The team spirit, and the administrative practices that were designed to encourage it, brought success and prestige to the Collingwood Football Club. Yet this very success could also create problems for the club. The policy of not making extra payments to star players caused many Collingwood players to listen to other coaching offers, and several left the club while they were still capable of being effective players. The administration's exclusive focus on the well-being of the club meant that the interests of individual players were at times taken for granted. While Collingwood's success won the admiration of other clubs, it seems clear that in some cases this was mixed with envy, especially at the administrative level. Collingwood usually won no favours when League delegates met to resolve disputes, and its players were often dealt with harshly by the League tribunal. As a result, football's happiest and most successful club could at times become a place of bitterness and disappointment.

The careers of Harry and Albert Collier are a perfect vantage point from which to observe these contradictions. The brothers were products of the Collingwood area and their loyalty to the club was total. But both were prepared to stand up to the administration to defend their or other players' rights. Albert went coaching in Tasmania for two years, when he was in his prime as a footballer, after the club was unable to find him a job and refused to make extra payments to him. Albert's case offers a clear piece of evidence that there was a limit to what John Wren could do, or was willing to do, to help the club and its players. The Colliers were hard but fair players but both received lengthy and almost certainly unjust suspensions from the VFL tribunal. Harry was improperly denied a Brownlow Medal on the grounds of a technical breach of the voting rules by an umpire. They gave their club magnificent service but, as their playing careers neared the end, they were treated insensitively by the administration.

Part of Collingwood

Albert and Harry Collier were grandchildren of Daniel Collier whose parents were from Guernsey. Born in 1852, Daniel was four years old when his mother made the voyage to Australia, accompanied only by her six children. When Daniel was aged 21 he married Kate Redmond, an immigrant from Ireland; the first of their nine children, Albert Augustus Collier, was born in Collingwood in 1873. In 1898, Albert married Hannah Binks and they rented a house at 13 Turner Street, Abbotsford. One of Albert's brothers, Harry Edward Collier, lived next door. The City of Collingwood rate books list Albert's occupation as a signwriter, and Harry's as a painter, and they may well have been in business together. Albert and Hannah's sixth child, Harry, was born in 1907. Another son, Albert Jr, was born almost two years later. Eventually the family grew to ten children, six of them boys.

Part of Turner Street runs along the outer side of Victoria Park, and the Colliers' house was near the turnstiles at the south-west corner of the ground. A single-storey terrace of only two main rooms, the house was small even by the standards of the Collingwood area, where houses were typically of three or four rooms. The Colliers' house would have had a lean-to kitchen and laundry, and perhaps a sleep-out in the backyard. Although the family later moved to a more substantial two-storey house with four main rooms, in Hotham Street, just across Hoddle Street in Collingwood proper, it is likely that the household remained crowded. Harry remembered that the last of the six brothers in bed each night had to sleep on the floor. Two of the brothers were twins named Ernest and Herbert, but dubbed 'Bluey' and 'Pinky' to tell them apart; Harry and Albert Jr could never remember the twins' real names. Albert Jr was almost always known as 'Leeter'. Some writers have suggested that this was a variation on 'leader', and would thus probably have been given to him after he became a League footballer. In fact, Albert Jr told Richard Stremski that the nickname originated shortly after his birth, when an Italian lady who lived in the same street visited him and his mother. She was later overheard telling people that 'Mrs Collier's had another little baby'. With her strong accent the word 'little' was interpreted as sounding like 'leeter'. The nickname stuck because it was used to distinguish him from his father.

The Colliers were a respectable working-class family. The children were taught to show consideration for others and address adults formally. Len Fitzgerald grew up in a nearby street, and he remembers that Harry and Leeter 'were terrific blokes. They were a terrific family and their parents were nice people as well'.

Harry and Leeter were inseparable. They went to school at Victoria Park State, across the road on the other side of the football ground, and they spent every afternoon and evening kicking a ball on the ground, and then watching training. 'You were part of Collingwood, in your own way, you thought', was how Leeter remembered his formative years. Like lots of other local kids, they continually tried to sneak into the training rooms to catch a glimpse of the players. On match days, they earned pocket money by selling VFL programs — then called the *Football Record* — outside the ground. They organised their own matches among the local kids and played football for their school. All of the Collier brothers played football — at one time all six played for Ivanhoe — but Harry and Leeter had most of the family's sporting talent. In summer, they played cricket and also took an interest in swimming and running. Harry represented Victoria in a schoolboys' football carnival in Sydney, and Leeter later captained Victoria's schoolboys' football and cricket teams.

After Harry won the club's best and fairest at Ivanhoe in 1924 he was invited to try out at Collingwood. Unfortunately, he injured his knee and was not fit to make his debut until early in the 1926 season. It was almost inevitable that Leeter joined Collingwood at some stage but, when he did join the club, it was under unusual circumstances. Leeter was playing cricket for the Collingwood firsts and as the 1925–6 season drew to a close the football club secretary, George Connor, asked if he would like to have a run and meet James McHale. 'Here's a young fellow who's been playing cricket,' said Connor when he introduced Collier and McHale. 'He's a pretty keen footballer, too. I'd like to see you give him a run, Jim.' Leeter later told Stremski that he remembered McHale pointing a finger, which had a pronounced bend in it, and asking him, 'How old are you, laddie?'

'I'm 15, Mr McHale.'

'Oh, you're too young to be playing here. I only started when I was 16.'

Leeter looked at Connor, who noticed the disappointment in his face. 'Well, he's brought his togs tonight, Jim,' Connor said. 'Let him go out on the ground and have a run.'

'Alright sonny,' said McHale. 'You can go out on the ground, but keep away from those big fellas, you'll get killed out there.'

Leeter recalled thinking to himself: 'you bloody old fool. If you can do something I can possibly do it . . . [On the ground,] I mowed into every big and small bloke as much as I could'.

Leeter Collier is probably the most precocious footballer ever to have played the game. Shortly after his first training run, Leeter was playing in the last cricket match of the season at Victoria Park. As soon as the cricket match finished, Collingwood footballers ran out onto the field for an internal practice match. One of the teams was one short and someone asked Leeter to fill in. He borrowed a bicycle and went home to get his gear. No-one was playing at full-forward, so he took the position and ended up kicking six goals. He was still aged 15 when he was selected for the seniors in the opening round of 1925. He caught the train to Windy Hill and although his 'guts were churning all the time' he was confident enough to attempt a long placekick for goal after taking his first mark. Despite his youth and his parents having taught him to show respect to his elders, Leeter was more than prepared to speak up and put himself forward in adult company if he believed that he was in the right. Towards the end of the 1925 season, Leeter was playing in the reserves and he and another player, George Clayden, defied Jock McHale by refusing to play in the seniors, and telling him so to his face, so that they could qualify to play in the reserves' finals. There were fully-grown men at Collingwood who were afraid of McHale; Leeter had only just turned 16. When Bruce Andrew played his first game, a Fitzroy player crashed him to the ground after he had taken his first mark. As Andrew looked up he saw the Fitzroy player lying on the ground, with Leeter Collier standing over him. 'Now look, son,' Collier said to Andrew, 'don't worry about these fellas. We'll look after you.' While that comment might suggest that Leeter was by then a seasoned veteran, he was in fact aged 18, and 17 months younger than Andrew was. Collier was a players' representative on the committee at 19. He won the Brownlow Medal in 1929 when he was 20 years old.

Leeter saw it as his job to protect his team-mates, especially the smaller ones. Carlton's Jack Hale, who played with him in interstate matches, recalled that Collier told him before matches that he would use a grunt to let Hale know that he was behind him, keeping potential opponents at bay. 'He was *tough*,' Hale told Mike Williamson. 'Never said too much, but he was there'. Leeter also expected his team-mates to come to each other's assistance. Alby Pannam remembered that he had stood back rather than become involved in a skirmish in his first match. 'You do that again,' Leeter told him, 'and you'll get a kick in the backside from me.' Leeter told Stremski that if a new player was in the side he would usually look for him to give him a handball 'to give him a bit of a go'. That also says much about Leeter's ability to read the game and the amount of time he had to dispose of the ball. Standing just a shade less than six foot tall and playing mostly at centre half-back, Leeter's kicking skills were superb and as a young player he was a brilliant high mark. In the final game of the 1930 Carnival in Adelaide, Leeter had 28 kicks and took 12 marks. *The Age* commented that his opponents 'seemed overawed at having to compete against Victoria's champion centre half-back'. After Leeter burst through a pack one day, McHale himself commented, 'God! Nobody could stop that, could they?'

There were good judges of football who thought that Leeter Collier was one of the greatest players, if not the greatest, of all time. Bruce Andrew, who was involved with football for around 60 years as a player, journalist and administrator, was of the opinion that:

> If you're going to ask me to name for you two players who could play anywhere, I would link Albert Collier — Brownlow Medallist at 20, centre half-back, in the ruck, centre half-forward, who could drop kick a mile, stab kick and make sure the lace hit you in the belly button. Magnificent all-round player, and of course, a protector. He had everything. Having played alongside him for all those years, I rank him right up with Teddy Whitten.

Norm Smith wrote in 1962 that:

> Forced to pick a VFL team from the all-time greats, I would make Collingwood's Albert 'Leeter' Collier my first selection. He was a brilliant footballer and the best team man I have ever seen. He could make his team revolve around him. I first saw him play at centre half-back. I can still remember his great pace, soaring high marks and wonderful kicking. He was still a great player when I started football in 1935. Then I was able to appreciate his inspiring team work. He was no longer the brilliant player I idolised as a boy, but his team work made him one of the greats of football. He could do more with a hand pass than most players. In a match he might have had less than 10 kicks in a day, but he would wreck his opponents with uncanny hand passing. He protected his team and did the bulk of the heavy work. The way he could make the team play around him was something to see.

Leeter was not the only Collingwood player to use handball as a method of team play. After the flick pass was outlawed in 1927, Collingwood adapted quickly to the requirement that the ball had to be struck with a clenched fist. Ivor Warne-Smith wrote in *The Argus* after a game in 1933 that:

> Collingwood on Saturday against Melbourne used handball to perfection, and at times had the opposition completely bewildered. The general plan adopted was simple. Collingwood has used the same method for many years, and still manages to succeed with it. If two or three of its men are chasing the ball and are followed by two or three opponents they allow one man only to go for the pick up and one man probably shepherds. All three opponents generally try to pounce on the Collingwood player who is picking up the ball, and, surrounded by all his opponents, this player punches it over to the third player, who has kept running and has obligingly been given a clear field. Should the third player be collared by anyone else in the vicinity the player who has been shepherding is generally following, still in the

> direct line for goal, and waiting to receive a hand pass from his team mate. This is following Collingwood's main system of backing up and taking the nearest straight line for goal. It wins many matches.

It is unclear what role Jock McHale played in the development of this handballing game. Several players from that era have acknowledged that Jock was not a great teacher of skills; rather, his method was to identify the particular skill that a player needed to work on, and then leave the player to work out how to perform and practise it. It may have been the club's most skilled players who passed on the basic features of the method to others. Leeter said that he and Harry acted as de facto 'assistant coaches' to McHale by ensuring that new recruits blended in and conformed to the team plan. Leeter used to encourage them to run past the senior players at training and call out for a handball. On the field he was equally at home in winning the hard ball, crashing through a pack and disposing of the ball creatively, as he was at shepherding and talking to his team-mates.

Collingwood's string of flags in the late 1920s and the 1930s was the work of a champion team. As 'Old Boy', *The Argus*'s football writer, commented after the 1928 grand final, 'Collingwood had no man in the colours who did not shine. Every man pulled his weight'. Even surrounded by such excellence, however, Leeter Collier's play stood out like a beacon. In six premiership-winning teams, only his performance in the 1930 grand final, in which he 'spoilt his play by undue attention to the man, and incurred the displeasure of the umpire and the crowd', was less than outstanding. *The Argus*'s football writers noted that he 'led the defence' in 1927, was 'specially commended' in 1928, 'did great work' in 1929, 'inspired the Collingwood team' in 1935, and was 'an inspiration in the ruck' in 1936.

Harry Collier was not the brilliant player that his brother was; in pace and skills, he fell short of the great rovers of his era, such as Haydn Bunton and Dick Reynolds. But he was adept at reading the play and crumbing the ball off packs, and he had accurate disposal skills. *The Argus* described his play in the 1929 grand final as 'clever, cool and reliable'. As his team-mate Percy Bowyer put it, Harry was a very fair player but if anyone got in his way he did not hesitate to meet him with a hip and shoulder. Like his brother, he always supported team-mates who were in trouble. Leeter recalled one game when a Fitzroy player threw a punch at him, which he just managed to avoid. In an instant Harry had knocked the Fitzroy player down; when he got to his feet he said, 'So, I've got to fight both the Collier brothers, have I?' 'That's right,' said Harry.

Harry was just the man to build and maintain team spirit at the club. He made sure that new players were welcomed, especially the 'strays', as he called them, who came from outside Collingwood's metropolitan area. The Colliers themselves were Protestants, living in a predominantly Catholic suburb, but the issue of sectarianism did not affect the club's unity or morale. As Harry put it, 'You were one way, you knew the other bloke was another way, but you were all cobbers'. Harry led the riotous celebrations at Victoria Park after the 1935 premiership, but later that night he crashed his car into the front fence of Archbishop Mannix's house. The players celebrated the premiership the following year in a quieter setting, at Hannah Collier's house.

Harry's greatest value to Collingwood was as an on-field leader. He was captain from 1935 to 1939 and in each of those five years the Magpies made the grand final. Harry told Richard Stremski that 'there were 18 blokes that could have been captain. All that was wanted was a bit of advice, I'd say'. He was being too modest. Teams at that time needed a good captain because coaches could not use a runner to send out messages, and had no opportunity to speak to their players from the time they ran onto the field until half-time. Syd Coventry led the 1927–30 teams with distinction, and Harry proved to be a worthy successor after Coventry left the club at the end of 1934 to coach Footscray. Collingwood captains were given free reign by McHale to make positional changes as they saw fit. Harry could think on his feet in match situations and listened and responded tactfully when other senior players suggested possible moves. Furthermore, his determined style set a perfect example for the rest of the team. Warne-Smith wrote after the 1935 grand final that 'Harry Collier, in his first year of captaincy, not only led the side capably to the premiership, but played a sterling game'. In 1937 Harry 'also played a captain's part, directed his team well, and led nearly every winning move. It was not his fault that Collingwood lost'.

Perhaps there was no better illustration of Harry's leadership qualities than his performance in the 1936 grand final. He had injured his shoulder and hand in the second semifinal, and had a quiet game in the grand final. Late in the last quarter the Magpies were clinging to a lead of only a few points when South's wingman, Jim Reid, gathered the ball forward of the centre and raced towards goal, with only Harry standing in his way. Reid tried to run around Collier but, as Harry put it, Reid 'ran into my arms'. Collingwood collected the loose ball and Leeter 'coolly passed over' to Phonse Kyne, whose goal gave the team a crucial break. It was one of many cases in which, as Warne-Smith had written the previous year, 'Collingwood owes a lot to the Collier brothers'.

Side by side they stick together

When Harry Collier first went to Collingwood as a player, he 'didn't think you got paid'. As Collingwood lads, the honour of receiving a black-and-white guernsey was in itself a huge reward and they probably would have willingly paid a fee to play for the club. However, the money the boys received from football was an important issue to the Collier family. Harry and Leeter both had jobs but they lacked the disposable incomes that would have enabled them to play as amateurs. Harry, who had worked at the Carlton Brewery since 1926, recalled that, before he married in 1930, he and Leeter gave around half of the money they made from football to their father and mother to help them support the family. The remainder of their football wages was banked, to keep it safe for a rainy day.

The Great Depression left manual workers like Albert Collier Sr vulnerable to unemployment and wage cuts. Harry and Leeter kept digging into their savings as their father found work harder to come by. Harry remained in work but by the end of 1930 Leeter had no job, possibly because he had been working as his father's apprentice. Another explanation for the family's precarious financial position may have been the health of Albert Collier Sr, who died in 1933 from a perforated ulcer and may have been unable to work for several years. Leeter was one of many League footballers who were unable to find work, but in these tough times Collingwood's team spirit remained strong. When the club reduced match payments from £3 to £2 10s during the 1928 season, the players met and considered a motion, which was seconded by Leeter Collier, that they refuse to play for £2 10s. But as Stremski writes, when Syd Coventry expressed his opposition to this, 'his adamant stand stifled dissent at the meeting, and the strong bond among the players prevented any recriminations'. There was a similar situation in 1932, when the players met just before a match after rumours began circulating that match payments were about to be halved. The players took the field anyway, and the reduction turned out to be only to £2 10s and was paid back at the end of the season. While the players were looking after their own interests, they remained loyal to the club. As Leeter Collier put it, 'We'd have played for nothing'.

In 1930, the VFL's Coulter Law set a maximum match payment of £3; clubs were also permitted to pay an allowance of £3 per week to players who were unemployed. This was not huge money, but at least it was possible for players who were out of work to receive an income of £6 per week, which was 50 per cent above the basic wage. Although the Coulter Law was designed to help the financially weaker clubs, only Collingwood and Carlton could afford to pay the full match payment of £3. During the Depression, North Melbourne could only afford to pay half this and Melbourne and Hawthorn did not pay their players at all. Although the Collingwood Football Club attempted to find jobs for unemployed players, the policy of equal pay for all players was adhered to strictly. Players who were unemployed received no allowances and when Leeter Collier was out of work his request for an allowance was rejected by Frank Wraith.

Leeter's response was to listen to an offer from Cananore, a Tasmanian club. It was a generous one — £9 per week as playing coach, plus a guaranteed job as a builder's labourer at £7 per week — but Leeter never really wanted to leave Collingwood. There was no doubt that the Magpies could have found the extra £3 per week to pay one of its most important players an allowance that would have kept him at the club, but refused to do so as a matter of principle. Leeter was not prepared to back down either so he went to Tasmania for two years. He won the Leitch Medal for the best and fairest player in the Tasmanian Football League in 1931 and coached Cananore to a premiership. When Leeter returned to Melbourne at the end of 1932, possibly to be with his ill father, Collingwood tried to find a job for him, but this proved difficult until John Wren pulled some strings at the Carlton Brewery, where a job as a painter was found.

It seems unlikely that there was any lingering resentment at the club towards the Colliers over this episode. While Leeter had been away, Collingwood had finished only in fourth and third positions in 1931 and 1932 respectively, and the club welcomed him back with open arms. Both the Colliers remained indefatigable defenders of their team-mates' rights. Leeter was moved into the ruck and willingly shouldered the burden of protecting other members of the team. In doing so he took risks which on occasions led to him being reported, and Harry, who by now was a member of the committee, was able to argue successfully that his brother was entitled to receive match payments while he was suspended. As a selector, Harry fought tooth and nail against dropping any player who was temporarily out of form. There is no evidence that the club regarded either of the brothers as troublemakers. Harry became club captain and Leeter took on the role when his brother was unavailable.

There was a healthy mutual respect between Leeter Collier and Frank Wraith. Leeter always knew that, beneath Wraith's penny-pinching, there lay a genuine concern for the well-being of Collingwood and its players. When Leeter was recovering from an injured knee in 1939, Wraith asked him if he would take over the job of coaching the seconds until he regained full fitness — the regular seconds' coach Hugh Thomas had left the club. Collier agreed, but was shocked when he received his next pay packet in which his wage had been halved to 30 shillings per week. When Collier asked Wraith about this he was told, 'Well, that's what the [seconds'] coach gets'.

Collingwood's wage structure was literally an open book, and when Leeter collected his pay one day he noticed on Wraith's ledger that some players were being paid expenses for travelling to and from training. Leeter told Wraith that he wanted to claim his travelling expenses. 'Alright Albert,' said Wraith, with a smile on his face. The secretary then calculated that if Collier took a tram ride from the brewery to Collingwood, which cost tuppence, and walked home after training, he was therefore entitled to the sum of fourpence per week in travelling expenses. Even Leeter laughed when he recalled that.

Shabby treatment

For the most part, football was good to the Collier brothers. They lived out their boyhood dreams by winning places in the local team that they loved, and became key players and leaders in one of the greatest teams of all time. They were idolised at Collingwood and won the respect, and at times admiration, of opposition players, officials and fans. Yet it is possible to identify four occasions when the Collier's football careers were adversely affected by decisions made by the game's administrators. Three of them were made by the delegates of the VFL, but the fourth was made by the Collingwood Football Club itself. In each case it seems clear that these decisions were unjust.

The first case involved the counting of votes in the 1930 Brownlow Medal. At that time, the umpires awarded only one vote for the best player on the ground. In 1930, when all votes had been declared counted, three players were tied on four votes each: Richmond's Stan Judkins, Footscray's Harold Hopkins, and Harry Collier. Leeter Collier finished with three votes. One vote, however, had been unrecorded. Umpire Bill Blackburn had simply written 'Collier' on one ballot paper. If the vote had been for Harry he would have won the medal outright; if the vote had been for Leeter the result would have been a four-way tie. When queried by the VFL's permit and umpires subcommittee, Blackburn said that he meant 'that little rover feller'. The subcommittee decided not to accept Blackburn's vote and it remained unrecorded. There were no League rules at the time to cover the event of a tie in the Brownlow Medal, and although the subcommittee recommended that no medal be awarded that year, the League president ruled on an *ad hoc* basis to award the medal to Judkins, on the grounds that he had played the fewest games that season. The VFL changed its Brownlow Medal voting rules the following season; umpires now had to vote for the three best players in each game, and record the surname, initial and number of each player. That was tantamount to admitting that there had been flaws in the 1930 vote count. There is no doubt that Harry Collier deserved to win a Brownlow Medal in 1930; although he was awarded one retrospectively in 1989 (as was Hopkins), he had to live almost 60 years of his life with the knowledge that he had been denied the game's highest individual honour at the whim of League officials.

Collingwood people could easily be forgiven for having thought that the actions of the League delegates were an expression of the resentment that the other League clubs felt towards the Magpies and their success. Those who subscribed to this view probably had their suspicions confirmed by three controversial suspensions in the late 1930s. Two of these involved the Colliers. At the time, reported players had their cases heard by a subcommittee of League delegates, rather than an independent tribunal. When Gordon Coventry was suspended for eight weeks in 1936, the fact that he had been provoked — his Richmond opponent had kept punching a crop of boils on the back of his neck in marking contests throughout the day — and had never been reported in a League career that by that time had extended to 287 games, apparently counted for nothing.

Early in the 1937 season, Leeter was walking off the ground at half-time during a rough match at North Melbourne. Next to the players' race, sections of the notorious Arden Street crowd were abusing and spitting on the Collingwood players. Leeter stayed close to one of his smaller team-mates to protect him, but as they walked up the race a woman swung an umbrella at them. What happened next is unclear, but the outcome was that a North Melbourne committeeman lodged a complaint to the League against Leeter for spitting on him. Leeter almost certainly said something to the crowd and in doing so spittle may have flown from his mouth. But, as Leeter stated in his interview with Stremski, it was not possible for him to spit intentionally because he played without his set of false teeth. The use of that simple defence would have been Leeter's wisest strategy, but before he appeared before the League's investigating committee Collingwood obtained legal advice that the investigating committee was not authorised under VFL rules to hear such a case. Leeter was instructed to make a statement to that effect to the committee, and then walk out of the room. When the chairman of the investigating committee, Lou Roberts, a Richmond delegate and former club president, insisted that Collier stay, Leeter walked out anyway. He was suspended for eight weeks for an unspecified offence, presumably one of misconduct for failing to obey a directive of a League official. The original charge of spitting was never heard.

At that time, the League was making a concerted effort to reduce the level of violence and foul play in what had become a very tough competition. That was certainly commendable. Leeter Collier was no angel: in 1936 he had been suspended for six matches for striking. But for all that, Leeter's suspension in 1937 must be judged as a scandal. Stremski writes that 'Wraith wanted to take the League to court over the matter since the arbitrariness and pettiness of the decision was an obvious denial of natural justice'. The club did not want to go to the expense of mounting a legal action, however, and let the matter drop. Leeter's suspension was served before the finals started, and during the time he was suspended John Wren paid him £5 per week. But for the rest of his playing career, and the rest of his life, Leeter had to live with the stigma that he was a 'spitter', which is a contemptible offence in the eyes of players and supporters. Years later, when he spoke to Stremski, Leeter remained upset by the issue and was convinced that 'I got six weeks for nothing'.

In 1938, the Carlton Football Club made an official complaint against Harry Collier on the grounds that he had struck a Carlton player as they were leaving the ground. Harry had been needled by a comment made by the Carlton player, who ended up with two stitches in his lip. Collier had been reported twice before — for kicking in 1929 and spitting in 1937 — but he had been found not guilty both times. Collingwood delegates were convinced that with Harry's record he would receive a reprimand or at the most a two-week suspension. Harry admitted the offence and apologised for his conduct. The League's investigating committee, again chaired by Lou Roberts, suspended him for the rest of the season, which ended up totalling 14 games.

Harry deserved some sort of penalty, but the harsh sentence he received was out of proportion to the offence he had committed. There was also a marked inconsistency between Collier's sentence and those handed out by the investigating committee during that season. In the 27 cases heard in 1938, 17 players were found guilty. Four of them received reprimands. Apart from Collier, 12 players were suspended and their sentences averaged 3.75 matches. Harry's 14 matches was the most severe suspension of the season. At a later League meeting, a Collingwood delegate tabled a petition signed by 2500 people requesting a review of the decision made by the investigating committee. This was defeated narrowly by a vote of club delegates. Harry's suspension stood, but the committee paid him full wages and Wren chipped in with £40 to help tide him over until the following season. The suspension was a double blow to Collingwood. The team missed Harry's leadership, especially during the grand final that year which was lost to Carlton by 15 points. McHale wanted Leeter to take over the leadership role, even though Leeter's game was restricted by a knee injury. Leeter did not want to play in the grand final but McHale insisted that he take the field.

Before the start of the 1940 season, the Collingwood committee suggested to the Collier brothers that it was time for them to retire. Neither wanted to but, at three-quarter-time in the final practice game, Harry and Leeter were told that they were going to be cut from the list. After the match it was announced that the Collier brothers had retired and that a testimonial fund would be established for them. Wren immediately contributed £200 and eventually £269 was raised through the fund. It is difficult to understand why the committee was so insistent that the Colliers were no longer required. They were clearly past their best but both were fit and Leeter was aged only 30. Once World War II started, the club struggled to put competitive teams on the field and, as Stremski concludes, 'the loss of the Colliers tore the heart out of the Collingwood side'. It is equally difficult to understand why the Colliers were treated this way when they clearly deserved something better after their years of devotion to the club. Harry was at least allowed to play one game in 1940 to qualify as a 15-year player, but when the senior coaching job became available at the end of 1949 the club failed to even acknowledge his letter of application. Leeter had become involved in club politics during the general election of 1939, but had done so as a supporter of the incumbent administration and remained a strong supporter of McHale and Wraith.

It seems likely that there was nothing personal in Collingwood's cavalier treatment of the Colliers. The administration was focussed on the well-being of the team rather than individuals. That philosophy served the club well during its golden era but, in the period just before World War II and then after it, Collingwood began to face tougher competition from other clubs. In an environment in which rival clubs, including those of the VFA and interstate, were competing to attract players, careful management of the well-being of players was needed to attract and retain quality recruits. During the 1940s, Collingwood was without the services of three champions — Ron Todd, Des Fothergill and Len Fitzgerald — who had left when they were in their prime but who might have been retained had the administration not taken the interests of individuals for granted. Collingwood did not win a premiership during this decade.

Leeter played for Fitzroy in 1941 before joining the RAAF while Harry captain-coached Essendon reserves to a premiership in 1941. When the VFA competition resumed after the war, Leeter was captain-coach of Camberwell and he took the perennially underachieving club to runner-up in 1946. At the age of 37, Leeter was still a fine player in a strong competition. In 1947 he left Camberwell to run a hotel and coach at Kyneton, and later that season Harry took over as captain-coach of Camberwell, despite being 40 years of age. Albert later took a coaching job at Sea Lake, where he met his wife, Mavis, who was a local nurse. Harry returned to Collingwood and served as a recruiter and talent scout during the 1950s and 1960s.

With players in tow he did countless road trips throughout Victoria and the Riverina, visiting schools and junior clubs to generate interest in Collingwood, and Australian Rules football in general. He served as chairman of selectors under Bob Rose and saw at close quarters the heartbreaking grand final losses of 1964, 1966 and 1970. He endured the other grand final losses of 1977, 1979, 1980 and 1981. Leeter passed away in 1988, but Harry lived to see Collingwood's drought-breaking premiership in 1990, the club's first in 32 years. After Harry died in 1994, his funeral service was held on the oval at Victoria Park.

Colden Harrison, as sketched by his daughter, Ruby Harrison, in 1884

Portrait of Colden Harrison (artist unknown)

Albert Thurgood 'brought art and culture into the game', as football historian C.C. Mullen put it.

Subiaco's 1913 premiership team. Captain-coach Phil Matson is seated behind the cup, fifth from the left.

A cartoonist's view of Matson the coach

A Collingwood selection committee meeting in 1937: (from left) Albert Collier, Harry Collier, secretary Frank Wraith, and committeeman Malcolm 'Doc' Seddon

Albert Collier, 'about to play on guts alone' with an injured knee, at the toss of the coin with Brighton Diggins at the start of the 1938 grand final

Albert Collier (left) at the Carlton Brewery, with foreman Jock McHale and workmate Brighton Diggins

A young Diggins, in action for Subiaco against East Fremantle, at Fremantle Oval

'On the ground you dream of playing on'. Brighton Diggins, in football boots, inspecting the surface of the MCG on the morning of the 1938 grand final

Port Adelaide's 1939 premiership team — 'perfectly coached', as one journalist recalled, by Bob Quinn (second row, third from right)

After his last game for Port Adelaide, the 1947 preliminary final, Bob Quinn is carried from the field by his vice-captain, Lew Roberts. West Adelaide captain, Johnny Taylor, offers his congratulations.

Bob Quinn

Bob Quinn is presented with his second Magarey Medal in 1945.

A club's tribute: the main stand at Port Adelaide's Alberton Oval

5

Brighton Diggins
(1906–1971)

Every man has a job to do and will not let Carlton down. We have no champions, but every player helps his team-mate and puts the team first.

BRIGHTON DIGGINS

When he was at school, Brighton Diggins was always getting into trouble. On the rare days that he was not sent to the headmaster to receive 'the cuts' — a leather strap over the palm of the hand — the headmaster would call into the classroom and ask, 'Is Diggins not at school?' It was not that he was a bad boy: he stayed out of serious trouble and as an adult became known and admired for his honesty, fairness and firm principles. It was not that he was unintelligent: as an adult he became an adept public speaker, a clear, perceptive writer and an excellent communicator. But as a boy Brighton was a problem for his teachers and parents because all he wanted to do was to kick a football.

Growing up in the sun and sand of Perth — then virtually a frontier town of scattered suburbs — Brighton led a Tom Sawyer-like existence. He and two of his brothers once stole some carrots from a Chinese market garden and, after the owner had chased them off with a shotgun, their father had to cut the pellets from their backsides with a penknife. The Indian Ocean at City Beach lay only about six kilometres from his house in the predominantly working-class suburb of Subiaco. Brighton and his friends used to walk there and spent hours swimming and playing games. They would often stay there all night, eating and sleeping in a tent they had pitched in the sand dunes. Even when Brighton left school — at the age of 14 — he would often run to City Beach after work, spend the evening on the beach, and sleep in his tent. When he arrived to play his first game of football for Subiaco, at the age of 20, he was in bare feet because he had never worn football boots in his life.

Brighton's father, Arthur Diggins, built a tennis court in the backyard of his home to give his family of eight sons and four daughters something to do and hopefully keep the boys out of trouble. Brighton put it to use by doing standing jumps over the net to improve his spring. The rest of his time at home, it seemed, was spent working a punchball and skipping. At City Beach he swam and ran up and down the sand dunes. He was a natural athlete: although he shot up to six foot in height and filled out quickly, he retained an extraordinary level of running ability. By the standards of the day he was a physical giant, but he had pace and he could turn and manoeuvre like a rover. After a few seasons at a local junior club called Jolimont, where the game was rough and ready and the players received no formal coaching, he was invited to try out with the district's senior club, Subiaco.

He had been born in 1906 and christened John Bryton Diggins. 'My parents started to call me "Brighton" when I was a nipper,' he told a reporter. 'I don't know exactly why, but I think it was after an uncle of mine of that name.' Arthur Diggins was a native of Victoria, whose parents had come out from England during the gold rush. Arthur had moved to Perth during the depression of the 1890s when thousands of young people left Victoria and headed for the goldfields of Western Australia. Arthur was an engineer working at a foundry when he married Lucy Mountain. They built a house in Subiaco, one of the Perth suburbs that boomed during the 1890s and 1900s. A high proportion of Subiaco's population was made up of Victorian tradesmen who built their own cottages in their spare time. Such people had headed west because jobs and opportunities were more plentiful there than in Victoria; ironically, by the end of the 1920s many of their children were ready to head to the eastern states because of the depressed and uncertain state of the Western Australian economy.

Brighton was one of several talented youngsters who made their way into the Subiaco team in the late 1920s. He made his debut in the opening round of 1927 and was a consistent performer, playing mostly on the back line. After only a few games, the *W.A. Footballer* predicted that 'his name should become a household word in the vastness of Subiaco and the State generally'. Later that season, when the Western Australian team was away at the carnival in Melbourne, Diggins was selected in a second Western Australian side chosen to playing against a touring Collingwood team. Still only 20, Diggins more than held his own against the Victorians and, by the time of the 1930 Carnival in Adelaide, he had developed into a ruckman. The Melbourne press noted his play approvingly, and in the game against Victoria he 'outmarked and outbumped' the opposition rucks.

By now, the effects of the Great Depression were biting hard. The Western Australian economy was particularly vulnerable because it was dominated by wheat growing, which was affected by falling prices and drought. Perth existed essentially as a commercial centre for its rural hinterland so was less industrialised than Melbourne or Sydney. Thousands of young men were out of work and depended on government handouts. It was inevitable that promising footballers, who in Perth played basically for the love of the game, would listen to the offers made by VFL clubs with money to spend on match payments and, more importantly, that could arrange jobs for recruits. In 1930, Subiaco's Len Metherall went to Geelong, as did Claremont's George Moloney in the following year. The Ford Motor Company had opened a factory in Geelong in 1925 and had a close relationship with the football club. Metherall and Moloney played in Geelong's premiership team of 1931, and this was the beginning of a large-scale movement of players from the West to Victoria.

A Perth reporter once wrote that 'Diggins seems to derive as much enjoyment from the game as do the spectators from his spectacular efforts'. The game had been easy and uncomplicated while he was growing up, but now there were deeper and more complex issues associated with it that had to be thought through. He had little formal education and his job of driving a delivery van for a department store was not secure. In 1929, Brighton had married Amanda Murphy. Their first child died as an infant and by the end of 1931 Amanda was pregnant again. Arthur Diggins was by now in poor health and needed financial assistance from his older sons to support his large family. Had jobs in Perth been plentiful, or had Subiaco been able to find him a job, Brighton might have stayed in his home town. But in 1931, Brighton simply could not afford to overlook any opportunity presented to him to use his football talent to secure his family's financial future. That meant he would have to move to Melbourne.

The best that money could buy

By the early 1930s, Archie Crofts had got into the habit of starting each working day by saying 'I wonder what my subjects will have to say about me today?' Crofts's kingdom was a chain of over a hundred grocery stores, each with lucrative wine and spirits licences. This business empire, which extended throughout Victoria and the Riverina and employed over 700 people, had started in 1905 when Crofts bought a grocery store in South Melbourne. Crofts was a loyal, community-minded citizen of South Melbourne, and it dismayed him that the rise of his grocery empire coincided with the steady decline of the South Melbourne Football Club.

When the first Crofts store opened, South Melbourne was the most heavily populated suburb in Melbourne. South had been a powerful VFA club and won its first VFL flag in 1909. The spacious Lake Oval, located in the heart of South Melbourne, was close to train and tram services and the club had visions of developing it into Melbourne's second major football venue. After winning the premiership in 1918, however, South's fortunes went into a downward spiral. Lack of success on the field reduced gate takings and memberships, which made it difficult to recruit and retain quality players. By 1929, the club was operating an overdraft of £780 and in the following year could not afford to pay its players until the end of the season. The club had not developed contacts with local businesspeople who could offer jobs to prospective recruits. A strong Roman Catholic element within the committee and the supporter base meant that the club was less than welcoming towards potential players and supporters who were not Catholic.

At the end of the 1931 season, club president Jack Rohan persuaded Archie Crofts to become vice-president. The club was in such a parlous financial state that the committee was prepared to overlook the fact that Crofts was a Protestant. As patron of the club, Crofts would use his personal wealth to pay players the maximum of £3 per game that was allowable under the Coulter Law, and more importantly, in an era when unemployment rates in Australia stood at around 30 per cent, provide jobs at his stores for recruits. Former Subiaco player John Leonard was appointed captain-coach, as much for his knowledge of and contacts with footballers in Western Australia as for his considerable playing and leadership abilities. Leonard was a Freemason and so was his first signing, Brighton Diggins. Another Subiaco player, Billy Faul, and Bert 'Bluey' Beard from Kalgoorlie completed a quartet of Western Australian recruits. The club would eventually attract so many Western Australians that the *Sporting Globe*'s football writer Hec de Lacy suggested that the club change its nickname to 'The Swans'. There were other recruits from closer to home, such as Jack Bissett from Richmond and 17-year-old Herbie Matthews from VFA club Northcote. In subsequent years, more recruits crossed from Western Australia, and from South Australia, Tasmania and country Victoria as well, and the team became known as the 'Foreign Legion'.

South Melbourne began the 1932 season wearing a new jumper, with a bright red 'V' replacing the red sash. Although the club was still known officially as 'the Bloodstained Angels', it began using a logo featuring a swan printed on its membership tickets. Under VFL rules the interstate recruits could not play until they had lived in Victoria for three months, but South still won its first ten games. The team already had several promising youngsters, such as 19-year-old full-forward Bob Pratt and rover Terry Brain, and some experienced players such as Austin Robertson and Peter Reville. Leonard added discipline to the team and encouraged it to play direct, long-kicking and attractive football. Under his coaching South's existing players improved and the recruits proved to be worth their salt.

Any doubts that may have existed about Diggins's ability to make the grade in Victoria were dispelled in his debut match, in which a crowd of 40 000 at the Lake Oval saw South take on the reigning premiers, Geelong. It was a thrilling game and Diggins later told reporters that 'I guess I've never seen that ball travel up and down the ground so fast before in my life'. South was trailing by three points with only a few minutes to go when Diggins 'leapt into the air, took a most spectacular mark and, with a prodigious punt, sent the ball sailing through the posts'. A further goal by Pratt increased the winning margin to nine points. *The Argus* commented that Diggins 'has height, weight, strength, and pace, and marks and kicks extremely well. For a big man he turns remarkably'. The following week another crowd of 40 000 was at Punt Road and, although the muddy conditions were not what Diggins was used to, 'he marked brilliantly ... and with forceful play repeatedly gave South the initiative'. One writer was of the view that:

> Perfectly built and very fast, Brighton Diggins ... is the nearest approach to the ideal footballer that the game has had in West Australia for many seasons. Standing just 6.0, he weighs 14.5, so that he is a follower that any club would welcome. There is nothing of the lumbering solidity about him, for he is dashing and forceful.

By the end of the 1932 season, South had lost its momentum somewhat, partly because Diggins had broken his leg, just above the ankle, and follower Peter Reville had a broken arm. The team was eliminated in the first semifinal but over the season its improvement was substantial. Leonard returned to Western Australia for work reasons at the end of the 1932 season and was replaced as captain-coach by Bissett. Recruiting was stepped up. The charismatic Laurie Nash came from Tasmania, as did Ossie Bertram and Wilbur Harris from South Australian club West Torrens. James O'Meara from Kalgoorlie, who had been out of work for 18 months, crossed the Nullabor to join the club and Johnny Bowe from Subiaco contacted his former team-mate, Diggins, about the possibility of playing and working in Victoria.

In contrast to their brilliant start in 1932, South struggled for consistency in 1933. The first eight rounds yielded only four wins. Diggins then learned that his father was seriously ill and he immediately caught a train to Perth. Unfortunately, Arthur Diggins died before Brighton arrived. Brighton then stayed with his family in Perth and missed three matches. When he returned, South needed to defeat Carlton, one of the top teams, to stay in contention for a place in the top four. Diggins only made it back in time for the game by catching a ride on an airmail plane to Adelaide and then boarding the express train to Melbourne. His game was inspirational, and Ivor Warne-Smith wrote in *The Argus* that 'he marked superbly, and tore through crushes, coming out with the ball. His pace was surprising'. Pratt kicked 11 goals and the other ruckmen, Bisset and Beard, also returned to form. Victory that day boosted South's confidence, and after another big win the following week it was reported that:

> In those two games, South played phenomenal football — all at bewildering speed, and with remarkable accuracy. All their big men have swung into top form. Their ruck is practically unbeatable. The small men, also, are in irresistible fettle. The defenders, while not brilliant, are a tough bunch. The side, in short, is perfectly balanced, and revealing superlative teamwork. South's forte is speed, and plenty of it. Very effective is their lightning-like position play from half-back or the centre to the deadly Pratt, who marks and kicks goals as only a champion can. The starting point of many a successful attack is the amazing Diggins. His marking and long-distance kicking, allied with speed and judgement, stamp him as a match-winner.

In the final home-and-away round, South played Geelong. The winner would move into second place and receive a double chance in the finals. By now, South was almost unstoppable. 'They played like a machine', as one writer put it, and thrashed Geelong by 109 points. The Foreign Legion was now ready to mount a serious challenge for the flag.

In the second semifinal South, aiming for its tenth win in a row, trailed Richmond by 26 points at three-quarter-time. 'In five thrilling minutes, the whole aspect of the game changed sensationally' as South slammed on three quick goals. The eventual winning margin was 18 points. Diggins, who had been outstanding all day, played at centre half-forward, changing in the ruck. In the grand final, South was far too good for the Tigers. The continuing good form of South's rucks again allowed Diggins to play at centre half-forward, where his pace and strength held him in good stead in his battle with Richmond's rugged key defender, Joe Murdoch. Diggins 'was a constant menace to Richmond', reported the *Sporting Globe*. 'He was supreme in the air, and his long kicks were very telling.' Nash and Diggins were star performers 'but the eighteen as a team played fast and clever football, and proved a better balanced side than Richmond'.

South Melbourne's 1933 flag triumph should have been the first stage in its re-emergence as a football power. Diggins, Nash, Pratt and Matthews had years of football left in them. As one of only two VFL clubs south of the Yarra River, South Melbourne could have reasonably expected to become the Collingwood of Melbourne's southern suburbs. Membership, which stood at only 1900 in 1929, had risen to 6000 in 1934, the highest in the League. However, South was not able to string together a run of premierships as Collingwood had done, and as a club it never came close to developing the team spirit and strength of leadership that were the hallmarks of the Magpies. Collingwood and South Melbourne epitomised the football truism that 'a champion team will always beat a team of champions'. The differences between the two teams were never more apparent than in the 1935 finals series. South played brilliantly during the home-and-away rounds, but in the grand final Collingwood rose to the occasion 'and matched careful organisation and teamwork against the skill and pace of the Southerners'. Close-checking tactics were used to crowd the play and prevent South's players from getting the ball out into the open where they could move the ball quickly. The Foreign Legion was capable of playing brilliantly as a team, as it showed in the 1933 grand final, but this was less likely to happen when the opposition was able to bottle up the game. In the 1935 grand final, many of South's players became rattled as 'play became crowded, tempers became frayed, and at times open hostilities occurred'. Norm Smith was able to observe that 'it always appeared to me that South's players played too much as individuals and not enough as a team' because in grand finals, the matches that counted, Richmond in 1934 and Collingwood in 1935 and 1936 beat South by continuing to play as a team once the game became physical.

Diggins was one South player who was not fazed by the pressure of the 1935 grand final. While his pace made him suited to a game in which play was open, he also had the strength and courage needed to cope with more physical encounters.

> Once again, Brighton Diggins was the outstanding South player throughout the game. Undisturbed by the vigorous encounters and manhandling, Diggins played on; his cool, complacent demeanour being an object lesson to the hot-headed and erratic players . . . In one of the unnecessary melees, two Collingwood players grounded Diggins. One of his opponents was apparently seeking trouble. South's burly ruckman calmly pushed his opponent, sprang to his feet, and pursued his all-day object — the ball. In the heated exchanges, with tempers ruffled, arms swinging, generally terminating in belligerent attitudes, Diggins was the peace-maker.

Jack Dyer called the Foreign Legion 'the greatest collection of stars I have ever seen gathered in a side', but its success as a team depended heavily on the contribution of three players: Nash, Pratt and Diggins. South relied on the marking, pace and brute strength of Nash at centre half-back and of Diggins in the ruck and at centre half-forward to win balls that were in dispute and bring other players into the game. Both were beautiful kicks who usually sent the ball long to the advantage of their team-mates. Most of the other players in the team preferred the ball to be out in the open where they could use their pace to run onto it. Any South player who had control of the ball forward of the centre would usually send a long kick in the direction of Pratt. As Hec de Lacy wrote, when Pratt made a run for the ball and leapt to mark it 'he was like a fighter plane taking off'.

When the triumvirate of Nash, Pratt and Diggins were all fit and playing well, as they were in 1933, South was close to unbeatable. But when any of these three players was absent or not able to perform at his best the team struggled to cover their loss. There was thus a brittleness in the Foreign Legion that was exemplified by its defeats in the 1934–35–36 grand finals. In round 2 of the 1934 season, Diggins landed awkwardly in a match at Princes Park. His ankle was broken and dislocated. He did not return until the final home-and-away round and even then he was limping noticeably. He played in the grand final and was named as South's best player but he was obviously handicapped by the injury. 'Two or three times during the game, he was noticed in a stooping position, tenderly rubbing his foot, after which he limped around the oval until the ball came his way, when he forgot the pain of his disability, and hurled his massive frame into the fight with a courage and recklessness that compelled admiration of friend and foe.' Diggins was one of the few players who did not deserve to be criticised for what was a tame South Melbourne performance. Before the grand final, Pratt had kicked 148 goals in 20 games, but Richmond played three defenders on him to crowd him and he scored only two further goals. In 1935, Pratt missed the grand final after being knocked over accidentally by a truck carrying a five-tonne load of bricks as he stepped off a tram the night before the game. In the first quarter of the 1936 second semifinal, Collingwood's Len Murphy hit Diggins in the jaw, for which he was later suspended for eight matches. Diggins was in a vulnerable position because his eyes were on the play downfield and his mouth was open as he shouted instructions to a team-mate. He was very groggy when the trainers lifted him and took him to the forward pocket. At half-time the club doctor found that Diggins's jaw had been broken in two places, and his jaw and teeth later had to be wired together. The grand final was a close one, and South clearly missed Diggins's presence.

Collingwood's team spirit contrasted sharply with that at South Melbourne. In 1935, the two clubs went on a mid-season tour to play exhibition matches in Brisbane, Newcastle and Sydney and on the return trip the teams found themselves on the same train. Harry Collier recalled that the Collingwood committee, realising that the trip could serve to strengthen the bonds between its players, had turned on beer, soft drinks and food for its players, while South's players had been provided with nothing. 'We shared with them — we were all cobbers in those days,' Collier said, but South's players could not have helped but notice that the Collingwood committee was taking much better care of the welfare of its players than the South committee did. South's administration may have tended to take its players for granted because it felt entitled to expect unquestioning loyalty in return for having provided players with jobs during difficult times.

The beginnings of Brighton Diggins's problems with the South committee can be traced back to the end of the 1933 season when Diggins was invited to join Melbourne as captain. The South committee persuaded him to stay by promising to appoint him as captain when Bissett retired. That was good enough for Brighton, and for the next three seasons he was happy to serve as vice-captain to Bissett and take over as coach when Bissett, who was nearing the end of his career, was injured. At the end of the 1935 season, the committee assumed that Bissett, who had fractured his skull and been badly concussed in the grand final, would be retiring. The position of coach was advertised, and Diggins, who was popular with the players and the choice of most supporters, was one of the applicants. Surprisingly, the committee reappointed Bissett. This did little to boost morale around the club and the 1936 pre-season 'was remarkable for its lack of spark and spirit'. A professional punter, Bissett did not play in the opening round because he had driven to the races before the game and returned too late to take his place in the team. When Bissett resigned at the end of season Diggins was once again one of the applicants for the coaching job, but the committee appointed Roy Cazaly as non-playing coach. Diggins could accept that, but the committee then reneged on its promise to give Diggins the captaincy when Bissett retired and appointed Nash instead. It was now perfectly clear that the South committee did not want Diggins as captain or coach under any circumstances, and that it had been less than honest in previous discussions with him about his future at the club. Diggins relinquished the vice-captaincy but announced that he would still like to continue as a player. South's response was to drop him from the team for the opening round of 1937. As Mark Branagan and Mike Lefebvre observe in their book, *Bloodstained Angels*, because the South committee knew that Diggins could not play for any other club without them giving him a clearance, it 'decided to nail him to the wall'.

This was madness. The team was in need of rebuilding and could ill afford to ignore a man with such impeccable leadership credentials as Brighton Diggins. The circumstances that had allowed South to assemble the Foreign Legion were now changing. By the end of 1936, the Depression was coming to an end and the promise of a job in a grocery store was no longer a wondrous lure to potential recruits. The VFL had extended its residential qualification period from three to twelve months, which made it more difficult to recruit players from other states. South needed a leader who would not only get the best out of the players, but also work hard at recruiting and developing strong links between the club and its local recruiting zone. Diggins was certainly willing to do that: he already took a strong interest in local junior teams, even coaching one of them. There was no more popular and respected player in League football. As one writer put it after a match against Carlton in 1935:

> 'Brighton Diggins'. The name that never draws anything but praise from friends or foes. 'Great fellow — great player, great sport' . . . The crowds are quick to sense a fair and manly footballer. In the hurly-burly of the rough and tumble at Carlton, Diggins kept his cool, worked like a Trojan, and set a splendid example of first-class football. As the dejected Southern supporters watched the departing athletes after the final bell, a special cheer went up from one group for the South Melbourne vice-captain. Continuing his trek to the rooms, Diggins looked around in search of Charlie Davey. From afar-off he espied Davey, and sent a cheery gesture of congratulations to his successful opponent. When this chap retires from the game, he will take away with him a reputation [as] . . . a gentleman of the game.

Unfortunately, the judgement of the South Melbourne administration was clouded at this critical time by sectarianism. Branagan and Lefebvre, who interviewed Pratt, concluded that, at South, Diggins and Pratt were always odd men out because they were Freemasons at a predominantly Catholic club. The players themselves seem to have had no problems with each other: for instance, Nash was a Catholic but Diggins got on well with him. But from some club officials there was an undercurrent of ill-feeling towards Diggins and Pratt that surfaced when their 'wives were ignored by committeemen at social functions or given the cold shoulder, [and] tickets were sometimes unavailable or misplaced'. The club's attitude towards Diggins would only have been strengthened when he and Amanda divorced. News of the divorce was kept out of the papers but was common knowledge to the South committee. Despite Diggins's 'performances and personal qualities, the committee was never as effusive about his talents and often kept him at arm's length'. When the issue came out into the open at the start of 1937, Diggins was told directly by the committee that a Freemason would never captain or coach the South Melbourne Football Club. There was no chance whatsoever that he would be able to fulfil his leadership ambitions at that club. The tragedy was that that information was kept from Diggins until he was aged 30. It was a shabby way to reward the five years of service he had given, and to run a football club.

'We have no champions'

When Brighton walked out of the Lake Oval clubrooms after being dropped, the only thing that he knew for sure was that he would never play for South Melbourne again. When he returned from work to his house at Albert Park the next day, he found that officials from nine VFL clubs had called and left their business cards, but his options were limited by South's refusal to clear him to play with another club and by him having only a few more years left as a player. Although Brighton was now single, he still supported his ex-wife and his daughter. He had already left his job with Crofts and was working at the Carlton Brewery where his foreman was Jock McHale. Brighton was happy there — he relished the hard labour of shovelling hops — and enjoyed living and playing League football in Melbourne. Nevertheless, it made sense for him to consider offers from football clubs outside of the VFL because these would have helped to set him up financially for the rest of his life.

A few weeks later, a party of Carlton officials including vice-president Kenneth Luke went to the Lake Oval and asked for permission to speak to Diggins. They were told that this was impossible as Diggins had returned to Perth. In fact, Brighton had taken leave from the brewery to visit one of his brothers in Perth who was seriously ill. Diggins spoke to officials of several Western Australian clubs and received an offer to become playing coach of Perth Football Club, which had already secured the services of his friend and former team-mate Austin Robertson. Perth's offer was a generous one — a substantial fee for coaching and a guaranteed job in a newspaper office — which Diggins accepted in principle but asked for more time to think things over. He told the Perth officials that his preference was to remain in Melbourne. He then received a letter from Ken Luke offering him the captain-coach position at Carlton. There were also approaches from country Victorian and VFA clubs to consider. It seemed that, everywhere he went, people stopped him in the street and asked him if he would be staying in Perth. To get away from it all, Brighton went back to his boyhood playground of City Beach and took long walks there while he made up his mind.

Diggins eventually chose to go to Carlton. He had known Ken Luke, a fellow member of a group of Freemasons called the Sportsman's Freemasons, for some time. Born in Brunswick in 1896, Luke served an apprenticeship as an engraver and left his original employer at the age of 24 to start his own firm based in a small factory in North Fitzroy. Eventually, Luke became the largest manufacturer in Australia of silverware, badges, hospital equipment and catering equipment. Although he was a flashy dresser, drove a black Buick and kept a stable of racehorses at his property at Romsey, Luke never lost the common touch. He employed hundreds of workers but mixed with them easily and seemed to know each of them by name, and many of them by nickname. As a supporter of the Carlton Football Club, Luke employed dozens of players over the years and provided temporary jobs for many country recruits when they first arrived in Melbourne. When Luke became president of Carlton in 1938, the club had not won a premiership since 1915 and he was determined to end the long drought. Many great players wore the navy blue guernsey during the 1920s and 1930s, but in pressure games the rest of the team fell away if any these champions was kept in check. Like South's Foreign Legion, Carlton was vulnerable to the tactics of 'champion teams' that manned up its stars and closed the game up with physical pressure. Luke's vision of how that trend might be reversed centred on recruiting a strong on-field leader who could teach the Carlton players how to cope with big-match pressure. Luke wanted Diggins as captain-coach and was finally able to negotiate his clearance from South Melbourne by exchanging one of Carlton's fringe players for him. In addition to his coaching fee, Diggins was promised a bonus of £150, paid out of Luke's own pocket, if he led Carlton to the 1938 flag.

Team spirit at Carlton was better than it had been at South Melbourne and players and officials of different religions had always got along well. Diggins had the total support of a stable, capable committee, but he still had to win the players over. Micky Crisp, one of the senior players, later wrote:

> Now, when Brighton came to Carlton he had had one or two barneys with South Melbourne. That's not my pigeon, but I say from what football experience I have had that a man who leaves a club in similar circumstances to those in which Brighton left South has to tread warily in his new surroundings. We all knew Brighton as an opponent, but Brighton as a team-mate — well, that was up to him.

Diggins earned the respect of the players simply by being himself, as a person and as a footballer. As Crisp put it:

> From the moment he walked into that training room he showed himself a gentleman. He was determined, he was forceful if needed. He never was a bully. His soft way of speaking might have suggested to some a lack of leadership — that was their funeral . . . Diggins was a man's man — that's where he succeeded this year. He drove us, he led us, but he always went with us. He was one of us. He was game. He never once asked us to go in where he would not go himself . . . I might have said, in shorter fashion, that he won our confidence.

Diggins worked hard to get the team fit. He started with himself: during the periods when he was inactive due to injury, he would usually put on around twenty kilograms and his bulk made it hard for him to get fit again. He hired a physical training expert to loosen and strengthen the players' muscles, concentrating on their abdominals and shoulders. Diggins's training routine included more running for speed and endurance than was the case at other clubs. He also used a technique copied from Geelong's Reg Hickey, which trained players for situations that were likely to occur in matches. This training helped younger players such as Bob Chitty, Ken Baxter and Paul Schmidt to mature, while older campaigners like Crisp, Jim Francis and Jack Wrout appreciated the novelty of Diggins's methods.

The 1938 Carlton team had the depth, evenness and strength that had been lacking in previous seasons. The defence was watertight. The ruck division, led from the front by Diggins, was solid and strong. Harry 'Soapy' Vallence had been Carlton's star full-forward for ten years, and although he was in his final VFL season the emergence of Baxter and Schmidt as productive forwards took a lot of pressure off him. The forward line also had a hard edge with Wrout at centre half-forward, and Rod McLean and rover Jack Hale resting in the forward pockets. Every Thursday before a game, Diggins would meet with Luke and his selection committee over lunch at Luke's factory to pick the team and discuss tactics. After the Blues showed their mettle with a one-point win in a rough game against Richmond, Warne-Smith commented that 'the side was not any better, individually or collectively, than it has been, but it stood firm against physical persuasion, came with a magnificent rally from behind to snatch a victory, and on doing so proved that Carlton as a team now has a courageous spirit'. To a man, the players now had confidence in themselves and in each other. After finishing on top of the ladder, they looked forward to running out onto what Diggins called 'the ground you dream of playing on' — the MCG at finals time. On the day before the grand final, Diggins told the press:

> Every man has a job to do and will not let Carlton down. We have no champions, but every player helps his team-mate and puts the team first.

The game once again pitted Diggins against a Collingwood team whose coaching, leadership and method of play he admired greatly. This time, it was Collingwood whose players were checked closely to prevent them from getting their teamwork going. Every Collingwood player was given an opponent who played him shoulder to shoulder and subjected him to physical pressure. Even Ken Baxter at full-forward played defensively, not moving from the goal square so that Jack Regan would be kept out of the game.

The one Collingwood player who was given no opponent was Albert Collier. Because Diggins worked with Collier, he knew that he was unfit and warned his players that anyone who touched Collier in any way would be replaced immediately. 'He's playing for us today,' he told them. Diggins was convinced that it was to Carlton's advantage to have a half-fit Collingwood player remaining on the field; Jock McHale's view was that his team needed a strong on-field leader, even one who was not fully fit, to have a chance of winning. Even though Carlton won the game, this does not necessarily mean that McHale was wrong: had Collier not played, Carlton might have won by a greater margin. (Contrary to myth, McHale did not attempt to gain an unfair advantage by ordering Diggins to work on the morning of the grand final: Diggins was photographed at the MCG that morning, wearing a suit and football boots, inspecting the playing surface.) One thing was undeniably true, however: in 1935 when Diggins had last played in a grand final, a key member of his team had been out injured; the year before that, Diggins himself had gone into the game carrying an injury. This time, when Diggins and Collier faced each other to toss the coin, it was Brighton who was fully fit and backed by a determined team. Albert was also leading a fine team, but his brother Harry was missing and he was the one carrying the injury and about to play on guts alone.

A record crowd of 96 834 somehow squeezed into the MCG to see the game. Thousands of people were locked out and thousands more sat on the oval between the fence and the boundary line. The game itself was thrilling. In Warne-Smith's words:

> The match was fought out on a man-to-man basis, in which no player was allowed to roam unguarded into open spaces. This style of play prevented an open and exhilarating game and the

> spoiling tactics helped to crowd the game and to make errors, but with it all the terrific pace, the brilliant marking, the splendid teamwork and shepherding of both sides, and the tense finish made an entertainment which will be long remembered.

Collingwood got close on several occasions and trailed by only a few points late in the game. Carlton was always able to absorb the pressure, often through the play of Diggins himself, and then counter-attack. Most commentators named Hale as the best player on the ground, with Diggins not far behind. 'Diggins exerted a dominating influence when he was in the play,' one wrote. His marking kept Collingwood out at crucial stages and, even in the last few minutes, when everyone else seemed to have stopped to a walk, he was still sending the ball forward with telling dashes.

When the siren sounded, Carlton was 15 points in front. So many people ran onto the ground that it took ten minutes for all of the Carlton players to leave the field. A crowd estimated by Hec de Lacy at 5000 people attempted to get into the Carlton dressing-room. Somehow, Albert Collier and a group of Collingwood officials made it in and generously offered their congratulations. Beth Lindau, whom Diggins would marry the following year, remembered that when Brighton left the field that was the last she saw of him for a week. There were no official engagements for the premiership team, and no social functions to which women were invited. Brighton jumped into a car with a group of Carlton players and ended up in Adelaide.

Leading a team to a premiership would have been a wonderful note on which to end a football career. Before the grand final, Diggins had announced that the game would be his last. He was paid his bonus by Ken Luke and used the money to help pay for six hectares of bushland near the beach at Mt Eliza. Luke managed to persuade him to postpone his retirement, however, and when the Blues finished fifth in 1939 it was the first time that Diggins had played for a VFL side that missed the finals. He continued to be dogged by bad luck with injuries and played only five games the following season before breaking his hand. By the end of 1940, Brighton was in the Army, teaching unarmed combat at the military training base at

Frankston. By the time the Army was demobilised, Diggins was in his late thirties and his playing days were well and truly over.

Brighton Diggins did not achieve the same legendary status in the game that people such as Jack Dyer and Albert Collier did. He played fewer than 100 VFL games; Dyer played 310 and Collier played 217. Dyer won six club best and fairest awards and Collier won a Brownlow Medal and three club best and fairests; Diggins never won a club best and fairest or a Brownlow. Yet when he was fit, Diggins could more than hold his own against Dyer, Collier or any other big man of that era. Through no fault of his own, Diggins was not able to sustain the quality of his best football over a long playing career. Nonetheless, Diggins achieved much as a player and playing coach, none of which should be taken for granted. He was a key figure in South Melbourne's last premiership and he turned the fortunes of an underachieving Carlton around. He remains the only Western Australian to have coached a VFL/AFL premiership team.

After his retirement as a player, Diggins had opportunities to make a further mark on the game through coaching, the media or club administration. He certainly had the credentials for a career in any of those fields. He coached Frankston in the Mornington Peninsula Football League and built a young, fast team out of local lads. He took them to the grand final in three consecutive years but they were beaten each time by a Hastings team that included a young full-forward named John Coleman, who was destined for greatness as a League player. Brighton then became a football writer for *The Argus* and arranged to cover the team that Carlton would play the following week so that he could write comprehensive weekly reports on opposition teams and players for the Carlton selection committee. In the late 1950s, there were suggestions at Carlton that he might be approached to run for a position on the committee, in the hope that his people management skills would bring to an end the factional brawling into which the club has descended.

Diggins decided not to follow up on any of these career opportunities. After his spell at Frankston he did not consider any further coaching offers. He quit his job at *The Argus* because he was unhappy with the editorial changes that were often made to his articles. He chose to stay out of Carlton's internal politics and visited Princes Park only a few more times, although he would always send a telegram wishing the coach and team good luck when Carlton was playing in a grand final. As a boy, he had grown up believing that nothing else mattered in life than playing football. As a youth and a young man he lived the life of his dreams in which football was not only fun but also a way of making a living. As he aged, Brighton simply grew tired of the game and ended his involvement with it altogether. He always had a radio tuned to a football broadcast, but his family home at Mt Eliza, rather than a football ground somewhere, had become the epicentre of his world. There he and Beth raised two daughters whom he allowed to use his football trophies, such as the cup he won for being South Melbourne's most consistent player, to collect tadpoles. The only trophy he wanted preserved was the medal he received as captain-coach of the 1938 premiership team. He gave it to Beth, asked her to look after it, and suggested that she might wear it when she went to the races to bring her some luck.

Brighton tried to stay in good physical shape: he never smoked and he kept his weight stable. But the bones he had broken continued to give him trouble and restricted what he could do. Heavy physical work was out of the question and he worked as a sales representative for Kraft. Eventually, he was unable to walk up a hill on their property without Beth's help. Beth, who was a nurse, would apply heated washing soda to his aching joints. He was tormented by persistent chest pains, which he took to be heartburn and refused to see a doctor about. Eventually angina medication was prescribed but Brighton also developed prostate cancer. Beth went out shopping one morning in 1971 and, when she returned home, a doctor was there. Brighton had died of a heart attack.

6

Bob Quinn

(1915–)

I'll be running out, and I won't be looking back to see who's behind me.

BOB QUINN

In May 1940, the war in Europe took a dramatic turn when Germany launched its *Blitzkreig* against Western Europe. Germany had been at war with Britain and France for over nine months without any major land operations, but now with their air power and tanks the Germans swept through Belgium and the Netherlands. British forces were evacuated from Dunkirk in May. By June, France had fallen and Hitler was strolling through the streets of Paris. These sudden victories stunned the world. Italy now declared war on Britain and France. Germany had earlier signed a non-aggression treaty with the Soviet Union, and the USA was not yet involved in the war, so Britain and its Commonwealth allies stood alone against the Nazi war machine.

One lunchtime in June 1940, a young man named Bob Quinn walked out of the Port Adelaide factory where he was working and enlisted. At the time, Australia had a system of two armies: one was a volunteer force that was eligible to serve overseas; the other, the

Citizen Military Forces, was a conscripted militia that could be called up to defend only Australia, New Guinea and Papua. Quinn could have served his country by remaining in the militia, thereby minimising the disruption to his personal life. At 25 years of age, he had a lot to look forward to by staying in Adelaide but Bob saw it as his duty to defend his family and his country. He was single but part of a large family that included five brothers and five sisters. His younger brother, George, who was too young to enlist, lied about his age so that he could join up. Bob was able to enlist because he was working in an occupation that was not essential to the war effort — the factory he worked for made handbags. When he walked into the recruiting office, officers wanted to photograph him for a recruitment poster, but Bob refused, saying that the decision to enlist was a matter of individual choice. Bob and George Quinn were part of a surge in numbers of Australians who volunteered after the German occupation of France. From June to August, 102 000 men enlisted and eventually the government halted recruitment in the overseas armed forces, fearing that too few were remaining behind to man the militia.

Bob Quinn joined the Australian Imperial Force and did his basic training in Adelaide, during which he was promoted to sergeant. After Christmas 1940, he boarded a troop ship at Port Melbourne bound for the Middle East. By March 1941, he had been promoted to warrant officer and was stationed at Tobruk in Libya. North Africa had assumed great strategic importance when Italy entered the war and used its colony of Libya as a base for an invasion of Egypt. Success there would have given the Axis control of the Suez Canal and access to the oilfields of the Middle East. Allied forces drove the Italians back and by February 1941 had advanced to the Libyan ports of Tobruk and Bengazi. The Allies then lost their advantage in unsuccessful campaigns in Greece and Crete. In March, the Germans' Afrika Corps, led by Rommel, launched a counterattack that drove most of the Allied forces back into Egypt. Despite being surrounded and outnumbered by German forces, around 22–25 000 Australian, British and Indian troops defended Tobruk from April to December until they were relieved by a British counterattack. The tenacity of the 'Rats of Tobruk', as the Germans dubbed them, denied Rommel a quick victory and prevented him from mounting a campaign to move further into Egypt.

Although the port of Tobruk could receive basic supplies by sea, the odds against the Diggers and Tommies holding their ground were formidable. The German troops were well trained and equipped with tanks and artillery. Fortifications and ammunition dumps that once belonged to the Italians had been booby trapped with mines and explosives. There were long periods of inactivity between intensive German air attacks and shelling. Dust, flies, fleas, poor quality water and inadequate rations added to the strain. Yet the soldiers of Tobruk rose to the challenge. The war correspondent Chester Wilmot wrote that adversity brought out the best in them.

> The pressure from without produced a solidarity within, which left little room for complacency or individual interest. Every man, section and unit grew to realize that the safety of the garrison in greater or lesser degree might depend on the success of his job, no matter how unimportant it might seem. Tobruk forged such a sense of unity that what happened to one small sector seemed to have happened to the whole garrison . . . This feeling underlay their determination to see the fight through together.

The one part of Tobruk that the Germans controlled was a hill, sloping upwards from the Allied positions, with a frontier of about eight kilometres. Retaining control of that hill, with its elevated position deep in enemy territory, gave the Germans their best chance of capturing Tobruk. Much of the Allies' resources were tied up in trying to hold this frontier. Protected by barbed wire, minefields and an anti-tank ditch, the Germans used concrete pillboxes for cover and were armed to the teeth with field guns, mortars, machine guns and grenades. They kept strengthening their defences while the Allies waited, in vain, for reinforcements.

During July the commanders of the Tobruk garrison began making plans for an assault on the German position. Scouting patrols attempted to ascertain the nature and location of the Germans' key defence points but they gathered only limited information. The infantry really had little idea of what was going to hit them when they began their charge, and how hard it was going to be to break through the German defences. One battalion would attack from the north, while another, the 2/43rd, would strike from the south. The 2/43rd Battalion, with 129 men, was divided into four platoons, 36-men strong, one of which was led by Warrant Officer Bob Quinn.

At 3.30 am on 3 August 1941, a heavy artillery barrage was launched, followed by an infantry charge. As Quinn's platoon reached the barbed wire, enemy flares illuminated the area and most of the platoon was mown down by machine gun and mortar fire. Quinn and the remainder of his platoon got through the wire and ran 50 metres across a minefield. Only eight men were left when they reached the anti-tank ditch that gave them some protection. From there they engaged in a grenade and gunfire duel with the Germans, with one grenade wounding Quinn in the leg. A reserve platoon went to Quinn's aid, but fewer than a dozen of them made it to the anti-tank ditch. For an hour, Quinn, the three other survivors of his platoon, and the survivors of the reserve platoon fought to gain control of the post, but there were too few of them to have much chance of breaking through. Quinn was wounded again, in the face. The official report filed in Quinn's defence service record states that when the order came for the platoon to retreat shortly before dawn, Quinn 'extricated it with coolness and judgement, and joined the remainder of the Coy. [Company] in the withdrawal from the post, refusing treatment until his men were clear'. Stretcher-bearers carried out Quinn and most of the other wounded. When it was light, the Germans allowed the Australian stretcher-bearers to collect their wounded and retrieve the bodies from the minefield.

Bob Quinn would later receive the Military Medal for 'courage, leadership and devotion' in the field.

He remembers being taken to a field hospital. The damage to his leg was extensive and life threatening. As he puts it, 'there was a hole in my thigh'. A tourniquet had been applied on the battlefield but it was still a miracle that he had not bled to death. He remembers the surgeon telling him to stay still, and that he may have to amputate. Quinn then asked: 'Will I play football again?'

Bob Quinn was, indeed, a footballer. A rover who stood 5 foot 6 inches (168 cm) tall and weighed just under 11 stone (70 kg), Quinn at the time he enlisted was one of the best footballers in Australia. He first played for Port Adelaide in 1933, and for three consecutive years, 1936–37–38, he had been voted by *The Advertiser*'s football writers as the likely winner of the Magarey Medal. 'None deserves the honour more than Quinn for his consistent brilliance,' the paper wrote in 1938. Quinn finished fourth in the Medal count in 1936, second in 1937 and won the trophy in 1938. He was a key member of the Port Adelaide premiership teams of 1936 and 1937 and was captain-coach when the club won the flag in 1939. His older brother Tom played in the VFL and became vice-captain of Geelong, but was adamant that Bob was a better player than he was. Interstate matches pitted Bob Quinn against Haydn Bunton and Dick Reynolds, but his game suffered nothing by comparison. For Jeff Pash, himself a Magarey Medal winner and then a journalist with *The News*:

> He was . . . the most accomplished footballer of the time. He had everything — including the most perfect disposal I have seen. Bob Quinn's stab pass was a high-velocity bullet.

Bob McLean, the Port Adelaide secretary who first played League football in 1934, wrote in 1971:

> I personally rate Bob Quinn as the finest exponent of Australian rules football that I have seen. Given an even break for the ball he was never beaten, he was an unerring foot pass and possessed grit, determination, daring and skill of a quality that has rarely, if ever, been seen in one player. It would be true to say that as a footballer and a leader, Bob Quinn became a legend in his own life time.

Before going to war, Bob Quinn had the football world at his feet. He was captain-coach of the reigning premiers and, although the financial rewards for footballers in South Australia were not great, the club had found a job for him at the factory of Arthur Swain, chairman of the club's management committee. After Tobruk, Quinn's career appeared to be over, but that was not to be the end of his contribution to Australia, or to South Australian football.

Before Tobruk

Bob Quinn inherited his dark, wavy hair and olive complexion from his paternal grandmother. Mary Sidoli was around two years of age when her parents migrated from Italy in 1853 and settled in the Port Adelaide area. Mary married a member of another immigrant family, Michael Quinn, at the Catholic Presbytery at Semaphore in 1873 and two years later the first of their seven children, John (Jack) Quinn was born. Jack worked as a wharfie and at the age of 27 he married 19-year-old Letitia Mary Kelly who was part of an Irish Catholic family and had been born in Adelaide. The Quinn's first child, a daughter, was born a year later in 1904 and Letitia would eventually give birth to five sons.

Robert Berrima Quinn, the last child of the family, was born in 1915 in Birkenhead, a largely residential suburb on the other side of the Port River from Port Adelaide. Birkenhead was by no means an attractive place, but it offered workers cheap housing close to the maritime, commercial and manufacturing jobs that were available in Port Adelaide. The houses in Birkenhead were modest, wooden cottages and, although big families like the Quinns would have found them cramped to live in, the neighbourhood was not overcrowded or lacking in amenities. The development of low-density suburbs, linked by tramways and railways, gave the Port district an unusual character for a seaport town. Its residents were not jammed into terraces or blocks of flats without good sanitation or clean drinking water, as their counterparts were in other port cities such as Liverpool and Dublin. There was plenty of open space around Port Adelaide and, as was the case throughout Adelaide, disposable incomes were higher on average than those in Britain, working hours were reduced over the course of the nineteenth and early-twentieth centuries, and a congenial climate encouraged large numbers of people to play and watch sport. There had been a football club in Port Adelaide since 1870. Formed by local tradespeople, the club had played at various locations in the area before making its home at Alberton Oval in 1881. From an early stage, Port Adelaide's location, some distance from Adelaide itself, fostered a mutual rivalry between Port and the other Adelaide clubs and local support for the club was one-eyed. Bob Quinn remembers the Port district as being 'football mad'.

Details of Jack Quinn's early football career are sketchy. He spent at least some of his early twenties in Western Australia, where work was plentiful; at the age of 23 he played a season with a club called White Feather, based at Kanowna, a boomtown not far from Kalgoorlie. By 1900, he had returned home and started playing for Port Adelaide. He would captain the club in 1904–05 and play in the premiership teams of 1903 and 1906. Jack Quinn was a crowd favourite, a rover who was 'as busy as a bee and very hard to catch'. After one match in 1901 he received praise 'on account of the brilliant rushes he made along the wings, sometimes taking the ball from near one set of posts almost to the other end of the ground'. Jack retired as a player in 1908, just as Port was about to enter one of its greatest eras. In 1910, a teenager named Harold Oliver made his debut for the senior team and soon developed a reputation as one of the greatest players that South Australia had produced. Tall and athletic, Oliver played at centre half-forward or centre half-back, or in the ruck. Port's other star player was Sampson 'Shine' Hosking, a centreman who in the 1911 Carnival had been used as a 'loose man' on South Australia's forward line. Hosking continued to use the tactic to great effect in League matches, continually running unattended into space to receive a pass from a team-mate. Oliver and Hosking were the key players in the teams that won premierships in 1910, 1913 and 1914, and were runners-up in 1911, 1912 and 1915. In 1912 and 1914, Port went through the home-and-away, or minor, rounds undefeated, and won 89 per cent of its minor round games from 1910 to 1915. At the end of the 1910, 1913 and 1914 seasons Port defeated the VFL premiers to claim the title of Champions of Australia. No team has ever dominated a senior competition to the extent that Port Adelaide did in 1914. As if to underline its superiority, at the end of that season Port also defeated a combined SANFL team. After 1915, League football in South Australia went into recess due to the effects of World War I. When the competition resumed in 1919, many of Port's great players from the prewar era came back to play but Oliver was now working in the country. Oliver played only a handful of games in 1919, 1920 and 1922, but when he was captain in 1921 he played a full season and Port won the flag.

Four of Jack Quinn's sons went on to play for Port Adelaide: Tom made his debut in 1928, Jack Jr in 1929, Bob in 1933 and George in 1940. Jack Quinn Sr did not hand out praise freely, and Bob remembers that after games his father was always telling him how he could improve. Bob's mother was more reassuring, simply telling him week in and week out, 'Don't worry, son'. Before joining Port Adelaide, Bob Quinn played a few seasons for Exeter, a local Port district club. By the time Bob had become a regular member of the Port Adelaide seniors, the Magpies were starting to develop a powerful team that would contest six consecutive grand finals from 1934 to 1939. Bob soon established a reputation as a player who could reproduce his consistent home-and-away form under the added pressure of finals matches. At the age of 19, he showed 'courage and intelligent disposal' in his first finals match, the 1934 second semifinal. Port lost the grand final that year by nine points to Glenelg, even though Bob kicked five goals. *The Chronicle* noted that 'like his more famous brother [Tom], he tempers even the most torrid exchanges with a coolness which enables him to perceive the right thing to do'. Although South Adelaide beat them by eight points in the 1935 grand final, Bob had another fine finals series. After the 1936 premiership win, *The Chronicle*'s verdict was that:

> No man contributed more to the Port Adelaide victory than Quinn. He ran himself to an extreme stage of exhaustion, but even then he fought grandly for possession and sent it with deadly accuracy and nice judgement to the man in the best position to score.

Such performances could hardly fail to make Bob a recruiting target for VFL clubs. Tom Quinn's excellent career at Geelong also strengthened Victorian clubs' interest in Bob. Tom joined Geelong in 1931, having impressed them with his play in the 1930 Carnival which was played in Adelaide. He was somewhat stockier than Bob but played the game in much the same way that Bob did. He was fast, courageous and a beautiful kick. The highlight of Tom's football career was his play during the 1937 finals series. 'With his roving, position play and deadly disposal', he was most football writers' choice as the best player on the ground in the second semifinal. The grand final between Geelong and Collingwood was one of the best ever played. Ivor Warne-Smith wrote that 'grand high marking, fine long-distance and accurate passing, cleverness, and team work of a high order predominated, and never has there been such sustained pace'. The young Geelong team was nervous early and trailed by three goals at quarter-time. Captain-coach Reg Hickey made a number of major positional changes, all of which were successful. By half-time Geelong had drawn level and in the last quarter raced away with the game to win by 32 points. In the rooms after the match, Hickey paid a special tribute to Quinn; because the captain-coach had played himself at full-back, Quinn was called upon as vice-captain to provide leadership around the ground. Tom did this and was clearly the best player on the ground. Warne-Smith wrote that 'Quinn's game could not be faulted. He played a lone hand for a long time early, and his passing and position play were always deadly effective'.

Several VFL clubs, including Geelong, approached Bob Quinn. However, he says that it was common knowledge that he was not going to leave Adelaide: Port Adelaide was his home town and he was happy living there. He felt a strong attachment and sense of loyalty to his football club which had provided him with a job. Tom's case was different because, in the depths of the Great Depression, the Geelong Football Club found a job for him at the Ford Motor Company factory in Geelong, and he stayed in Geelong after his playing days ended. Tom died in a motor accident in 1969.

Under 'Shine' Hosking's coaching, Port's play was marked by smooth teamwork, much of it originating from Bob Quinn's effective combination with ruck-rover Allan 'Bull' Reval, a tough ball-winner who used handball creatively to bring others into the game. Another important playmaker was Lew Roberts, a champion centreman. Bob Quinn, Reval and Roberts used a 'play-on' style that kept the ball moving. Normally, only one handball would be delivered in any given passage of play: it would be used to put a player in the clear who would then pass the ball short to a loose man, or send a long drop kick to a position where a team-mate would have a good chance of taking a mark. Port's best forward during these years was Albie Hollingworth, a high-marking centre half-forward who kicked 78 goals in both the 1936 and 1939 seasons. Overall, the side was disciplined and played as a team. After they won the 1937 flag, it was noted that:

> Port Adelaide was always a little the faster side and displayed a keener sense of co-operation. There seemed always to be a Port Adelaide player at hand to take a hand-pass from or to jump in to assist a team mate in difficulty.

Football in South Australia was not at this time a very physical game. The emphasis was on skills and accurate disposal of the ball. Bob considered the game not to be rough at all: 'you'd get a crack [be hit] occasionally,' he says, but players tended to even up during the game and then out of the umpire's earshot would say, 'now we're even'. After that, the matter would usually be forgotten. Brawls were rare and feuds that might have continued throughout matches and kept simmering over several seasons did not develop. In that sense Bob Quinn, who was a determined but fair player, typified the era during which he played.

Bob led Port to another flag in 1939, his first season as captain-coach. This was the season in which the AFC reintroduced the boundary throw-in, and in a masterstroke Port recruited 'Big Bob' McLean from Norwood to bolster the rucks. As a coach, Bob Quinn was not a tactician; his method was to lead by example and he liked his team to play an attacking game in which midfielders would try to create a loose man rather than concentrate on 'standing' or playing close to their opponents. In the grand final the Magpies carried no passengers, and although its kicking for goal was poor — 16.28, with Quinn kicking 1.5 — it still beat West Torrens by 47 points. It was a team that was on the verge of greatness when Quinn decided to enlist. In retirement, *Advertiser* writer Brian Barry reflected:

> Whither the 1939 team had the war not cut so cruelly across everything? . . . I feel Port in 1939 began a new era in which it would have been highly successful in terms of premierships such was the talent, zest and experience of this side . . . Perfectly coached, brilliantly led, abounding in talent . . . it should always be remembered.

After Tobruk

After being evacuated from Tobruk, Bob Quinn spent ten weeks in hospital and a convalescent depot in the Middle East. He rejoined his unit, underwent officer training and was promoted to lieutenant. In March 1943 he returned home for five months' leave, during which he rested his leg, and when he was able he began running to gradually restore his strength and fitness. He married May Walker and in the following year their first child, Pam, was born (three more children were born in later years: Margaret in 1946, Robert Jr in 1947 and Greg in 1954). These were good times, but there were sad and worrying events as well. Bob's brother, George, had been killed at El Alamein. May's brother, Charlie, an Australian cricketer who had toured England before joining the RAAF, was killed over Germany. From late 1941, Japan advanced aggressively through the Asia-Pacific region, with Australia itself being protected by only a thin defence force.

By the middle of 1943, the war with Japan in New Guinea had reached a stage where the USA had established air and sea superiority over the region. Australian ground forces were given the job of clearing the Japanese from the Huon Peninsula. In September 1943, Australian and US forces launched a combined land, air and sea attack on the Japanese at the port city of Lae. Quinn was part of the infantry that fought in the savage battle that followed. He received a bullet wound in the right forearm that resulted in a compound fracture: he still remembers seeing the bone sticking out of his arm. A soldier who came to assist him was killed instantly in the gunfire.

When he got back home, Quinn rested before deciding to make a comeback just before the start of the 1944 season. During the war years, League football had continued in South Australia, but the eight teams were reduced to four as clubs merged with their closest neighbours. Port combined with West Torrens. When the team ran out onto the Adelaide Oval for the opening game of the season, Quinn received a wonderful ovation from all parts of the ground. Making a brilliant debut that day was a small, left-footed centreman, Bob Hank. Hank would go on and win Magarey Medals in 1946 and 1947, but unfortunately for Port he was a West Torrens player. Hank, whom Quinn describes simply as 'a gentleman', embodied the ideal of sportsmanship and became the most widely admired footballer in South Australia after Quinn retired.

During the second semifinal in 1944, Quinn took a knock to the part of the arm that had been shot at Lae. Bob McLean later wrote that:

> Quinn remarked to me during the three-quarter-time break that he thought he had broken his arm and he busily wrapped sticking plaster around the suspected break. Upon resumption at the centre bounce the ball broke in his direction and he punched the ball towards our goals with the injured arm, followed through himself, gathered in the ball, and from the resultant kick, scored a goal. An X-ray confirmed that his arm had been broken and he was in plaster for many weeks.

'Yes, it did hurt a bit,' Quinn said in a modest and matter of fact way when he confirmed the story. He played the rest of the last quarter with his broken arm held in to his side. Port–West Torrens won the game, but without Quinn they lost the grand final.

In 1945 Quinn was appointed captain-coach of Port Adelaide. The Magpies dominated the home-and-away rounds that season, losing only two games, but lost the grand final to West Torrens. That was a huge disappointment but Quinn himself had a stellar year. He captained South Australia to a win over Victoria at the Adelaide Oval and was awarded a trophy for being South Australia's best player. He won the Magarey Medal, polling votes in 14 of the 17 games he played in. Port was again runner-up in 1946 and, although Quinn had a fine season, his former team-mate Bob Hank won the Magarey Medal. Quinn won Port's best and fairest in his final season, 1947.

During his final years as a player, Quinn not only played fine football but also retained his ability to lead others by setting a fine example. Even in his final season as a player, his selection as South Australia's captain-coach for the 1947 Carnival was regarded in football circles as 'a foregone conclusion'. After Quinn's retirement, West Adelaide's captain, Johnny Taylor, named Quinn as 'the best captain I've seen and the best the State has ever had'. Quinn's greatness as a leader was illustrated during a remarkable match between Victoria and South Australia at Princes Park in 1946. Before a crowd of 30 000, Victoria adapted well to the wet and slippery conditions and led by 39 points at half-time. During the break, Quinn gave his team what the Melbourne press described as 'a rousing speech'. 'I called them gutless,' Bob remembered. He said to them, 'I'll be running out, and I won't be looking back to see who's behind me'. South Australia then fought back through 'splendid handball, with men rushing into position for the passes'. Quinn, his fellow rover Jack Oatey, and Hank, 'weaved with deadly effect in and out of the packs'. During the last quarter, South Australia still trailed by 13 points before Quinn kicked a goal. South Australia then 'transferred play in a flash for Quinn, now irresistible, to screw a clever left-foot goal, making the difference one point'. South Australia then ran up a lead of four goals, but Victoria rallied and drew the game.

Bob Quinn's last game of League football was the 1947 preliminary final. He was aged only 32 when he retired, and Len Fitzgerald, who had seen him play against Victoria the previous season, remembers that although he had probably lost a little of his pace he was still 'a beautiful reader of the play, who knew how to be in the right place at the right time'. However, Quinn recalls that by this time he was not coping well with the physical stress of playing. He was still feeling the effects of his war wounds and felt that they were 'tearing me up inside'. Although Port appointed him as non-playing coach in 1948, he decided instead to take over a country hotel at Kadina. Bob played and coached at Kadina until he broke his pelvis and decided to give the game away. Quinn was appointed coach of South Australia in the 1953 Carnival, even though he was no longer a League coach.

It took Port some time to find a leader to replace Quinn. Lew Roberts was captain-coach in 1948 but he retired at the end of that season. Jack McCarthy, a former coach of Port colts (juniors) was non-playing coach in 1949, but the committee decided that a playing coach was what the club needed. Their first choice, Jim Deane, was refused a clearance by his club, South Adelaide. Port then appointed Fos Williams, a rover from West Adelaide who had played under

Quinn and with McLean in the 1947 Carnival, even though he had no coaching experience at all. McLean retired as a player and became club secretary in 1949 and he and Williams set to work building the Port Adelaide of the 1950s. Quinn liked Williams, but he chose not to resume an active involvement with the club after he returned to Adelaide in 1969 to take up a hotel at Thebarton. In 1951 he had helped the club out by giving a lecture to a group of schoolboy footballers from the Port area. But as far as the senior team went, Bob's attitude was that he had had his turn and he was happy to let Fos get on with the job. He followed the team and enjoyed the success it had under Fos's coaching, but never went into the rooms to speak to the players.

Bob retired from the hotel industry in 1977. He played golf, was an active member of the RSL, was involved in community activities, and kept in contact with many of the friends he had made through football. He enjoyed his retirement, but it seems clear that beneath his good-humoured exterior lay the mental scars of war. Like many men of his generation, he tended to keep things bottled up and he gave few clues to how the experience of combat had affected his psyche. His daughter Pam says that for years he never talked at all about the war, and only began speaking of his experience in recent years. Once, Pam and her family were travelling with Bob and when passing through Canberra they took him to the Australian War Memorial. Bob had no objection to this but, once inside, the experience and the memories that it stirred was too much for him. He became so emotional and upset that his family had to take him out of the building.

Bob Quinn achieved so much as a footballer that it is easy to overlook the effect that World War II had on his career. Quinn actually took the field for Port Adelaide 185 times and played 15 games for South Australia. However, in the SANFL records, a player's game tally includes the number of games that his club played while he was unavailable due to war service. As a result, Quinn's official game total stands at 248. That figure makes it seem as if the war reduced Quinn's career by only around 20 per cent. But the four years that Bob lost when he was away at the war, and recovering from the wounds he suffered, were when he would have been at his footballing peak. The long-lasting effects of those wounds also shortened his career, forcing him to retire at an age when he was still capable of playing consistently good and, at times, brilliant football. Had his football career continued uninterrupted, there is no telling what he might have achieved. The war changed his life; he lost beloved family members and he himself bore mental as well as physical scars. But Quinn never lost the selflessness and bravery he showed when he volunteered to defend his family and his country. Quinn's was a story that was played out, in differing circumstances, by tens of millions of people during the war years.

In some respects, Quinn was the typical South Australian footballer of the 1930s and 1940s. His style — fast, hard but fair, with an emphasis on finding a team-mate through accurate disposal — defined the way that South Australian football was played during these years. Every club had players who played that way, such as Laurie Cahill (John Cahill's uncle), Jack Cockburn and Max Mundy at South, Jeff Pash and Ron Phillips at North, Vic Bateman and Alby Wundersitz at Sturt, Bill McCallum and Jack Oatey at Norwood, Torrens's Bob Hank, and West Adelaide's master of handball, Jack Broadstock. Such players were distributed so well around the League, thanks to the electorate system and the practice of paying players only a few shillings a week, if at all, that each of the eight clubs won at least one premiership between 1933 and 1947, the years that Quinn's career spanned. In five of the 12 seasons that Quinn played, the team that won the premiership had not made the finals the year before. There were lots of good players in South Australia, but Quinn was one of exceptional talent and consistency. He took the skills of the game to a level that made him clearly the best footballer in South Australia and, arguably, Australia. In that respect, Bob Quinn was incomparable.

In the mid-1960s, a new stand was built at Alberton Oval. It provided much-needed seating, and administration and social facilities, including a large banquet room. Unlike many pieces of architecture from that period, the stand has aged well. In recent years a stylish, contemporary entry foyer, bar and restaurant have been added at the rear. As John Kennedy puts it, this is a modern, forward-thinking football club, 'but with respect for tradition bolted onto it'. All through the stand there are team photos and other memorabilia that commemorate the club's history. The stand overlooks the playing field where countless people have had their ashes scattered by loved ones, such was their love of the club and its oval. Engraved brick pavers, showing the names of Port Adelaide supporters, some of them families spanning several generations, who wish to record their devotion to the club, have been laid on the asphalt standing area in front of the stand. This is sacred ground, where the semi-amateur Port Adelaide of the twentieth century meets the professional club that entered the twenty-first century as a member of the AFL. At the front of the roof is the name given to the stand when it was opened, still clearly visible in clean, white letters:

ROBERT B. QUINN M.M. GRANDSTAND

Admiration for Quinn extended well beyond Port Adelaide. 'I *like* Bob Quinn,' says Len Fitzgerald, a former Sturt player, with warmth in his voice. 'He volunteered to defend his country when he was at his footballing peak . . . Marvellous man.' He is a member of the AFL Hall of Fame, and in 2002 the SANFL honoured him by establishing the Bob Quinn Medal which is awarded each year to the best player in the League's Anzac Day match.

Part 3

Modern football

Len Smith (1912–1967)
and Norm Smith (1915–1973)

John Kennedy (1928–)

Jack Oatey (1920–1994)

AFTER WORLD WAR II, the Australian economy enjoyed a period of economic growth that lasted until the early 1970s and transformed the geography of its major cities. Before the war, jobs and working-class housing were clustered in dense cores around ports and central business districts, with the outer suburbs being home to predominantly middle-class commuters who used public transport to get to work. Rapid population growth after the war — the population of the capital cities more than doubled between 1947 and 1971 — and an economy with high levels of government assistance encouraged multinational companies and local suppliers to build new factories, which were located in outer suburbs where land was cheap. Working-class families moved to outer suburban areas where jobs were plentiful and houses on large suburban blocks were affordable. Increasing rates of car ownership allowed suburbs to be built away from public transport routes. However, the car was only one of a range of consumer goods, including refrigerators and TVs, which became cheaper and more freely available. Leisure became increasingly privatised — first through television, and later through videos, electronic games and the Internet — and kids increasingly played inside their homes. Almost half of the capital cities' increase in population was the result of the arrival of immigrants from overseas. This wave of immigration included not only people from Britain, traditionally the major source of migrants to Australia, but also large numbers of Italians, Greeks and eastern Europeans who brought their own cultures with them and, in many cases, an enthusiasm for the sport of their homelands. The local game, Australian Rules, was virtually unknown to them. Migrant families, and later affluent young people, moved to the old inner-city areas where football clubs were located, while suburbanisation encouraged fans of the game to live further away from the grounds.

These changes had the potential to reduce the demand for watching Australian Rules football. In many ways, the game was stuck in the past, operating under conditions that had evolved when football depended on strong support from local communities. Its battered old grounds were no longer within walking distance of where most fans lived, and administrators were generally slow to appreciate that they lost valuable revenue by playing all home-and-away games at club grounds. The problem was highlighted in Melbourne on the King's Birthday holiday in 1949, when 46 000 people crammed into Richmond's Punt Road Oval; when the gates were closed, 20 000 were still outside. A short walk away, the MCG — the only ground at which most spectators did not have to stand in the open — stood empty. VFL players were subject to a maximum wage that was eroded in real value by inflation during the 1950s, and a set of transfer rules that created, as Bob Stewart puts it, 'a master–servant relationship'. Recruiting zones applied to Melbourne but, outside the metropolitan area, clubs, could compete for recruits, a system that gave enormous advantages to the most prestigious clubs. The Coulter Law prohibited the payment of signing-on fees so, to lure prospective recruits, clubs which complied with that law had to offer non-monetary rewards, such as the opportunity to play under a famous coach or in a premiership team. Country leagues retained some of their best players and recruited experienced League players to coach their teams by offering them rewards greater than those available in the VFL. Clubs in Adelaide and Perth lost few of their star players to the VFL, and the high standard of play in their leagues was demonstrated by the creditable performances of their club and state sides against Victorian opposition.

The two VFL clubs that did not need to offer financial inducements to sign young players were Melbourne — which played on the MCG, the Mecca for football followers, and was coached by the great Norm Smith — and Collingwood, football's most famous and popular club. From the early 1960s, other clubs attempted to close the gap on them by flouting the Coulter Law. Recruiting officers now arrived at the family homes of young footballers with bundles of pound notes stuffed in paper bags or in boxes of chocolates. Geelong brought 'Polly' Farmer and Denis Marshall across from Perth and St Kilda signed Tasmanians Darrel Baldock and Ian Stewart. When Carlton recruited Melbourne captain Ron Barassi as captain-coach in 1964, the football world was in uproar as many fans perceived that club loyalty was becoming a thing of the past. Barassi was perhaps the first player and coach whose salary reflected the value he added to his club and his contract with Carlton was a clear sign that football was changing. So too were the transformations of St Kilda and Richmond, which moved to new grounds in 1965 and would soon reap the rewards of aggressive recruiting. Work had already started on the VFL's own stadium, at Waverley in Melbourne's outer south-east, the brainchild of League president Kenneth Luke.

A gap was starting to open up between the clubs that adapted to and took advantage of these changes, and those clubs that did not. Television coverage promoted interest in the game in general, but its benefits were felt most by the popular and successful teams. They were seen more often on TV, and sponsors used their star players to advertise products. Competition between clubs to recruit the best players drove up costs, and the VFL responded by abolishing the Coulter Law and extending zoning at random across country Victoria. Zoning was expected to advantage weaker clubs by giving them automatic rights to recruit players who lived in their zones. However, some zones had more young people and their populations were growing faster than others, so zoning put some clubs at a major disadvantage.

While the economic structure of the game was changing, so was the nature of play on the field. A number of coaches took basic ideas about how football should be played and found ways to make them work more efficiently. Norm Smith and Hawthorn's John Kennedy had learnt the value of teamwork and discipline by following Collingwood as boys, and as coaches they introduced new levels of fitness and aggression to the game. Geelong's Reg Hickey and East Perth's Jack Sheedy built teams that used the handpass to move the ball quickly. Jack Oatey at Sturt and Len Smith at Fitzroy and Richmond constructed game plans that helped players to perfect their decision-making skills and move the ball on with handball and precise kicking into space. These coaches took players who were paid next to nothing and got them to play the game their way; in doing so they raised the standard of football and influenced generations of future coaches.

By the early 1970s, the average League footballer was fitter, faster and more skilled than his pre-World War II counterpart and just as tough. Administrators also helped to make the game quicker and more exciting by changing the rules to award free kicks against players who kicked the ball out of bounds on the full, and imposing a 15-yard penalty against players who failed to return the ball on the full to opponents who had been awarded a mark or free kick. A centre diamond (later a centre square) was added to reduce congestion at centre bounces. These changes opened up play, and faster movement of the ball made things easier for full-forwards of the calibre of Carlton's Alex Jesaulenko, Collingwood's Peter McKenna, Geelong's Doug Wade and Hawthorn's Peter Hudson. The attractiveness of the game was reflected in attendances: in 1947, the average match attendance in the VFL was around 18 000; by the early 1970s, the figure ranged from 22 000 to 23 000. The ability of the game to retain its existing fans and attract new ones was perhaps most pronounced in South Australia because the standard of play there was high and clubs were able to retain nearly all of their star players. By 1974, attendances at all SANFL matches were about double what they had been in 1949, which meant that the average Adelaidean was just as likely to watch League football as his or her counterpart had been at the end of World War II.

7

Len Smith
(1912–1967)

and

Norm Smith
(1915–1973)

I have reached the conclusion that some footballers or teams succeed because they cheerfully pay the price of success, and others, though they may claim ambition and a desire to succeed are unwilling to pay that price.

LEN SMITH

You just do not lose grand finals.

NORM SMITH

In its almost 150-year history, the Melbourne Football Club has enjoyed two eras of success. The first was when it won three consecutive flags from 1939 to 1941. The club was transformed after 1932 when, in a recruiting coup, Richmond's secretary Percy Page was enticed to cross from Punt Road to the MCG, and coach Frank 'Checker' Hughes made the same move the following year. Page and Hughes introduced to Melbourne a professional, will-to-win attitude that was noticeably lacking at what was then a gentlemanly, virtually amateur club. It was Hughes who changed the club's nickname from the 'Fuchsias', which he considered to be effeminate, to the 'Demons'.

A master coach who knew when to give his team a dressing-down and when to give individuals a quiet word of encouragement, Hughes had great tactical sense and his teams benefited from regular injections of new, versatile players, obtained through Page's astute and energetic recruiting. The club's depth was remarkable: on grand final day in 1941, 12 of Melbourne's senior players were unavailable due to injury or war service, while its opponent was almost at full strength. That victory was probably the finest achievement in the club's history. A further premiership, coached by Hughes, came Melbourne's way in 1948.

Melbourne's second period of greatness was from 1954 to 1964, when the Demons played in eight grand finals and won six flags, including a hat trick in 1955–56–57. Their loss in the 1958 grand final cost them the opportunity to win six flags in a row. At this time the club's recruiting was done by secretary Jim Cardwell and recruiting officer Ken Carlon. In an era when footballers who lived outside the metropolitan zones could join any League club, Cardwell was unmatched in his ability to sell his club to prospective recruits and their parents. Like Percy Page, Cardwell had no extra money to offer to a young boy as an inducement to sign: Melbourne and Collingwood remained the last clubs to adhere strictly to the League's Coulter Law on player payments. Sincerity and a gentle approach were Cardwell's selling points. Joining Melbourne gave a boy the opportunity to be part of a winning team, to play in finals and to play on the MCG every second week. With selection on the senior list came honorary membership of the Melbourne Cricket Club. Other clubs could offer money but none could offer the range of advantages that Melbourne did. Cardwell's door, either of his office at work or of his family home, was always open to players who wanted to talk about a problem. Efficient country recruiting, together with a strong metropolitan zone and the operation of the father–son recruiting rule, enabled Melbourne to replace its players as they retired or took country or interstate coaching jobs. Although the 1955 premiership team was young, only six of its members played in all of the five flags won between 1955 and 1960. In all, 39 players were needed to fill Melbourne's premiership teams during those years, and the 1964 team contained 11 players who were playing in their first premiership.

One of the things that the teams of these two eras had in common was the involvement of Norm Smith, as a player in the first era and coach in the second. Smith was a fine full-forward who played over 200 games. He could kick big tallies of goals — he led the VFL goal-kicking with 89 in 1941, and kicked 80 or more goals in two other seasons — but was also known for his ability to bring others into the game with handball and 'decoy' leading. *The Argus* commented that:

> Norman Smith, the Melbourne full-forward . . . moves beautifully when required, can kick long distances, and is the most dangerous and effective forward in the game today. He has the strange complex for a full-forward of not wanting to kick goals himself, and is quite happy as long as someone else is putting the ball through.

In the remarkable 1948 finals series, Hughes brought Jack Mueller, who had been coaching the seconds, out of retirement to replace a suspended player. While Mueller kicked 20 goals in three games playing in a forward pocket, it was Smith's play as a decoy full-forward that 'directly or indirectly, was responsible for most of these goals'. As Essendon's captain-coach, Dick Reynolds, wrote after the grand final replay:

> Norm Smith was the best player on the ground. He was the brains of the Melbourne attack, and rarely wasted an opportunity of unselfishly sending the ball forward to Mueller.

Smith's first year as Melbourne coach, 1952, came after the team had finished last the previous year. Hughes was still involved in an advisory capacity but Smith was very much the man in charge. Two years later, Smith's young side finished runner-up, and in 1955 the Demons defeated Collingwood in the grand final. When the siren sounded, Smith was ecstatic. 'I felt a giant that day,' he later wrote. Smith was aged only 39 at the time and his thirst for success on grand final day remained unquenched in subsequent years.

The magnitude of Norm Smith's contribution to Melbourne can be illustrated by the following point: Melbourne's first hundred years as a VFL/AFL club produced only two flags in the 70 seasons that Smith was not involved as a player or coach; in the 30 seasons in which Smith was actively involved with the club, it won 10 flags.

The sacking

Of course, all this makes the decision of the Melbourne committee to sack Smith midway through the 1965 season unfathomable. Melbourne was the reigning premier, had won its first eight games that season and was very much in the running for a finals spot. In a dramatic few days, the committee fired Smith, declaring in their letter of dismissal to him that this was necessary 'to prevent any further disruption of the club's activities', but then changed its mind. The relationship between the committee and coach remained strained and as a coach Smith probably lost a great deal of his self-confidence. Melbourne missed the finals in 1965 and won only three games the following year. In failing health, Smith retired at the end of the 1967 season.

Most explanations of the sacking have centred on Smith's quick temper and the effect that this had on his dealings with many members of the committee. Even his devoted wife, Marj, conceded that 'Norm is argumentative at times'. Hassa Mann remembered that 'Smithy demanded that at the end of a game we had to be totally exhausted, or else we weren't fair dinkum'. Smith could not tolerate what he perceived to be a lack of commitment and when he became enraged he was a man to avoid. On one occasion at half-time he grabbed a Melbourne player by the throat and pinned him against a brick wall in the dressing-room. He once also did this to Jim Cardwell while yelling 'when you get me players, get me players with guts!' In an era when players who were replaced by a nineteenth or twentieth man could not return to the field, and when coaches could not come onto the ground to speak to players at quarter-time, coaches had less tactical scope to get the best out of their players than today. They really had only the half-time and three-quarter-time breaks to work on motivating their players. Full-forward Barry Bourke remembers that:

> If you didn't play the game the way he wanted you to play, he'd let you know, and *by hell* he would let you know. He was a very tough man . . . a very tough man. He just demanded everything

> out of his players. A lot of players at that time fell by the wayside because they couldn't handle the heat, but because Melbourne had a very strong list at that point in time they were able to pursue that path because if some fell away there was someone else to take their place.

Bourke also recalled a match against Footscray, in which he was beaten in the first half by the Bulldog's full-back, David Darcy. At half-time Bourke was goalless and Melbourne was trailing. Smith 'ripped into me . . . he called me everything and said, "You have got to get in front"'. In the second half Bourke did that, kicked five goals and Melbourne won the game. After the match Smith and 'Checker' Hughes went around the rooms and spoke to each player.

When Smith got to Bourke, he asked, 'how many'd you get?'

'I got five, Norm.'

Smith turned to Hughes and said, 'the bastard's got five', and walked away.

Smith's hard exterior was balanced by his sense of fairness and honesty, and a genuine love of spending time relaxing and talking football with his friends and other football people. In those days, every club used to hold an after-match function for players, coaches and officials of both sides. Even the umpires attended. It was simply considered the done thing to attend these functions; besides, six o'clock closing meant that this was the most convenient way for football people to have a Saturday night drink. Melbourne's home games were followed by a dinner dance in the evening. Here Smith, once he had unwound with a few beers, would show the softer side of his character. Norm could usually be seen in a corner somewhere, talking football with his own players and his opponents until around midnight. During the evening there would be a sing-along which Norm would lead. He knew how to let his hair down, and could drink large quantities and hold it very well. In these situations Bourke found Norm to be 'the best company in the world'. As Bob Skilton remembers:

> There were times during a game if you heard a player getting a blast from Norm Smith you would say that those two guys would never speak again, but he had that wonderful capacity to the same night have you eating out of his hand again.

Smith cared deeply about the welfare of his players and their families. He never forgot a name and knew each player's family members by name. He never shirked the unpleasant task of telling a player that he was unlikely to make the grade and was being cut from the list. One player who was told this news broke down in tears; Norm spent the next two hours talking to him, and ended up crying with him.

Norm was an intelligent and articulate man. His formal education was limited but, when he spoke about football, Smith was able to use words with precision. His speeches were well thought out and constructive, rather than impulsive and abusive. His voice would boom, but he would rarely, if ever, curse. The impact of Smith's words was heightened by the players' knowledge that at all times the coach was speaking with sincerity.

Norm Smith's Melbourne teams won multiple flags, not through individual brilliance, but by playing as a team and carrying few passengers. They had few 'star' players — Ron Barassi and Hassa Mann were perhaps the only exceptions — and had no out-and-out champion ruckmen, centre half-forwards or full-forwards. These were even, fit, physically strong sides that won matches by getting numbers to the ball and contesting every issue. When a Melbourne player brought the ball out of defence, he could count on at least a couple of team-mates being close by to shepherd and talk to him. The ball would then usually be kicked long into attack; a fast-leading full-forward would then receive a pass or act as a decoy to create space for other forwards. Barassi, whose own desire to get to every contest bordered on the fanatical, roamed the ground at will, inspiring and exhorting his team-mates.

Melbourne's Achilles heel was that every member of the team needed to be focussed on the task at hand. Thus, in the 1958 grand final, Collingwood was able to pull off the greatest upset in football history by using niggling tactics and hard tackling to put the Demons off their game. Murray Weideman threw his weight around, and the close tagging of Barry 'Hooker' Harrison caused Barassi to lose his concentration. Other Melbourne players seemed unsure whether they should retaliate or follow Smith's instructions and concentrate on the ball. Smith was devastated and told Mann that 'you just do not lose grand finals'. Two years later, Melbourne again played Collingwood in the grand final. Again, it was a wet day and Collingwood tried to unsettle their opponents. Smith didn't even mention what had happened in 1958, but his players were absolutely committed to playing football, regardless of what Collingwood threw at them. When Weideman hit Barassi in the mouth at a boundary throw-in — so hard that it damaged a nerve in Barassi's upper lip, causing it to tingle for the next 25 years — Barassi's response was simply to look at Weideman. The Demons won easily, holding the Magpies to only four scoring shots, a score of 2.2. Mann recalled that after the game Smith was upset that Collingwood had been allowed to score even two goals.

While Smith's coaching methods worked well with nearly all of his players, they were not always appreciated by the club officials he had to work with. Exactly when Smith had his first argument with a Melbourne club official is not known. It seems certain that Norm would have expressed views contradicting those of others in a forceful way on innumerable occasions but, with Ivor Warne-Smith as the club's chairman of selectors, any difficulties arising from differences of opinion were smoothed out. Norm got on famously with Warne-Smith and respected his judgement, but after the latter died in 1960 his calming influence was missed. Smith himself thought his relationship with the committee first started to deteriorate when, in a post-match outburst in 1963, he told a radio interviewer that the field umpire that day had been 'subconsciously biased towards the underdog'. Norm's son, Peter recalls that Jim Cardwell listened to a tape of the interview and approved its release for broadcast. When the umpire brought libel action, Smith was disappointed when the committee refused to give him any financial support. Smith later wrote that, after this episode, 'I felt that certain committeemen had not backed me and I found I could not tolerate them'. From that point on, Norm found it increasingly difficult to work with an administration that in his opinion had become soft and complacent after years of success. Norm's reaction was to devote his energies to building a closer, more productive relationship with his players, while attempting to keep club officials at arm's length.

The situation deteriorated further when Ron Barassi sought a clearance to captain-coach Carlton at the end of 1964 and Norm supported his application. Barassi was more than just Smith's protégé: they and their families had been close for years. Ron Barassi Sr, a team-mate of Norm's, had been killed at Tobruk in 1941 and, when young Ron was invited to train at Melbourne in 1953, his mother had remarried and wanted to live in Tasmania. Ron was only 16 at the time and, because he was not blessed with enormous natural talent, he would have to work hard to make it in the VFL. Smith suggested that he live with him and his family to have the best opportunity to become a Melbourne player. For four years Ron lived in a bungalow in Norm and Marj's backyard, and by the time he had moved out to get married he had already played in two premiership teams. By 1964 Barassi was Melbourne's captain and still its most important player. His clearance application sparked accusations of greed and disloyalty within the club, but Smith saw things differently. He later explained: 'I felt that the boy had given us such service ... he'd done well for himself and wanted to improve himself and I was not going to stand in his way'. Melbourne agreed to release Barassi once it became clear that he could not be persuaded to stay, but within the club there were people who accused Smith of acting to get rid of a potential rival for his coaching position. This talk was not only factually incorrect — Smith had offered to retire as coach to keep Barassi at Melbourne — but also a slur on the character of a man who had devoted most of his life to the club. This time, wounds were inflicted that could not be healed by the parties getting together and talking football over a few beers. Norm's comments on Channel Nine's *Tony Charlton's Football Show*, shortly after he was sacked, revealed how deeply he was hurt by the accusations made about his part in Barassi's clearance, and to this day the issue still rankles Ron Barassi and Peter Smith.

After eight rounds of the 1965 season, Melbourne was undefeated. But most of these victories were against weaker teams, and in five games the winning margin was a goal or less. During this period there were rumours circulating around the football world that Norm Smith had been approached to coach Richmond. Norm's brother Len, who had stepped down for health reasons, had been coaching at that club. Jack Titus was acting as caretaker coach and did not want the job the following year. It is not known whether there were any formal negotiations between Norm and the Tigers' administration; however, at the end of 1964 Richmond officials had held secret talks with Ron Barassi about him becoming playing coach, with Len Smith as his assistant. It was Len's idea and Ron wanted to talk further about it but Richmond's president, Ray Dunn, decided not to pursue the matter; he was engaged in negotiations to move his club's home games to the MCG and wanted to preserve a friendly relationship with the Melbourne football and cricket clubs. For the same reasons, Dunn confirmed that Richmond was not seeking Norm Smith's services as coach, even after Melbourne sacked him. In any case, Smith's first loyalty was to Melbourne. When Tony Charlton asked him if he would consider taking the Richmond position, Smith replied, simply and with obvious sincerity, 'I'm Melbourne ... I'm Melbourne through and through'.

In round 9, in front of 72 000 fans at the MCG, St Kilda thrashed Melbourne by more than ten goals. It was the strongest evidence to date that Melbourne's golden era had come to an end and that hard decisions about rebuilding the club needed to be made. Words were exchanged after this game between Smith and club officials based on the coach's judgement that the club was slipping. After a loss to Richmond in round 12, Norm was summoned to a meeting with the committee the following Wednesday. He could see the writing on the wall and told Len that he would resign at the meeting. Len told him: 'Don't be a fool. You owe it to the boys to keep coaching. Eat humble pie'. Norm kept his cool at the meeting, admitted that he had said the wrong thing at times, and promised to stop speaking out against the committee and the selection committee. Smith also agreed to tell the players that he supported the committee fully. The committee put these undertakings into a letter that Jim Cardwell handed to Smith before training the following night. Norm took the letter, shoved it in his pocket without reading it, and walked onto the field to address the players. There are conflicting reports about what happened next. Several players later came forward and said that Smith had said nothing derogatory about the committee; Smith had stated that, while individual members of the selection committee could put forward differing opinions, once a vote had been taken he and the selection committee had always closed ranks and put on a united front for the good of the club. Hassa Mann said that he had interpreted this as praise for the committee and the other selectors. As the players walked off the field, committee members approached them and asked them what Smith had said. Cardwell later told Barassi that one unnamed player, perhaps misinterpreting what Smith had said, told the committee that the coach had not made a statement of his full support for the committee. Smith's letter of dismissal arrived the following evening.

Blood brothers

Norm Smith's quick temper and his desire to always say what he thought made a rod for his own back in his dealings with club officials, but it is worth noting that Len Smith also had continuing problems with a club committee when he was coach of Fitzroy. Len was a gentle man who was quieter and more even tempered than his younger brother. Graeme Richmond, who was club secretary at Richmond when Smith coached there, called him 'the finest man I ever knew. He was a man of no malice'. If a man like Len Smith could have problems with the committee at Fitzroy, it is likely that Norm Smith's personality was not the central issue in his disputes with the Melbourne committee. It seems clear that in both cases the disputes between coach and club officials were symptomatic of deeper problems at the Melbourne and Fitzroy clubs.

Len and Norm Smith's father, Victor Smith, was born in 1883 and their mother, Ethel Brown, in 1886. Both came from large, working-class families: Victor was the twelfth of thirteen children and was born in Hotham (North Melbourne) a few years after his parents and family had returned to Melbourne after living for around ten years in Ballarat; Ethel was the third of ten children and was born in Collingwood. They married in 1910: Len was born in 1912 and Norm in 1915; a sister, Marj, was born in 1918. The family grew up in Northcote. Victor Smith was a lover of all sports and was more than willing to buy equipment for his children (and later grandchildren) and go along and watch them play. Len's mother recalled that when he was aged two he was given a soccer ball 'and it became the treasure of his young life'. Norm was given a new football each year and 'until the novelty wore off he used to take it to bed with him'. With their father's encouragement, Len and Norm excelled at football and cricket. The surviving members of the Smith family who knew Victor 'Pop' Smith remember a man who was gentle, kind and generous (those words are invariably used by people in general to describe Len also). 'He drummed teamwork into us all the time,' Norm recalled. 'His motto of teamwork being greater than the individual is reflected in both our coaching techniques.'

The Smith boys' world was centred on their family, football and work, and each of these things gave them a consistent message about the importance of teamwork and hard work. Despite their age difference, Norm and Len hung around together and kicked a football with other kids in a rough paddock in Northcote. 'I never remember Len saying a cross word,' Ethel Smith told Hec de Lacy. 'Never once has he answered me back.' But 'as a youngster Norman was always wrestling some bigger boy, and he was such a full-blooded kid that he always seemed different'. Though his father and brother were Essendon supporters, and both went to watch them play each week, Norm became a Collingwood fan and went to Victoria Park regularly to watch the great Magpie sides of the late 1920s and early 1930s. 'Their teamwork made an everlasting impression on me,' he later wrote. Victor Smith had a small engineering business which manufactured parts for prams, and both Len and Norm did engineering apprenticeships. Norm recalled the influence that his first foreman had on him:

> I thought he was tough at the time. But I know now that the discipline he taught me was the discipline I have passed on to the players in my teams . . . You have to slave and slog. Don't be ashamed of failing, as long as you can get up and go on trying.

When his father died in 1943, Norm took over the family business — Victor Smith's probate record shows that at the time of his death he was working as a metalworker. Norm had married Marjorie Ellis in 1940, and their only child, Peter, was born in 1947.

By 1932, Len had made his way into the strong Northcote team, which won five VFA flags between 1929 and 1936. Len played in three of these, in 1932, 1933 and 1936, mostly at centre half-forward. Northcote's captain-coach during those years, Percy Rowe, was a former Collingwood premiership player and it seems reasonable to surmise that Rowe would have passed on to young Len the ideas about the importance of teamwork that characterised Collingwood teams of the 1920s. Lightly built and standing just under six foot tall, Len preferred to use his leap and avoid body-on-body contests in marking. When 'Checker' Hughes and Percy Page visited the Smith household in 1933, it was Len they had come to sign but his father asked that they also consider Norm, who was then playing for Dennis in a local competition. Len played 18 games for Melbourne in the mid-1930s, and after another spell at Northcote he resumed his League career at Fitzroy, where he played 75 games. To those who saw the Smith brothers play, it was something of a puzzle why Len's League game tally fell well short of Norm's. Hec de Lacy, for one, was convinced that Len had the greater natural ability. But Len was unlucky with injuries and he was not able to settle into one position while he was at Melbourne.

Len married Flo Wiseman in 1933 and they had three children: Barbara, Norma and Kevin. From 1940 to 1945 Len served in the RAAF as an engineer based at Laverton and Darwin. After his discharge he became a foreman at Millers Rope Works in Brunswick, and also took on the job of coaching Fitzroy's thirds. Len coached them to a premiership in 1955 and in the following season he also worked as chairman of selectors for the seniors. At the end of the 1957 season, the senior coaching job became available and club secretary Ward Stuchbury contacted Len, who was holidaying in Queensland, asking him if he was interested in the job. Len returned to Melbourne to be interviewed by the committee and was appointed as senior coach.

Len, Norm and their wives loved the club's social activities. Family, football and friends were just about the extent of their interests. Marj watched every game that Norm coached and was a member of the Melbourne Football Club social committee; Flo was also interested in football and enjoyed watching it. Len didn't drink alcohol — his beverage of choice was lemon squash — but he was certainly no wowser and bought drinks for others when it was his round. Norm was a teetotaller until the age of 32 when, near the end of his playing career, he developed a taste for beer. But Norm drank in social situations only and never at home on his own. Len smoked; Norm did not. Len's only other vice was that he would eat a quarter-pound (113 gram) block of chocolate in bed every night. Neither of them was a churchgoer, nor very much interested in politics. Norm and Marj had a holiday house at Rosebud which during the Christmas break was an open house to Melbourne players and other football people. Norm had a trailer made to hold 20 dozen bottles of beer, which he took to Rosebud so that supplies would be on hand during the Christmas–New Year rush when people came calling. Regular visitors included Fred Fanning, a former team-mate; John Coleman, who lived nearby; Ken Hands, who coached Carlton in 1959–64; Mike Williamson, the TV football commentator; and their families. Peter Smith remembers one New Year's Eve when 29 people stayed the night at the holiday house, and recalls in his early teens being sent to the local fish and chip shop with an order for four dozen hamburgers. Len and Flo usually took their family to Rosebud also, staying at a friend's holiday house. As Ron Barassi puts it, the brothers were close 'without being in each other's pockets'. Both of them dedicated their lives to football: when Len was coach of Fitzroy's thirds and chairman of selectors, he was also coach of the Brunswick amateur team that played on Sundays. This meant that he was involved with football seven days a week. Neither of them made much money out of coaching: Barassi thinks that given Norm's habits of buying birthday presents for players and their families, and frequent rounds of drinks and providing meals for visitors, he probably lost money out of coaching.

Both Len and Norm were sticklers for fair play, honesty and discipline. Norm insisted that his players always be humble in victory, and although he hated losing he would always be the first to congratulate the opposition. Morris Reid, who played with the Fitzroy thirds in 1955, recalls Len always telling his players that if they did the right thing and made the ball their objective, the umpire would look after them.

Ron Barassi tells the story of how he lost his temper in a match against Fitzroy after an opponent's raised forearm struck in him the throat. Ron chased the player and decked him; Fitzroy's Kevin Murray then flattened Barassi in retaliation. All this happened behind play. Like Len, Ron worked at Millers Rope Works and on the Monday morning Len called him into his office and lectured him about the unacceptability of his conduct, which Barassi accepted without argument. Norm had a similar ability to impart his attitudes towards life and football to the men he coached. Max Walker, who had come from Tasmania to play football with Melbourne, once stayed overnight at the Smith house after he and Peter had a late night celebrating a successful day's play of district cricket. When the boys arrived home, Peter went into his parents' bedroom to kiss his mother goodnight, fell across the bed and accidentally kneed his father in the groin. The next morning, Peter left the house in tears after Norm's tirade, and then Walker was quietly but firmly ordered to sit down at the kitchen table. For twenty minutes, Smith spoke to Walker about the negative impact that drinking might have on his career. Max did not touch alcohol for six years after that.

For all their similarities in tastes and values, however, there were fundamental differences in Len's and Norm's dispositions. Both loved talking about football but Norm was wary of being bailed up by members of the public who wanted to put forward ideas about coaching and how to play the game. For that reason, Norm avoided places such as pubs and golf courses, and took his recreation in the backyard tennis courts at his home and holiday house. When mixing with football people, however, Norm was more outgoing. Len Fitzgerald, who made his debut for Collingwood in 1945 at the age of 15, remembers that Norm would advise him on the field, in a good-natured way, how he could improve his game. When he became a coach, Norm was happy to give that sort of advice to other coaches and players after the match. He was friendly with many of the other coaches of his era, in particular Geelong's Reg Hickey (the two even organised a Melbourne–Geelong family picnic that was held annually for at least a decade), Hawthorn's John Kennedy, Coleman, Hands and Collingwood's Phonse Kyne. Len Smith was more inclined to think about strategies and write notes about them, but he was never secretive and was happy to share these notes with anyone who asked to see them. After home games, Len had each of his players go into the opposition rooms, find their respective opponents and bring them back for a drink. Len then remained in the background while the players chatted. He was a happy man with a sense of humour and a giggle that was at times uncontrollable; Norm usually took a more serious view of things. Len never argued or raised his voice, but simply approached people and told them what he thought should be done; Norm said what was on his mind, sometimes bluntly and with force. When other people failed to do what Len thought was right, he usually hid his disappointment and tended to bottle his feelings up; Norm wore his heart on his sleeve. Len had a pleasant, warm exterior but remained a strong, determined person inside; Norm had a hard exterior but was soft underneath.

While Norm saw himself as a father figure to his players, Len used to refer to his players as 'my boys'. There was a subtle but significant difference here: Norm was an authoritarian figure who ruled fairly but with a rod of iron; Len was like a more patient parent who mentored and inspired in a quieter way. At half-time in one match at Brunswick Street, when Len was coaching Fitzroy and Norm was coaching Melbourne, Norm's scathing dressing-down of his players could be heard through the wall dividing the two teams' dressing-rooms. 'Listen to that, boys,' Len said quietly with a smile. 'How would you like to be coached like that?' Yet there was warmth and great mutual respect between the two brothers, who referred to each other as 'Normie' and 'Lennie'.

Len Smith never coached a League team to a premiership, and for that reason he was always in the shadow of his brother in terms of achievement on grand final day. But Len did not have the raw materials to work with that Norm did. The only time Len coached a team with a large number of star players was when he coached Victoria in the 1961 Carnival, a job he did so well that, at the end of his career, Essendon's Jack Clarke named him as the best coach he had played under 'by far'. Len also had a key influence over the way football developed in the 1960s, and what it would become in subsequent years. Early in his coaching career, Len's main strategy was to have his players play on at all times and run to where the ball had gone after they had kicked or handballed it. This helped his teams to move the ball quickly and keep possession of it, and Morris Reid recalls that when the method worked Len 'would dance with delight'. Over time, Len developed his tactics systematically and he wrote a list of playing principles that became known as 'The Golden Rules'.

When they were finally published in 1995 in Robert Pascoe's book *The Winter Game*, the golden rules hardly seemed profound and could almost have been called banal. Although anyone with much experience at playing the game would have known what these rules were, no-one had ever written them down. But the simplicity of the rules was deceptive. Though written roughly in pencil in an exercise book, Len's notes were virtually a textbook on how to coach and play the game. After Len died, Norm worked at revising them for publication but unfortunately this did not eventuate. Len's core idea was that at any stage in any game, a freeze frame would show one of three situations: team A would be in possession of the ball or about to win possession of it; team B would be in possession of the ball or about to win possession of it; or the ball would be in dispute. For each of these situations, Len identified a set of principles that he thought would help players make the best choice of action under match conditions. If his team had the ball, Len's rule was to 'get the ball through the goals in the quickest possible manner', by heading directly towards goal if forward of the half-back line, and by playing on quickly from marks or free kicks, with a kick or handpass. At least three team-mates were to be together near the ball at all times: one in possession of the ball, the others close by to talk, shepherd, back up, or receive a handball. The ball had to be kept moving to avoid packs. For Len, 'congestion is the ruination of football in as much that teamwork is nullified'. To receive the ball, team-mates had to play in front, and call clearly and intelligently for the ball. If the opposition had the ball, players had to play close to their direct opponents, punch the ball away from them, harass them and tackle them, and prevent them from playing on by standing on the mark and, if necessary, by holding up play, even at the risk of giving away a 15-yard penalty. If the ball was in dispute, the instruction was to get to contests to pick up crumbs, and to hit or kick the ball out of packs towards a team-mate calling for it in the open.

The use of these ideas by coaches brought about a significant change in the way that football was played. Traditionally, after defenders had taken a mark, they took a few leisurely steps backwards and kicked the ball long, towards or over a pack of players near the boundary line. If the opposition marked the ball, they would kick it back to a pack in the forward line. As a result, play was often slow and predictable. A great individual player like Albert Collier could bring other players into the game by marking the ball and distributing it with a handball; the rest of the team would then move the ball with stab kicks and handballs. Reg Hickey's Geelong teams, which won premierships in 1951–52, used handballs to create a loose man, starting their attacks from a dashing back line, led by back-pocket Bernie Smith and full-back Bruce Morrison. But these teams still depended on the contribution of champion key forwards to act as targets and kick match-winning scores. At centre half-forward, Collingwood's Frank Murphy (1927–30) and Phonse Kyne (1935–36) were fine premiership players. Geelong was served well by its captain, Fred Flanagan, at centre half-forward and George Goninon at full-forward. Len Smith's contribution was to apply the same method to every player on the team. His teams did not need champion forwards to play winning football: indeed, Len often rotated the players on his forward line to confuse the opposition, so that a rover might play in the full-forward position against a slower opponent for part of the game. What counted was a consistent, team-oriented contribution from all 18 players.

What was also unorthodox about Len's method was that it required footballers to think differently about the way they could contribute to their team's success. According to conventional football thinking, 'defenders' were those who played on the back line, having the job of keeping the ball away from the opposition's forwards. As Allan Jeans puts it, back-pocket players were at the time 'little grunters' who got the ball and kicked it straight back to where it had come from

(Bernie Smith, who ran with the ball and looked for a team-mate when disposing of it, was a brilliant exception). Players only considered themselves to be 'attacking' when they were in the act of shooting for goal. In most players' and coaches' minds, teams were made up of three types of players: defenders, forwards and those who took the ball from the defenders to the forwards. Under Len's model, teams were made up of either 18 defenders or 18 attackers, depending on the situation play was in. If Len's team had the ball, he wanted every player to follow his rules about getting the ball towards the goal as quickly as possible. Players were expected to use other team-mates to set up play, even on the back line. As soon as the ball was in dispute or possession went to the opposition, every player was expected to act as a defender and follow the appropriate rules for that situation.

To play the game Len's way, players needed to be fit. His method required players to be near team-mates who had the ball so that an effective handpass could be given. This placed an emphasis on fitness and led to the emergence of the 'running game' that began to dominate VFL football from the mid-1960s. Len's ideas about training — especially the measurement of players' fitness through monitoring pulse rates, and the introduction of training sessions the day after matches to help players recover and retain their flexibility — were years ahead of their time. To speed up movement of the ball, Len re-introduced the 'flick pass', a method of handpassing by which the ball was struck backhand with the palm of the hand, and which to most observers was indistinguishable from a throw. Footscray, whose captain-coach Ted Whitten was a master of the flick pass, was another team to build its game around it. Len devised drills so that players could practise this and other skills under match conditions. Players who made skill errors at training were required to do push-ups as a penalty.

Len's notes also set out his ideas on the importance of concentration and confidence. For Len, success in football came to teams in which all members were prepared to work hard, support each other, and concentrate fully on the job at hand. Overconfidence, the belief that victory can be taken for granted, and lack of confidence, when players become resigned to situations when things are going against them, were seen as destructive to team performance. Len considered that, if players kept following his rules, they would have a chance of turning things around even if their opponents were playing well. The need to maintain a high level of desperation and determination in the face of adversity was what Len called 'the price of success'. 'I have reached the conclusion,' he wrote in his notes, 'that some footballers or teams succeed because they cheerfully pay the price of success, and others, though they may claim ambition and a desire to succeed are unwilling to pay that price.'

At Fitzroy, Len's methods brought an instant improvement from the underachieving club. In his first year as coach, Fitzroy finished third at the end of the home-and-away rounds, having come second last the previous year. This was achieved without a single new recruit. Smith's Lions won the night premiership in 1959 (then contested at the end of the season by the teams that had missed the finals) and lost the 1960 preliminary final by five points. After Fitzroy lost its first three games in 1961, however, there were reports that for the past two years a feud had existed between Len and two committeemen about criticism of his coaching style. These committeemen were also members of the selection committee, with which Len had persistent disagreements over the selection of one particular player. Norm Smith had captain-coached Fitzroy in 1949 and was non-playing coach in 1950–51. His team (then unfortunately known as 'The Gorillas') was certainly competitive, but missed the finals each year. Norm's relationship with the Fitzroy committee was far from harmonious. Brian Hansen, a journalist who knew Norm well, later wrote that 'there were obstinate officials at Fitzroy and [Norm] Smith repeatedly argued with them. He felt some were holding the club back and he disliked the idea of officials interfering in his coaching plans'. Len encountered much the same problem with Fitzroy's management. Like Norm, Len did not achieve the kind of success at Fitzroy that would have forestalled internal criticism of his coaching methods. Len's methods were so radical that the passing of each year without a premiership gave more ammunition to his critics.

At the start of the 1962 season, one the club's most valuable players, captain Alan 'Butch' Gale, retired but the club's lack of vigour in recruiting meant that fresh talent did not arrive to replenish the team. As Ron Barassi later wrote: 'Fitzroy's country recruiting efforts were the poorest in the competition and no help at all to a coach'. After the team lost its first three games, the committee refused Smith permission to appear as a panellist on *Tony Charlton's Football Show*, but Len defied the committee, stating that he had appeared regularly on the show for the past four years and was going to continue to honour his commitment to it. Len probably would have been sacked at this point had he not enjoyed the complete loyalty of his players and a very high level of popularity among the rank and file supporters. 'Butch' Gale once wrote that:

> I resented him when he came along. I treated him with suspicion. He took over from a friend of mine — Bill Stephen [who left the club to captain-coach country team Yarrawonga] — and I thought he was too soft, too sympathetic . . . But he won me over to his way of thinking in just four or five weeks.

At the height of the dispute over Len's appearances on TV, the players met and passed a vote of confidence in their coach. Smith did not solicit this vote and when he learned of it he told the players to keep out of the dispute. When the president and secretary placed a newspaper advertisement stating that the players had passed a vote of confidence in the coach and committee, the players were incensed and told the press that the vote related to Len Smith only. In the *Truth*, Brian Hansen reported that 'Fitzroy players have told me that they are fed up with the pin-pricking war against Smith'. Hansen also argued that the committee was unwilling to sack Smith because they 'know that they would not see out the next election if they took this step. So it raises the question: Are they trying to goad him into leaving?' This does seem to be hard on Fitzroy's management: after all, Smith had handed in his resignation earlier in the season and the committee had not accepted it, and the people who Len was having trouble with were removed from the selection committee. Ward Stuchbury, club secretary, remained a loyal supporter of Len. These were not the actions of a club administration that was looking for any excuse to change its coach.

Len retired as coach of Fitzroy at the end of the 1962 season. In his statement to the press, he said that he felt too old and too tired to keep coaching. This was probably true, given his poor health and the strain that events at the club would have placed on him. However, his letter of resignation, which the club did not release, suggested a deeper problem. Len wrote:

> I feel that a younger man is needed for this most difficult job and he will need the fullest support and loyalty of every member of the Committee to carry out this job successfully. Unfortunately, I believe that this most necessary support and loyalty has not and would not be available to me. I am fully aware that [two members of the committee] have been criticizing my coaching, such criticism being typical of them . . . I am also most disappointed that recruiting was not carried out during the year.

Ward Stuchbury's reply, which has never been published, read in part:

> Len, please accept my sincere appreciation for the four wonderful and happy years you not only gave to me but to the Club generally. Full credit must be given you for our success . . . However one felt that success often brings complacency on the part of Officials and in this case is indicative.

One of the strongest critics of the club at this time was Alan Fitcher, a former Fitzroy player who was a writer for *The Sporting Globe*. Fitcher wrote that for a long time, at least back to his playing days in the 1930s, a 'cancer' of internal strife had affected Fitzroy. His conclusion was that Len Smith 'had been crushed through lack of support'.

Exactly why the Smith brothers had problems with their respective committees will probably always remain two of football's mysteries. Yet looking back on these episodes, two things are abundantly clear. First, the actions of the Melbourne and Fitzroy committees were based on massive errors of judgement.

Norm Smith was judged to have acted disloyally, when in fact his loyalty to Melbourne was complete. He was judged to have been acting in his own interests, when in fact Smith was clearly an unselfish and generous man. Finally, Smith was judged to have acted dishonestly, when in fact honesty was one of his strongest characteristics. Fitzroy's error of judgement was to think that Len Smith could be successful with less than complete support, and that he could be replaced as coach without any adverse impact on the club. Kevin Murray, at the age of 24 and with no coaching experience, was thrown in at the deep end and left to flounder by Fitzroy's passive recruiting policy.

Second, the internal disputes with the Smith brothers marked crucial turning points in the histories of the Melbourne and Fitzroy clubs. After Norm Smith was sacked, Jack Mueller predicted that 'I don't think we'll be able to replace Smithy at Melbourne for many, many years'. Alan Fitcher warned the Fitzroy committee 'that in Len Smith they have one of the top coaches in Australia, and if he goes the bottom will fall out of the club'. Both Mueller's and Fitcher's comments were prophetic. Melbourne would not make the finals again until 1987, and to date Norm Smith is still the last man to have coached Melbourne to a premiership. When Len Smith was appointed coach of Fitzroy, the club still had legitimate claims to be a major League club. It had won eight flags — the same as Carlton and Essendon — and the last of these had been in 1944, still within living memory. After Smith left the club, Fitzroy was immediately under pressure to survive as a League club in its own right and in the next six seasons won only 14 games and lost 97.

'This is madness! . . . they're all on the ball'

Allan Jeans was aged 21 when he was persuaded to come down to Melbourne from his home town of Finley in the Riverina to try out with St Kilda. It was his second attempt at League football: four years earlier he had played a few practice games at Carlton. At St Kilda he found a club that was wracked by disunity and badly in need of reform. During his first season at the club, the Saints won only one game. 'It was a poorly administered club,' he recalled.

> There were so many divisions in the club. When I arrived they had a president, secretary and committee of the First XVIII, a president, secretary and committee of the Second XVIII, a president, secretary and committee of the Third XVIII, a president, secretary and committee of the former players' association, a president, secretary and committee of the social club, and a president, secretary and committee of the cricket club. They were all going in different directions.

The pivotal event in the reform of the St Kilda Football Club was the appointment of Alan Killigrew as coach in 1956. Killigrew was St Kilda through and through, having been born and raised in the suburb, and had played with the club before his promising career was ended by World War II, during which he contracted tuberculosis. As a coach, Killigrew's mission was to ensure that St Kilda would 'cease being football's buffoons and to make other teams respect us'. He cut all but 16 players from the 1955 playing list and, with the assistance of new secretary, Ian Drake, and a young committeeman, Graham Huggins, began trawling country football districts looking for playing talent. They were prepared to flout the VFL's Coulter Law by offering financial inducements to recruits, and Huggins recalled that because the club made no funds available to them — the social club had surplus funds but insisted on retaining them to sponsor social activities — they had to dip into their own pockets and use the money that the club had paid them to reimburse their own travelling expenses. In the opening round of 1956, ten players made their debut for the club. Killigrew changed the colours of the sleeves and back of the St Kilda jumper from angelic white to a more menacing black. As a coach, Killigrew is most well known for his powers of oratory, but he also had a deep knowledge of the game and was one of the first coaches to place an emphasis on the use of the handball as an attacking, rather than defensive, weapon. His ideas about the handball were strongly influenced by those of Jack 'Cracker' Knight, a former Collingwood player of the 1930s, who was then coaching St Kilda's reserves.

By the end of the 1958 season, St Kilda's improvement under Killigrew was obvious: from last in 1955, the club had risen to eighth and won the night premiership. This was a minor honour but the first team trophy in the club's history. It was certainly an indication that under Killigrew the club was on the right path. But Killigrew was never given the chance to finish the job he started. Sectarian trouble had continued to brew at the club and boiled over at the end of the season. Killigrew, a devout Roman Catholic, resigned when he learned that a faction within the committee wanted him to be replaced, and took up the coaching job at Norwood. Jim Francis, an ex-Carlton champion and coach, replaced him, but he was very much an 'old school' coach who emphasised kicking and foot passing skills. By 1959, Jeans had risen to the position of vice-captain, but a rib injury forced him to retire at the start of the following season. Huggins, who by that time had become club president, arranged a coaching job at Sandhurst for Jeans, but Jeans was unable to obtain a transfer in his job in the police force. Instead, Jeans filled in as St Kilda's reserves' coach when Brian Gleeson could not continue the job due to work commitments. When the senior coaching job became available at the end of the season, Huggins and other members of the committee encouraged Jeans to apply. Religion was not a major issue to Jeans: he was a Protestant but he had married a Catholic. 'They got me because they wanted Killigrew's ideas,' Jeans says, 'but they couldn't get Killa back into the coaching role.'

Jeans found the early going as coach difficult. He was aged only 27, had little coaching experience and was in charge of players who had recently been his team-mates. After games he would spend time talking to opposition coaches, and developed a strong rapport with Norm and Len Smith. 'I think Norm and Len felt sorry for me because I was so young and took me under their wing,' Jeans recalled. St Kilda made the finals in Jeans's first season as coach, but was eliminated in a close game against Footscray. A few days after the game, Jeans received a letter from Len Smith, congratulating him on his achievement. In part, the letter read:

> Commiserations are no bloody good to a losing coach, as no matter what I say about St Kilda's wonderful effort in the Semi you yourself are still stuck with the disappointment of losing, and will be stuck with it until you settle down again. May I suggest

> that when you do settle down, don't look for any excuses Alan [sic], look for the reasons and then become determined to correct the weaknesses both in yourself and in your team so as you can go one better next year.

Len's idea that when things go wrong a losing coach should analyse what he has been doing, learn from past experience, and re-set his goals accordingly struck a chord with Jeans's way of thinking. The principle would serve Jeans well throughout his coaching career.

The Saints missed the finals narrowly in 1962 and at the end of that season two experienced players, captain Neil Roberts and defender Eric Guy, retired. But Ian Drake's recruiting continued to bring fresh talent to the club, and in the opening round of 1963 the team included four new players: Carl Ditterich, Ian Stewart, Bob Murray and Jim Wallis. Ditterich, Stewart and Murray became star players, but unfortunately Wallis had his career cut short by a knee injury. Ditterich and Murray were from St Kilda's metropolitan zone and several fine players came from this source.

But St Kilda's most important recruit during these years was Tasmanian Darrel Baldock. Baldock, who had resisted earlier offers from VFL clubs, was aged 23 when he joined the Saints, having captained his state in the 1961 Carnival. After only one season, Baldock was appointed as captain of St Kilda. Despite being only around 5 foot 9 inches (175 cm) tall and not a great high mark, Baldock played at centre half-forward. His assets were his ball-handling and recovery, and his disposal by stab-kicking and handpassing — skills he had honed as a boy through countless hours of kicking a ball hard against a brick wall and collecting it on the rebound. Baldock himself once said, 'The ball, because of its shape, never rolls or runs straight and that is why I also developed my somewhat ugly running action — a rock and roll style that keeps me low to the ground and always over the ball'. To win the ball, Baldock needed it to be delivered in front of him and in his fellow Tasmanian Ian Stewart, who played in the centre, he found a perfect foil. Stewart's vision and disposal complemented Baldock's ability to read the game, and both players were of immense value to St Kilda. In Jeans's judgement, 'when Baldock played well we never lost'.

In 1965 the Saints moved from the Junction Oval to the home ground of VFA club Moorabbin. (The original plan was for the two clubs to merge, but this fell through. Moorabbin was expelled from the VFA and disbanded.) At the Junction Oval, the football club's relationship with the ground manager, the St Kilda Cricket Club, had been deteriorating for some time. As was the case at many League grounds, gate money from football provided the bulk of the revenue, but a substantial part of this was diverted to the coffers of the ground manager (either a cricket club or city council) with little being returned in the way of improved facilities for spectators. Moving to Moorabbin would give St Kilda control over its finances and the amenities for its spectators. The club's new home was in the heart of a large market of potential fans in Melbourne's fast-growing southern suburbs. By the time a new grandstand and terracing had been built — financed largely by members of the St Kilda committee taking out mortgages on their homes — the Moorabbin Oval had been almost completely reconstructed. Close to a train station, and with plenty of room for further expansion, the potential of the venue was enormous. A crowd of 51 370 saw the opening game on Easter Saturday against Collingwood. With a brand new ground and a young, charismatic team, St Kilda Football Club had become chic. To thousands of people growing up in Melbourne's southern suburbs, St Kilda Football Club was as much a part of the 1960s as the Beatles were.

When St Kilda made the grand final in 1965 — the club's first since 1913 — no-one at the club had any prior experience in preparing for a match of such importance. When Jeans asked Norm Smith for advice he was told: 'Oh, go and talk to Lennie — he's smarter than I am'. Len had written to Jeans:

> I remember you saying that you were finding it hard to think of new things to talk about at your players meetings and I have jotted down in an exercise book home here quite a few points that I have used at lectures and players meetings and it is at your disposal if you think it will help give you new ideas.

Jeans went to Len's home and the two went through Len's coaching notes. Jeans was particularly impressed with Len's ideas about confidence and the importance of players working hard and concentrating in situations in which the match was not going in their favour. Jeans took his own notes and a summary of these was given to the St Kilda players at a team meeting.

Even with Len's wise counsel, inexperience cost Jeans and St Kilda dearly in the build up to the 1965 grand final. There was huge excitement around the club and several players were distracted by having friends and relatives arrive from out of town to see the game. During the season, Jeans had prepared for a crucial match against Melbourne by holding a team meeting at which the players watched films of Melbourne matches. The Saints had a huge win in that match, which confirmed in the players' minds that they now had the Demons' measure, and before the grand final Jeans decided to repeat the strategy and held a similar players' meeting on the Friday night. At the meeting the players built up and expended a lot of nervous energy and by the following day they were mentally tired. They started the grand final badly and were unable to peg Essendon back.

St Kilda's preparation for the 1966 grand final could hardly have been worse. The issues that Jeans had to deal with kept piling up. First, one of St Kilda's most important players, Carl Ditterich, missed the entire finals series due to suspension. Second, three weeks before the finals, Darrel Baldock strained his knee ligaments and was advised by a doctor to have his leg put in plaster for six weeks. Third, three regular senior players, Kevin Roberts, Ross Oakley and Des Kennedy were unavailable for the grand final due to injuries. Last, Collingwood's ace, Des Tuddenham, had run riot during the second semifinal, kicking seven goals and St Kilda had no idea who to play on Tuddenham in the grand final.

Baldock's injury was the most serious problem. He attempted to keep alive his chances of playing again that season by having his knee bandaged and undergoing intensive sessions of physiotherapy and strengthening the knee with weights. In the final home-and-away round, the Saints needed to win to make the finals. Baldock was still unfit and went to the races at Sandown to watch one of his horses run before the game. Against the orders of his medical staff, Jeans included Baldock as twentieth man at the last minute. The match was at Moorabbin and against lowly Hawthorn, but just before three-quarter-time the Saints were trailing. Jeans rolled the dice and put Baldock on, and within a few minutes he kicked a goal and helped to inspire his team to a narrow victory. At the last training session before the grand final, Baldock injured his knee again. Jeans brought training to an end immediately and had the players go off in a group so that no-one watching would know about the captain's injury.

Baldock played in the grand final, although needless to say he was a long way from being fully fit. He had a long shot for goal in the early minutes, and 'it felt like my knee went further than the ball!' Solutions to St Kilda's other problems more or less fell into place: Brian Mynott and Alan Morrow shouldered the ruck burden well to cover the loss of Ditterich; Jeans decided to play only one rover, with Ross Smith running on the ball all day and utility Daryl Griffiths playing close to the centre to support Stewart; second rover Ian Rowland was left out and John Bingley, who would play only eight games in his VFL career, was given the job of tagging Tuddenham.

The match was close all day, with neither side able to take control. About five minutes from the end, Baldock ordered all but a few key position players onto the ball, in the hope that his team would be able to get control of the ball and work it towards their goal. From Channel Seven's TV commentary position, 'Butch' Gale bellowed: 'This is madness! ... They're all on the ball'. One of his co-commentators, Ted Whitten, doubted the wisdom of the move. But the tactic worked and probably won St Kilda the game. With only a couple of minutes to go, scores were level and a boundary throw-in took place next to a Collingwood behind post. The ball was knocked over the back of the pack and three Collingwood players had a clear run at it. One of them seemed sure to get it and have a shot at goal. Baldock somehow was able to position his body between his opponents and the ball, tap it forward and clear the ball with a long kick. The ball was then sent to the St Kilda forward line where a crush of players caused Collingwood to lose possession, allowing 18-year-old Barry Breen to grab the ball and kick the winning point.

After the siren sounded, there were scenes of great emotion, many of them captured by Channel Seven's cameras and its commentary team. The most moving was a wonderful display of sportsmanship by Collingwood coach, Bob Rose, who made a point of working his way through a crowd of people to shake hands with Allan Jeans. Sitting a few rows behind the St Kilda coaching bench was Len Smith. A few days later, Len wrote and told Jeans that:

> I am not ashamed to admit that I had to use my hanky after the final siren, so glad was I that Alan [sic] Jeans and St Kilda had made the grade . . . I went home a happy man knowing how happy you would be . . . I guess you must know by now how much you have earned the respect of everyone connected with our great game.

'. . . Yellow and black!'

In 1963, Len Smith spent a happy year coaching VFA club Coburg. Then came an invitation to apply for the Richmond coaching position. Twelve months earlier, when he had resigned as Fitzroy coach, Smith told his friend Ward Stuchbury that 'I find now that the physical effort required of a coach is getting beyond me'. When the Tigers first approached Len, his response was that his views had not changed and he was no longer interested in coaching at League level. Nevertheless, the club's new president, Ray Dunn, and secretary, Graeme Richmond, persuaded him to change his mind. Dunn and Richmond were committed to reinventing almost every element of their club: its administration, its recruiting, its playing list, its playing style, and even its image. They needed a quality coach to bring about all of these reforms. At first, the Tigers had approached Bob Rose, who had been coaching Wangaratta Rovers, and then Essendon's captain Jack Clarke. But Rose was appointed coach of Collingwood, and Essendon refused the Tigers permission to interview Clarke, who was still a required player and would later coach the Bombers from 1968 to 1970.

Richmond had been one of the power teams of the League in the 1920s and 1930s and had built up bitter rivalries with other inner-suburban clubs, especially Collingwood and Carlton. By the 1960s, large numbers of Richmond people and their descendants were living out in the suburbs, giving the club an army of latent support. However, Richmond's long years as one of the chopping blocks of the VFL had reduced the number of people buying Richmond memberships and watching the club play. The club had not made the finals since 1947 and, in 1960, the year Len Smith took Fitzroy to second place on the ladder at the end of the home-and-away rounds, the Tigers won the wooden spoon. Recruiting players from outside the metropolitan zone was difficult because the club was not likely to play in the finals. The Punt Road ground was narrow and often muddy, and Richmond teams had developed a close-checking playing style in response to these conditions. The ground and its facilities were badly run-down and its future was threatened by plans to widen Punt Road itself.

The first action of the new administration was to establish a network of recruiting officers and scouts. Ray Jordan was appointed thirds' coach and would do the job with great success. John Nix proved to be a fine coach of the seconds. Once a potential recruit had been identified, Graeme Richmond, often accompanied by Jack Dyer, would visit the lad and his family and attempt to gain his signature. Richmond and Dyer usually arrived bearing gifts such as a small television set (which would be packed up and taken away if the player chose not to sign) and carried a bag with hundreds of ten-shilling notes which would be tipped out onto a table or the floor; despite this, the Tigers did not in fact offer prospective recruits much money. Royce Hart famously agreed to come over from Tasmania in return for a suit and a few shirts. Dick Clay received a used car for his signature when North Melbourne's hold on him expired. What was really being offered was the chance to be a part of a future premiership team. The Tigers could now sell themselves convincingly as a club with a future because they were making bold plans to play their home games at the MCG.

Len Smith was being offered what he had been denied at Fitzroy for years. As coach, he would be given plenty of raw material to work with because of the Tigers' aggressive recruiting and emphasis on developing junior talent. Furthermore, Len was promised that he would receive the complete support of the club's administration.

Ray Dunn told the club's annual general meeting that the 'Richmond committee will back Len Smith to the full'. The administration kept its word. As Norm Smith later wrote:

> When Len went to Richmond he received the utmost co-operation from Ray Dunn, Graeme Richmond and the committee. They gave him a free hand with his planning, accepted his principles of coaching almost without question, and helped him to get the type of player he wanted to develop a fast, play-on game for the MCG.

For a man like Len Smith, this was too good an opportunity to pass up. Such was Len's desire to take the job, and the Tigers' determination to have him as coach, that both sides were prepared to overlook any doubts they had about Len's age and his health.

Len's working relationship with Graeme Richmond soon developed into a personal friendship. Graeme Richmond, who died in 1991, was one of the most enigmatic figures in the history of Australian football. Richmond, who had played for the Tigers' thirds and seconds before his promising career was cut short by a knee injury, possessed a fanatical loyalty to his club and a steely ambition to take it to the top and keep it there. To many football followers he will be remembered for his ruthless, 'Godfather' image and his part in the infamous brawl at half-time during a game at Windy Hill in 1974; but many Tiger players recall fondly the genuine concern he showed for their welfare. In later years, Graeme Richmond would fall out with some of his friends and colleagues, as he did with Ray Dunn, for example. Not every Richmond coach would in the future enjoy the complete loyalty of the committee. But Graeme Richmond and Len Smith remained friends for the rest of Len's life. When Mike Williamson once asked Richmond what the best thing he did in football was, Richmond replied, without hesitation, 'signing Len Smith'. The secretary's unwavering support, and his dynamic boosting of the club, made him the perfect foil to Len's coaching.

As an administrator, Graeme Richmond played an enormously influential role in the transformation of the Richmond Football Club. Not only did he recruit nearly all of the members of the premiership teams of the late 1960s and early 1970s, but he helped to get the best out of those players by his use of a range of motivational tactics. Kevin Bartlett remembers that, before a match against a traditional rival such as Collingwood or Carlton:

> He would address the players like a general speaking to an army. He'd talk about going up Punt Road and crossing Victoria Street. 'There they'd be — the enemy. They're across there and we're going to hit 'em head on'.

He manipulated the media by feeding stories to his friend, Alf Brown, the leading *Herald* football writer, that were designed to 'needle' Tiger players. He also arranged to have photos of boom recruits, or of star players like Bill Barrot, a muscular, long-kicking showman who epitomised the new image of the club, appear in the newspapers often. This publicity generated enormous interest in a club that seemed to be going places, with a young, dynamic team.

Because Richmond's rise coincided with Melbourne's decline, potential recruits who wanted to be part of a successful team that played on the MCG were now more likely to listen to Graeme Richmond's sales talk than they were to Jim Cardwell's. The move to the MCG, where the facilities for spectators were far better than at Punt Road, made it easier for Richmond supporters, old and new, to come along and watch the team. In 1965, Richmond's first season of playing at the MCG, attendances at Richmond games were almost double what they had been the previous season, and from 1966 to 1969 more people watched the Tigers play than any other club. In 1960 a Richmond supporter named Jack Malcomson wrote the words to a new theme song (*We're from Tigerland ...*) and offered it to the club. This rousing song — easily the best of the VFL club songs — became part anthem, part battle cry for a new army of Richmond fans.

Len got to work quickly building a new team. The first change that Richmond players noticed was a greater level of intensity at training. Roger Dean, who had first played with the seniors in 1957, recalled the fairly easy regimen of Tuesday and Thursday night training before Len arrived. 'Len had different ideas on fitness — he was much more demanding — and we wondered what struck us when he came.' Smith took stock of his playing list and at the end of the 1964 season retained only 21 of the 47 players in his squad. Space had to be found for the players that Graeme Richmond had recruited and for likely types from the metropolitan zone. Len's preference was for 'big, fast men. I prefer 6ft. flankers, even wingmen, to smaller men, but they must have pace'. Francis Bourke and Dick Clay (recruited as a full-forward) would meet those requirements perfectly, and with Bill Barrot in the centre they formed probably the greatest centre line in the history of Australian football. Barry Richardson, who stood 6 foot 3 inches (190 cm) tall, was played as a half-forward flanker, although like Bourke and Clay he later became a key position player. Len knew that the process of grooming youngsters would take time, and predicted that it would not be until 1966 that the Tigers would be a genuine premiership contender.

Before that happened, Len had to develop in his players 'a will to win' and an attitude that 'when they were beaten, it hurt'. Len wanted the Tigers to play with a team spirit that meant that 'instead of going out on the ground expecting defeat, they expected to win'. He asked his players to think of each other as brothers, reasoning that they would be more likely to help out, to shepherd and talk to their brother than they would to someone who was not a brother. Len drummed his golden rules into the players, pointing out that if they all concentrated on following them the team would be more likely to develop just the right amount of confidence needed to win matches. When Richmond started winning premierships, the confidence of the players was one of its signatures. The Tigers epitomised a team that was prepared to pay 'the price of success'.

On the day before the opening round of the 1964 season, Len Smith suffered a heart attack. Len had first had a heart attack in 1958, four weeks before the finals. 'Butch' Gale filled in then and Len was able to resume coaching in the finals. After his second heart attack in 1964, Dick Harris, Richmond's reserves' coach, took over the job temporarily. Len spent about three weeks in hospital and was back helping Harris in an advisory capacity in round 6, even giving a pre-match address to the players. Two weeks later, Smith was given medical clearance to resume coaching. It was at the end of the 1964 season when Len suggested the club recruit Ron Barassi to captain-coach the team with Len acting as his assistant. When that plan fell through, Len resumed full control of the coaching job, despite his family's reservations. Len was aged only 52 but, for a person whose father had died of heart problems at the age of 58, and who smoked, the warning signs were not good.

Early in the 1965 season, Len called a young lad named Kevin Bartlett over for a chat during training. Bartlett, an 18-year-old from Richmond's local area, had been playing in the reserves. After asking how Bartlett was going, Len told him:

'You'll be on the bench this week.'

Bartlett was respectful — he thinks he may have called Len 'Mr Smith' at that time — but he could not hide a look of disappointment.

'What's wrong?' asked Len.

'Well,' said Bartlett, 'I thought I'd been going OK. I didn't think I'd deserved to be dropped.'

'No, no. You misunderstand me. You're going to be on the bench in the Seniors.'

In Bartlett's debut match, against St Kilda, he came onto the ground just before three-quarter-time and picked up about eight or nine kicks. After the game, Len asked Allan Jeans:

'What'd you think of my little boy today?'

'Well, he's pretty quick,' Jeans replied.

'We think he'll go a long way in the game.'

That was the last game that Len Smith coached. After training and a selection committee meeting the following Tuesday, Len had another heart attack. This time the doctors were adamant that he should retire, and the committee appointed Jack Titus as his replacement. After his convalescence Len remained involved as a selector. Although Titus had last played in 1943, he did a fine job, taking the Tigers to fifth place. But Titus did not want to continue beyond the end of the season, so a new coach had to be found.

Tommy Hafey had been a tough, hard-working back pocket for Richmond in the 1950s. When his League career came to an end, Hafey was appointed captain-coach of Shepparton and took them to three flags. Hafey liked and respected Len but his role model as a coach was Norm Smith. 'Melbourne's style during the 1950s was the greatest of any era I can remember — no nonsense, no frills, no finessin' — very, very direct.' Hafey's achievement at Shepparton was that he could take a group of young kids and get them to play the style of game that he wanted. That style, based on hard running, vigorous contesting for the ball and long kicking into the forward line, was modelled on that of Norm Smith's Melbourne. For Hafey's liking, Len's playing style required players to handle the ball a little too much and so run the risk of losing the ball. Hafey, a fitness fanatic who neither drank nor smoked, trained the Tigers hard. He took them to Percy Cerutty's training camp on Mornington Peninsula and led them on runs around The Tan, the gravel track that runs around the outside of Melbourne's Botanic Gardens. Tommy Hafey himself showed the same level of determination and honesty that he demanded from his players, and the respect he earned from his players as a result helped him to get the best out of them as footballers. Kevin Sheedy called him 'the best person I have met in football', and Kevin Bartlett believes that the players played more for Tommy Hafey than they did for the Richmond Football Club.

Len Smith passed away after another heart attack in July 1967, aged 55. He never got to see the team he helped to build — 'the best League side with which I have been connected,' he told a reporter — translate its potential into achievement. By coincidence, Richmond played Fitzroy the following Saturday, and everyone at the ground observed a minute's silence after the Last Post was played. The football community mourned Len's death widely and with sincerity. Harry Beitzel, a former umpire who then worked as a radio commentator, paid one of the best tributes:

> Football lost one of its greatest gentlemen, thinkers and lovers of the game with the sad passing of Len Smith. Len was always doing or saying something constructive for the good of the game and the players. Quiet, unobtrusive, analytical but a fantastic tactician and teacher, Len was welcome everywhere . . . To have known him was an honour — to count him as a friend a privilege — to have the chance of talking football with him an education.

A few months later, the Tigers edged out Geelong in a brilliant grand final. The team had a few veterans but by and large it was made up of young players, some of whom had long careers ahead of them. The Tigers blended skill with ruthlessness and a 'them and us' mentality that boosted morale and united the players. As the team approached the peak of its powers, even rejects from other clubs could be slotted in to fill gaps with great effect. One such player was Robbie McGhie, who was let go by Footscray, and filled the key centre half-back position in the 1973–74 premiership teams. McGhie was tall, fast and a long kick, with a streak of unpredictability that often interfered with the opposition's concentration — everything that Hafey was looking for in a player. The Tigers had a great record in grand finals, winning in 1967, 1969, 1973 and 1974. Their only grand final loss was in 1972 when they were shocked by a Carlton team that played brilliant football on the day, kicking the highest grand final score ever. Although the Tigers did not win the flag in 1975, the players were convinced that they were the best team in the competition that season. Hafey's coaching record is an impressive one and had Richmond won flags in 1972 and 1975, his record would have read six flags in a 10-year period, the same as Norm Smith achieved at Melbourne.

Of course, there is no way of knowing whether Len Smith, had he lived longer, would have had the same success at Richmond as Tommy Hafey did. Among Richmond people of that era, opinions are divided: on one hand, there are those who argue, as Graeme Richmond did, that Len 'set the whole philosophy, the whole style of game, gave us fresh thoughts and just regenerated a rundown Richmond Football Club'; on the other hand, Kevin Bartlett points out that Richmond under Len would have played a very different style of game from the physical, aggressive, long-kicking style they played under Tommy.

Although Tommy Hafey regards Norm Smith as his most important influence, he still maintained some important features of the coaching and playing style that Len introduced to Richmond. Hafey retained Len's concept of using tall, fast wingmen, believing that they could drop back into defence to make things difficult for the opposition's taller forwards. His instructions that players kick the ball long and move it quickly by playing on where possible followed Len's golden rule number 1 — 'Get the ball through the goals in the quickest possible manner'. Hafey insisted that Richmond get numbers to the ball, and used to tell his players that whenever he saw a photo of a match he wanted to see more Tigers around the ball than opponents. This was what Len was getting at in golden rule number 2 — 'Two men together at all times'. In his notes on golden rule number 6 which emphasised team spirit, Len wrote: 'Do things for each other without thought of reward'. Tommy was a master at building morale, loyalty and unselfishness in his player. Len instructed that when the opposition had the ball, rules 7–10 about minding your opponent and tackling and harassing him had to be followed by all players, including forwards. Hafey played tough players like Neil Balme and Ricky McLean on the forward line. Len would certainly have frowned on Balme's rough play in the 1973 grand final, but Richmond's aggression towards opponents with the ball was a logical progression from the ideas set out in the golden rules. While Hafey was Richmond's coach, copies of the golden rules continued to be handed to recruits when they arrived at the club.

It is taking nothing away from Tommy Hafey to say that Len Smith's influence lived on at Richmond long after he died. Tommy took many of Len's core ideas, married them with his own and produced a playing style that in many ways was different from the style that Len used in his own coaching. Len's ideas were powerful enough to be reshaped and re-created in a different context, and yet still remain recognisable. Tommy Hafey certainly deserves his status as one of the great figures in football history, but in his coaching the presence, even the ghost, of Len Smith can be detected. Tommy called the shots, but Len certainly remained an invisible part of the coaching panel.

Pride

A few weeks after the death of his brother, Norm complained of shortness of breath at training and went into hospital for a set of medical tests. Norm told the press that a cardiograph had shown his heart to be in good condition, but those close to him knew that coaching was now placing him under a great deal of stress. Len had tried to persuade Norm to give up coaching because it was clear, as Norm put it, that 'I was becoming more and more flattened by matches'. Marj had told him that she wanted him to retire. A few weeks before the end of the 1967 season, Norm received medical advice that he should enter hospital for a series of further tests. These showed a heart problem for which Norm received treatment. He decided to retire as Melbourne coach and his assistant, John Beckwith, took over. Norm told the press that 'I don't expect to have any yearning to coach again'.

Later in the year Norm felt his health improving and decided to run for a place on the Melbourne committee. Most of the other candidates put Norm last on their how-to-vote cards and he was unsuccessful. After the election meeting, acrimonious words were exchanged between Norm and some club administrators as the Smith family walked out of the MCG through the Members' stand. Norm had been given a testimonial dinner by the club but was insulted by the election snub. As had been the case when the club had sacked him in 1965, Norm felt that his record of service had entitled him to more loyalty from his club. He and his family severed all ties with Melbourne; his son, Peter, then a promising forward, went to Carlton.

Norm went along to watch some of Melbourne's games in 1968, sitting in the Members' stand. He also wrote a set of articles for *The Age*, one of which discussed some of the difficulties faced by the coaches of weaker sides:

> The main criticism I make is of the lower teams who do not put enough thought into their play — both team play and individual effort. And of some teams that have, over the years, been on the losing end of the stick, and do not develop enough club spirit and loyalty. Defeat becomes common to them, and they take it for granted. These clubs must try to build up a winning tradition, and develop to the highest degree a fierce pride in their team. If the club is not a proud one, it has little chance of success … A coach's role in rehabilitating a club is a vital one. And once having been given the job, everyone in the club must be behind him, accepting his policies and methods.

Norm was given a chance to apply those ideas the following season when South Melbourne offered him the coaching job. Marj did not want him to return to coaching, but there was no stopping Norm. The challenge was to lift a club that had not made the finals since 1945 and was in a precarious financial position. South's depth of player talent was thin: they had the great Bob Skilton, who was nearing the end of his career and had missed the entire 1969 season with a torn Achilles tendon; a champion defender, John Rantall; and a very promising centreman, Peter Bedford. The rest were competent League footballers, battlers and young hopefuls. The club supported Smith fully and understood the need for active recruiting, but the funds needed to chase big-name interstate players were lacking. Apart from John Murphy, a ruck-rover from Sturt, South's new players were from its metropolitan and country zones.

Even though the club was operating on a shoestring, Smith insisted that the training facilities and clubrooms be refurbished and painted. Norm trained the players hard and insisted that they refuse to accept defeat. Skilton remembers that while some players were motivated by a fear of Smith, others responded to the coach's hard driving by thinking, 'I'll show you, you bastard'. In 1970, Norm led South to fourth place in what was arguably the finest performance of his coaching career. As Skilton puts it: 'There were a lot better sides out of the Four than us in 1970, but Norm got the best out of us'. In the first semifinal, South led by five points after a thrilling first half but was overpowered by St Kilda in the second half.

South was not able to sustain that form in subsequent years. As players retired, the club could not find the new recruits needed to replace them. In the 1971–72 seasons, the Swans won a total of only five games. Norm wasn't sacked by South Melbourne, but at the end of 1972 the club told him that they were going to advertise the coaching position and that he was welcome to apply. Norm did not want to go through the process of applying for his own job, and resigned as coach. He then joined North Melbourne as an advisor to their newly appointed coach, Ron Barassi. Over the summer, Norm became ill with a brain tumour, and was unable to attend any matches in 1973.

Norm Smith died in July 1973 aged 57. Many tributes were paid to him, but one that is particularly worthy of note is that of Des Tuddenham. Tuddenham had been appointed captain-coach of Essendon in 1972 and had phoned Norm every week for advice. Although Norm had problems of his own, with South's poor form and his own deteriorating health, Tuddenham found that 'he was wonderfully generous. He always gave me constructive and thoughtful answers to my problems'. Tuddy's comments were an appropriate summary of Norm Smith the man:

> Norm generated tremendous personality and authority which brought him the respect of everyone in the game. But more than that, he put an enormous amount back into football.

Inheritors

Towards the end of the 2001 season, Geoff Kingston wrote in Adelaide's *The Advertiser* that:

> Allan Jeans is the greatest influence in the history of Australian football . . . Consider this. Four of the eight coaches in the finals were nurtured by him. And seven of the 16 AFL coaches learned the game from him when he masterminded the Hawthorn dynasty in the 1980s. True leadership is about influence long after you have gone like the ripples created when you drop a pebble into a pool.

Kingston knows his football: he is an excellent, respected journalist and a former All-Australian player. Jeans deserves to take his place in the elite company of the game's most influential coaches. There are not many people for whom that claim can be made. As Bob Skilton puts it:

> Most of us [players and former players] love the game. Many want to coach and pass on their knowledge to others. But there is only a small, hard core of people who are *able* to impart their knowledge to others.

But Allan Jeans's roots, and those of his protégés, are deeper than Kingston implies. In finding ways to get across to players his message on how the game should be played, Jeans used ideas from several sources that he had come across in his playing and coaching career. The ideas that worked would be retained and used again, perhaps in a slightly different form; those that were not successful were discarded. In Jeans's formative years as a coach, Len and Norm Smith passed on to him some basic principles and ideas about the game, many of which served well throughout his long coaching career. When Gary Ayres was asked in 2001, when he was coaching Adelaide, to recall the key features of Jeans's coaching, he said, 'He talked about sacrifice and being willing to pay the price to succeed'. That philosophy is derived from Len's ideas about confidence and concentration which Len shared with Jeans in the early 1960s. In his half-time speech in the 1989 grand final, when Hawthorn was trying to win back-to-back flags but was hampered by injuries to several players, Jeans took Len's idea about the price of success and presented it in a different way. He told the players a story about a boy who went to buy a pair of shoes and bought a cheap pair rather than pay the higher price for good-quality ones. The next day, Jeans told them, the boy's feet hurt and he wished he had paid the higher price, but by then it was too late. Jeans then asked his players to 'pay the price' that day. They were inspired — some had tears in their eyes — and they won the game by six points. Len's identification of the fundamentals of the game was embraced by Jeans who told his players that only three situations were possible in the game: 'They've got it; we've got it; its in dispute', as Ayres puts it. Jeans's belief that football was a simple and unchanging game was the basis for his most famous saying that the fundamental elements of football, however they were presented, were 'like sausages'. 'You can fry them, curry them, serve them with apple sauce, but whatever way you cook them, they're still sausages.'

Jeans was not the only person who used Len's and Norm's ideas as building blocks for a coaching career. When Ron Barassi took up the Carlton coaching job, he took Norm's ideas about discipline and teamwork and Len's ideas about training drills and the use of punishments for skill errors during training, and added several of his own, such as an insistence that players develop the ability to use both sides of their body for kicking and handballing. Ron's ability to get his ideas across to his players won him two premierships at Carlton and two at North Melbourne. In turn, Barassi's coaching would help to shape the ideas of a number of coaches, notably Robert Walls, Malcolm Blight and Denis Pagan. Similarly, a lineage exists between the game and philosophy of Tommy Hafey, which in themselves were influenced by the Smith brothers, and those of Kevin Sheedy and Mick Malthouse.

Len's and Norm's ideas had an impact on these and other coaches because they themselves had thought deeply about the game, could enunciate a set of ideas on how it should be played and, most importantly, were able to impart this wisdom to their players and anyone else who cared to listen. They were intelligent people who developed an interpretation of the fundamentals of the game that has proved to be enduring. Many of the ideas that Len came up with — such as the rotation of players on the forward line and using recovery training sessions shortly after matches — are now standard practice at AFL clubs. Norm's coaching philosophy — which emphasised teamwork, commitment and pride — can be identified in every football team, at every level, that plays the game successfully.

In 1979, the VFL paid tribute to Norm by introducing the Norm Smith Medal to be awarded each year for the best player in the grand final. The inaugural winner, Carlton's Wayne Harmes, was Len Smith's grandson. Although Norm had little time for individual awards, it is appropriate that his name will continue to be associated with players who can perform on the grand final stage.

8

John Kennedy
(1928–)

My modest contribution was to establish a tradition of having players who would go in and *get the ball*, at all costs.

JOHN KENNEDY

At the end of the working day, middle-class Melburnians who travelled home from their city workplaces on the train to Lilydale could see clearly the industrial landscape and crowded housing of Richmond. After the trains crossed the Yarra River they reached the station at Hawthorn, a village that marked the beginnings of Melbourne's eastern suburbs. From its birth as a suburb during the 1880s, Hawthorn retained its status as a place of genteel residence. Not all of its breadwinners were middle-class commuters and pockets of light industry and working-class housing developed. Nevertheless, churches and areas of substantial detached housing were prominent features of the landscape. Coffee palaces competed with hotels. When the City of Hawthorn opened a 10-acre sporting complex at Glenferrie in 1905, it was bounded to the north by Linda Crescent, a quiet residential street, and to the south by the clatter of a railway line. The oval and reserve were long and narrow and, when the grade of the railway line was raised after World War I to eliminate level crossings, the trains ran almost along the top of a narrow bank of terracing. Yet Glenferrie Oval retained a quaint charm even after the Hawthorn Football Club was admitted to the VFL in 1925. In the 32 seasons between 1925 and 1956, Hawthorn was virtually just making up the numbers in the competition: the club finished last or second last 21 times and won an average of four games per season. As club historian Harry Gordon wrote, even the club nicknames of the 1930s and early 1940s — 'the Maybooms', 'the Mayflowers' and 'the Mustard Pots' — 'tended to lack a certain belligerence'. Glenferrie Oval was a place where the home supporters, and even the players and officials, had learnt not to worry too much about the score. Graham Arthur, who joined the club in 1955, recalled that 'it was regarded more as a social league club. People enjoyed the cup of tea and cream cakes at half time'.

Although it was the only League club located in Melbourne's eastern suburbs, Hawthorn faced an uncertain future in the early 1950s. The club was administered well and had turned around an awkward financial situation that existed before World War II, when it could not always afford to pay its players; nevertheless, it remained vulnerable to assertions that on the field it was not up to League standard. In 1950 Percy Taylor, writing in *The Argus*, suggested that other clubs could assist Hawthorn by transferring some of their seconds' players. Three years later *The Sporting Globe*'s Hec de Lacy attacked the club's 'lilywhite approach to football ... At Hawthorn they have approached their commitments with kid gloves, without showing the vigour of other clubs'. For de Lacy, the time had come to ask whether the interests of the VFL clubs, and the game in general, would have been better served by having Hawthorn leave the competition and replacing it with either a strong VFA club, such as Port Melbourne or Coburg, or a new team called Eastern Suburbs, located further out on the suburban fringe.

Within ten years, however, Hawthorn had shed forever its friendly, gentlemanly image. The name 'Hawthorn' was now associated with virtues such as commitment, loyalty and courage and the club had earned the respect of the football community that it craved. The

Hawks' first finals appearance in 1957, and first premiership in 1961, was evidence of how far the club had come. After 1961, Hawthorn won another eight premierships before the end of the century, the same number as Collingwood, Melbourne, Geelong and Richmond put together during that period. Graeme Richmond probably spoke for all the other League clubs when he said, 'It grieves me to admit it, but we'd all like to be like Hawthorn'. This transformation was a team effort, brought about by a group of people, working in the same direction and with a common goal, who achieved more than they could have done as individuals. It became part of the Hawthorn ethos that success was the work of the many rather than the few, and that credit for what had been achieved was to be shared by all ranks at the club rather than bestowed on individuals. Nevertheless, it is impossible to overlook John Kennedy's contribution to the making of this football club. As captain of the club during the early years of team building, and coach of its first three premierships, Kennedy left an imprint on the Hawthorn philosophy that is still clearly visible. Kennedy's mentors and role models helped him to develop his ideas about football and coaching, his players and staff helped him implement them, and the players that he coached extended and applied them in new ways when they became coaches themselves. Yet the way in which Kennedy listened and spoke to, and interacted with other people was such a product of his own values and upbringing that it is difficult to imagine another coach producing teams that would have played in the same way that his did. Don Scott, who was club captain in 1976, Kennedy's last year as Hawthorn coach, told Channel Seven's Mike Williamson in an interview that Kennedy's football philosophy was deceptively simple. The basic message — 'go and get the ball, and when the opposition has the ball do something about it' — was straightforward, but there were several ways in which they could have been put into practice. The methods that Kennedy developed were designed specifically to counter the strengths of Melbourne and Collingwood; they also brought into the game new standards of intense training and hardness in competing for the ball. Until other clubs copied them, these methods were unique to Hawthorn.

Hard times

John James Kennedy was born in 1928 when his father, also named John James Kennedy, was aged 42. His mother, Margaret Cochrane, was 13 years younger than his father. Two more children, Leo and Margaret, would follow. The Kennedys were a Catholic family that lived in Camberwell. John Kennedy Sr worked as a cigar maker but, when the Great Depression hit, his firm began laying off workers, first the unmarried ones and then those who were married. After Kennedy lost his job he was out of work for two years. John Kennedy Jr was aged only 15 when his father died. Hard work and the support of a strong family — both immediate and extended — enabled the Kennedys to cope with this tragedy. With the assistance of Margaret's family, who were market gardeners, they were able to keep the family home. John Jr completed his education and, although he initially wanted to study Law, he took up the financial assistance available through an Education Department studentship and did teacher training. He became a teacher of English and History in technical schools.

All of the Kennedys were interested in football but although they lived in Hawthorn's territory, John Jr was a Collingwood supporter. Kennedy later recalled that even as a boy he admired the way that the Collingwood committee demanded the loyalty of the players. John was an independent and self-contained young man, and still at Teachers' College, when he was approached by Hawthorn and invited to try out with them in 1949. He declined the invitation, but the following year he walked into the club unannounced having decided 'to see how I would go'.

A new coach was in charge at Hawthorn when Kennedy joined the club in 1950. Bob McCaskill was a coach whose contribution to the development of the game has been overlooked unjustly by historians. Born in 1896, McCaskill played 36 games for Richmond in the early 1920s before taking up a coaching job at Sandhurst in 1926. In his first season, he took the Bendigo League club from last to runner-up, and eventually coached there for 15 years, winning nine premierships, six of them in a row. In 1941 McCaskill was appointed coach of North Melbourne. His coaching career there, which ended in 1947, was interrupted by war service in 1942–43, but in 1945 he took the struggling club to the finals for the first time. McCaskill's credentials were impeccable but his health was failing due to chronic inflammation of the kidneys. Hawthorn's reserves' coach, Jack Hale, became McCaskill's assistant, and when the coach's eyesight began to deteriorate Hale had to tell him what was happening on the field. They made a fine coaching team, with Hale gradually taking more of the workload and becoming acting coach when McCaskill was hospitalised at the start of 1952. Hale had been a champion player at Carlton before his career ended prematurely due to a serious knee injury, and he had coached South Melbourne in 1948–49. After McCaskill died during the 1952 season, the Sandhurst Football Club paid tribute to a man who 'taught our youth the fundamental requirements of real manhood . . . courage, self-reliance, determination and tolerance'. Dr 'Sandy' Ferguson, who was then Hawthorn's medical officer, described McCaskill years later as a man of 'immense personal integrity'.

It was almost inevitable that such a coach would have a significant impact on John Kennedy. McCaskill 'was strong on discipline', Kennedy recalled, 'and was a magnificent speaker. I was at an impressionable age when he came into my life and ready to be influenced by someone'. In Hale's words, McCaskill was 'a good bloke, brash at times, hard as iron. He was an army man and very tough'. He was determined to rid Hawthorn of its 'social club' mentality and he made sure that the players were trained hard. It was at McCaskill's insistence that the club's uniform be changed from dark brown with a gold 'V' to one of brown and gold vertical stripes, because he believed that the new uniform would make the players look bigger. McCaskill demanded that his players remove all traces of personal feeling from their game; he wanted players to show neither fear nor malice and be prepared to play on after being injured, if possible. His emphasis on discipline, hard work and unselfishness struck a chord with Kennedy's own values, which had helped his family to cope with adversity.

McCaskill wanted to build a winning attitude at Hawthorn. 'What I think has kept Hawthorn down most has been inability to feel the satisfaction of hard-won success following sustained endeavour,' he told *The Sporting Globe*. That, too, was something that Kennedy could relate to. John was sportsmanlike but underneath he did not accept Hawthorn's losses well and soon tired of comments made at after-match functions by well-intentioned opponents who told him year after year that 'you'll have a good side once you get a couple more good players'. Kennedy remembers getting onto a tram one day and being spotted by two young schoolboys who recognised him as a Hawthorn player. The boys were talking to each other, but John heard one of them say, 'That's Kennedy', to which the other responded, 'Yeah, too bad he's with a club like that'. Such incidents, and the generally negative light in which the Hawthorn Football Club was portrayed in the media, strengthened the resolve of Hawthorn people to have their club win a greater level of respect among the football community and the general public. For McCaskill, this could only be built on the foundations provided by a strong administration. There was no point in the coach expecting players to show commitment to the club, at the risk of personal injury, unless the administration operated to standards of honesty and loyalty that would make the club worth fighting for. Kennedy thought that McCaskill was right, and argues that the quality of people such as Ferguson, Ron Cook and Phil Ryan — all of whom gave long, financially unrewarding service to the club in various capacities, including terms as club president — helped to build a strong club spirit at Hawthorn.

Bob McCaskill had a game plan, built around three ideas, that was years ahead of its time. The first idea was that players who won the ball and had their back to the goal were to handball backwards to a player who was facing the goal and 'who had the picture', as McCaskill put it. Players with the ball would thus not have to turn, and perhaps break a tackle, and would give the ball to a player who was in space and had a clear view of goal. Years later, this method would form part of what became known as 'backplay' at Jack Oatey's Sturt. It is now a standard feature of modern football.

Second, players were instructed to kick the ball into space to where a team-mate would be leading. This also became a feature of the Oatey game plan. McCaskill told his players to take risks and kick the ball across goal rather than to where play would be crowded. 'If the play is on one side of the ground, then your opportunities are on the other side,' he used to say. This, too, is now a common football tactic.

Third, players were instructed to play on and keep the ball moving at all times. In the early 1950s, teams such as Geelong made use of play-on tactics, but McCaskill's game 'was much more daring', as Kennedy recalled, as it required players to play on regardless of the circumstances.

There was little if any improvement in Hawthorn's playing fortunes during McCaskill's tenure as coach. The team lacked quality players, lost every game in 1950 and won only four the following season. But Kennedy never forgot what he learned from McCaskill about the way that football should be played. When he became Hawthorn coach, Kennedy used part of the McCaskill game plan — the emphasis on play-on football, risk taking and constant movement — and made it the cornerstone of his own style of play.

The most traumatic situation that the club had to deal with during Kennedy's years as a player was when Alec Albiston and Col Austen left the club in 1950. When McCaskill was appointed, Albiston, who had been captain-coach for the past three seasons, was happy to step down as coach but wanted to retain the captaincy. Apparently, certain members of the committee promised this to him. During the practice matches, McCaskill became convinced that Kevin Curran, a strong player with a distinguished military service record, was the man to lead the team. When it was announced that Curran had been appointed captain by a unanimous vote of the committee, both Albiston and his friend Austen sought clearances (Albiston went to North Melbourne and Austen went to Richmond). Kennedy remembers the situation as being 'terrible', as the players involved were all fine men whom the club could not afford to lose. His view was that the whole sorry episode caused the administration to take stock and resolve that 'from now on no one makes any promises to anybody off the top of his head. We do things as a committee'. It was certainly a turning point in the club's history. Sandy Ferguson recalled that when he became president in 1953:

> I was determined that the events which hurt us so badly at the start of 1950 would never happen again. I adopted it as one of my principles that there were no secrets in the club, that everyone knew what everyone else was doing . . . I made it clear that if grievances occurred and they always must — they had to be settled in private. The big thing about 1950, though, was that it forced the realisation that something had to be done, that all aspects of the club needed to be looked at.

Because Curran was a Catholic and Albiston was from a prominent Protestant family, there were suspicions, which have never been substantiated, that the club's treatment of Albiston was motivated by sectarian bias. Kennedy is adamant that sectarianism was not a major issue for McCaskill, but Hale was troubled by the potential divisions within the club, having seen how destructive they had been when he was coaching at South Melbourne. Hale decided to tackle the issue head on, by having Catholics and Protestants compete in teams against each other during match practice and training exercises. Hale, a Freemason of Scottish descent, led the Protestant group, while Kennedy emerged as the leader of the Catholics. New recruits were sometimes perplexed when Hale asked them: 'Whose side are you on? Are you a Christian like me, or an Irishman like Kennedy?' Though Hale and Kennedy were each committed to their individual faith, the absurdity of the competition between the two groups turned the whole sectarian issue into a joke. There was light-hearted banter between the groups at the club, rather than mistrust and resentment.

This was typical of the general sense of fun at the club. After home games, players were required to attend a social function in the clubrooms, at which everyone was expected to take his turn at singing a song or telling a joke. One of the players, Roy Simmonds, was a gifted musician and he accompanied these performances on the piano or banjo. Kennedy recalled one night after training that he was talking to a visitor in the clubrooms and Simmonds ran through the rooms at top pace, stark naked. Closely following Simmonds was Jack Hale, also naked, but toting a bucket of water.

On Monday nights the players met at Hale's house in Bentleigh to discuss the previous Saturday's match. Using pennies and shillings to represent players, Hale would demonstrate tactics on a table. Hale was being paid £8 per week for coaching the club, but his wife was spending around £4 each week on tea, sandwiches and cakes for the players. The players who were single would also go to Hale's house on Sunday night and discuss football over soup and toast. Kennedy was a part of this bachelor group until he married Dulcie Delbosco in 1957. (They would have four children: Maureen, John, Bernard and Patrick.)

Hale continued the work that McCaskill had started. As a coach, he was just the man to instil both the values he had learnt at Carlton about the importance of winning, and those of Ferguson, who wanted every person who had become involved at Hawthorn to be the better for the experience. Though Hale had been a tough player and remained a belligerent person as a coach, he made sure that underage players did not touch alcohol while at the club. His demand that players show courage at all times, even when in pain, seeped in to the team's playing style. The administration supported Hale's team building through aggressive recruiting. Like most other clubs, Hawthorn ignored the Coulter Law ban on paying signing-on fees to new recruits. Clayton 'Candles' Thompson, a giant ruckman from Sturt, was paid a huge fee of £700 ('petrol money' was how Hale later described this, with a smile), while Graham Arthur, whose father had played for Essendon, received £250 for joining the Hawks from Sandhurst. Hale's finest hour as a coach came in 1957 when he led Hawthorn to the finals and in the first semifinal they defeated his old club, Carlton.

Although John Kennedy won four club best and fairest awards, it is fair to say that he was not a champion player: as a ruckman he was somewhat awkward and relied on grit rather than athleticism to make his way around the ground and win the ball. There was a lack of fuss and flair about his play that reflected both his ability and personality. But he learned from his mistakes and picked up tricks of the trade from opposition ruckmen. Kennedy was the embodiment of the McCaskill principle that footballers had to be prepared to play on while in pain for the good of the team: in one match he played with a broken arm, strapped up, before going off at three-quarter-time. He had learnt from McCaskill how to protect himself and he played with a vigour that sometimes raised the ire of opposition supporters. 'When the Melbourne members hooted that sounded like a Beethoven symphony to me,' he says. Nevertheless, he was never reported — 'not even cautioned', as he put it — in a League career that spanned ten seasons. He was a true sportsman, with a genuine sense of fairness, something that was revealed in a story told by Sandy Ferguson to Mike Williamson. In the 1957 preliminary final, Kennedy broke his hand early on in a marking contest. As a result, he had a poor game and his opponent, Melbourne's Bob Johnson, was the best player on the ground. After the match, Kennedy told Ferguson, who had strapped John's hand, 'don't you tell the press about this'. Kennedy wanted Johnson, whom he admired, to 'have his day' and he wanted to make sure that nothing distracted people from that. Ferguson, who would serve as club president until 1967, got to know Kennedy well over the years. At the end of the 1980s, Ferguson was still adamant in his view that 'John Kennedy is the greatest man I've ever met'.

Kennedy was a natural leader, despite his introverted nature, because he set an example for the rest of the team through his preparation and play. As early as 1952, McCaskill had identified Kennedy as a future Hawthorn captain, telling Phil Ryan that 'with responsibility he'll really blossom'. Kennedy was one of a group of players that included Arthur, Simmonds (who had invited himself to try out at Hawthorn because he thought that it would be easier to get a game with the bottom club) and John O'Mahoney (who later became the club's chairman of selectors) who met with Hale under the showers after every match and discussed what could be done to lift the team's performance. The group's post-mortems would often continue in the rooms until about 7 pm. After Kennedy became captain in 1955, Hale would sometimes use him as a target for personal criticism to stir the team up. The first time this happened was during a half-time break when Kennedy began to make a suggestion and Hale cut him off and delivered a burst of invective about his game. Kennedy was furious with Hale but when he confronted him later the coach simply smiled and said, 'We won the game didn't we?'

'No place for timid souls'

At the end of 1959, the committee appointed Kennedy to replace Jack Hale. Hale was still highly respected but a majority of the committee decided that he had taken the team as far as he could and that it was time for a change. Kennedy got the job ahead of Horace 'Tubby' Edmonds, a former Collingwood player who had coached Hawthorn reserves to the flag in 1958. Though the margin in favour of Kennedy was only one vote, the club was united in its desire to earn the respect of the football world through achievement on the field. In the VFL of the early 1960s, success would only come to teams that could find a way of beating Melbourne. That was a tall order, but at least Hawthorn could trouble Melbourne with the brand of hard, play-on football that McCaskill and Hale had developed. Almost invariably, however, the Demons and other strong teams such as Collingwood were able to move away from Hawthorn towards the ends of matches. Kennedy observed that:

> Melbourne were a great side and a very successful side, with a lot of skill, the best coach ever [Norm Smith] and a terrific leader [Ron Barassi] — they had a lot going for them. The papers used to write all about their skills, but we used to worry Melbourne a bit, particularly at Hawthorn. I used to notice that in a tight last quarter Melbourne would beat us, but it wasn't because they were more skilful, it was because most of their players were *bigger* than our players. [Ian] Thorogood, Geoff Case and these men were bigger than our men. They didn't go out of their way

> to bowl them over, they just kept boring in at the ball and the sheer physical size of them knocked us rotten. And so I thought 'if ever we're going to get anywhere we're going to have to match that size'.

For Kennedy, the logical response to this was to make his team fitter and stronger than any other in the League and to develop a method of play that would enable his team to exploit this advantage. Graham Arthur recalls that the first thing Kennedy said to the players as coach was:

> I don't believe that VFL footballers have scratched the surface as far as physical fitness is concerned. We're going to go after it and that's where our strength will lie, regardless of skills.

Under Norm Smith, Melbourne had led the way in physical fitness and strength but now Kennedy intended to take Hawthorn past that standard. In addition to a heavy program of running and match practice, Kennedy made use of circuit training, a routine of stretching drills and exercises which had been introduced to the club by Brendan Edwards, a player who was then a physical education student. At first, Edwards had done the drills on his own in the clubrooms after training, but in 1958 Kennedy and Arthur joined in and, in the following year, Hale ordered the entire team to participate. For David Parkin, who joined the club in 1961, the Hawthorn of that era 'set a new standard in preparation that had never been seen before'. At that time somebody in the press dubbed the team 'Kennedy's Commandos'.

Kennedy's instructions to his team were to get the ball, knock over opposition players (with hip and shoulder bumps) if they were in the way and move the ball on quickly by playing on at all times. Kennedy wanted the ball to be kept moving even when the opposition had it and told his players to throw the ball back to them immediately if it was their kick. It was not attractive football because, as Parkin put it, 'everyone was on the ball'. Arthur remembered that with Kennedy in charge 'nobody would dare run off the line of the ball'. Kennedy's view was that such a relentless style of play would wear the opposition down and allow Hawthorn to take control through their superior fitness. The club supported him with an active recruiting campaign, which was in the hands of a sub-committee headed by Ron Cook. This produced some skilful players, but also others, like 'Delicate' Des Dickson who, as Parkin commented, 'you wouldn't want to see coming the other way'. This recruiting meant that Kennedy could add bigger players to the team, like Ian Mort who was as big and strong as many ruckmen in the League. Kennedy played him as a half-forward flanker.

Although Kennedy wanted his team to prevent the opposition from controlling the ball, his game plan was not totally defensive. He asked his players to take risks, especially when they were trailing on the scoreboard. He told the players that if they simply played close to their man they wouldn't win the game, arguing that that was what had happened during the Great Depression when people tried to avoid risks by hoarding their money and thus making the crisis worse by taking money out of circulation. 'We've got to spend our money,' he would tell them when they were behind, by handballing and playing on, to get back into the game.

Success did not come immediately. The Hawks lost the first five games of 1960 and the committee was concerned about Kennedy's obsession with play-on football, as the tactic often backfired during games. At one stage the committee wanted Kennedy to make a comeback as a player so he could offer direction on the field. Hale was asked by the committee to speak to Kennedy about modifying the play-on style, but the coach refused to alter his method. The players believed in their coach and kept trying and, after breaking through for a win in round 6, the Hawks won five in a row. They won the last six matches of the home-and-away round but missed the finals on percentage. Both Kennedy and Arthur are of the view that Hawthorn would have won the flag in 1960 had the team made the finals. Parkin believes that in the following season Hawthorn would have beaten a combined VFL side because they 'were hell-bent on achieving what no other Hawthorn side had done'.

Over the years Kennedy developed a warm relationship with his coaching rival Norm Smith based on mutual respect. After games the two would stroll onto Glenferrie Oval or the MCG and talk about football in the darkness. Norm was never secretive and Kennedy was well aware that Norm instructed his players to make a special effort when they were playing Hawthorn. John knew that Norm always told his team that Hawthorn 'will hit you hard, so get in first'. The 1961 second semifinal, in which Hawthorn defeated Melbourne by seven points, was the toughest game that Kennedy had ever seen. 'It was no place for timid souls,' he told Williamson. After the week's rest, the Hawks were fresh again for the grand final. In the second half they powered away from Footscray, and Kennedy later commented that at the celebrations afterwards he realised for the first time what an important part of many peoples' lives football was.

Kennedy's image as a tough, stern disciplinarian who stood for no nonsense was created, at least in the minds of many of his players, by incidents such as that told by Garry Young, a member of the 1961 premiership team. After the round 2 games of 1960 were postponed due to bad weather, Young heard the news on the radio and went with his wife to the movies on the Saturday afternoon. When he arrived at training on the Tuesday, Young learned that the players who had gone to the club on Saturday had been taken on a 24-kilometre run. 'Then Kennedy gathered us in the training room,' Young told Harry Gordon, 'and in that harsh, schoolmaster's voice of his boomed: "All players who attended here on Saturday go to the right side of the room . . . those who missed go to the left!"' Only Young and full-forward John Peck had been absent on the Saturday. 'Kennedy glared at us and snapped: "Off with your boots and socks and meet me on the oval in two minutes"'. Kennedy, also in bare feet, simply said that the three of them were going to run 30 laps. As they ran through the cold mud, Young remembers being 'freezing, miserable and in pain'. As Kennedy and Young started the last lap, Kennedy ordered that they sprint to the end. Young had to be helped up the race by a trainer; by the time he had recovered, the coach had showered and gone home. Young wandered down the race and saw that Peck still had a couple of laps to run.

The incident reveals much about Kennedy as a coach and as a person. Young and Peck accepted their coach's command without complaint; it would have been difficult for them to do otherwise because Kennedy himself had also taken part in the run. (In fact Kennedy was the only person who had gone on the runs on both Saturday and Tuesday.) Kennedy's response to the errant players is also instructive. Norm Smith would have probably shouted at them, but it was more in keeping with Kennedy's character to speak to them hardly at all and then have them undergo the penance of physical exercise, which he also participated in. It would have been reasonable to assume that Kennedy was a tough man, given his Spartan training, his insistence on high standards of discipline and self-sacrifice, the way he used his deep, powerful voice to get his message across, and his total lack of flamboyance. In fact, what people thought was toughness was, as Don Scott put it, 'just the aura that he created and the image he put forward'. Kennedy the man was quiet and reserved and, although he had a warm sense of humour, his preference for avoiding social situations meant that he never got to know his players as well as Norm Smith did. He was not the sort to go to the social club after games and he always spoke to the players as a group. He had learnt from Len Smith that once the game was over 'it was time for the coach to *shut up*' and leave the players alone to relax. 'I don't think John had a one-on-one conversation with any of us in all the time I was there,' said Leigh Matthews, who played for Hawthorn for 17 seasons. The rapport between coach and players came from the team doing the things that Kennedy asked it to do, and everyone sharing the satisfaction of victory afterwards.

In 1962, the Hawks fell to ninth place, winning only five games. At the time it was difficult to pinpoint the reasons for the slide, but Kennedy later reflected that 'the emotional commitment in '61 was so great that it might have left us a bit flat next year'. Kennedy took much of the blame for this himself. He told Williamson in 1990 that:

> The intensity of the thing is good up to a point, but you've got to be able to go and have a chat to the players individually, which I don't shine at, and I think that would have helped to get the players going on a more even keel.

Hawthorn bounced back in 1963, but Geelong was too good in the grand final. The Cats' Western Australian ruckman 'Polly' Farmer, who due to injury had played only six games in his debut VFL season in 1962, made all the difference.

'Your troubles start when you get to the top'

Relations between the Hawthorn and Geelong clubs had been tense during 1963. After the teams met in the final home-and-away round, the Cats' coach, Bob Davis, told the media that 'Hawthorn is the worst and dirtiest team I've seen'. Geelong, with Farmer and a host of other brilliant players, was a team for the purists and their style was the opposite of Hawthorn's. During Hawthorn's 'social club' days, Geelong and the other clubs would have regarded the team as a good bunch of blokes, but began to view them with hostility when the Hawks became harder to play against and beat rival clubs. Kennedy did not care about that, but he did regard the accusation that Hawthorn was a dirty team as unfair. Although he admitted that things happened on the field that he 'was not proud of', he and his club never condoned deliberate foul play. For Kennedy, the aggression of his players was directed at the ball and any opposition player who stood between them and the ball. There was nothing vindictive or personal about the physical contact that followed. Some clubs accepted this as a normal part of the game; others did not.

Regardless of whether they hated the Hawthorn style or not, it was clear that Hawthorn's success created a new set of challenges for opposition clubs. To be competitive, clubs had to rethink their training and coaching strategies and become more active in recruiting. Some clubs failed to rise to this challenge, but others reinvented themselves and became serious premiership contenders. St Kilda, Geelong, Carlton and Richmond were no match for Hawthorn in 1961, but in subsequent years they became much more difficult opponents. As McCaskill had told Kennedy, 'your troubles start when you get to the top'.

After the 1963 grand final, Kennedy and Ferguson were invited to Geelong's premiership dinner. Kennedy was happy to go, but he told Ferguson that he would not be apologising for the way his club played the game. John was greeted warmly by Bob Davis and Reg Hickey, who had coached Geelong's last premiership team. He was then asked to say something as opposition coach:

> I congratulated them on being a great side and having a wonderful win. I said, 'As far as Hawthorn is concerned, there have been certain things said about Hawthorn by this club, but if you think or anyone here thinks that Hawthorn, while I have any say, will change one little bit, they're wrong. We'll go harder and tougher and fiercer than ever'. The whole place stood up and cheered. That's Geelong — I mean, that would have been greeted at Carlton or Collingwood by sullen silence.

Kennedy wanted to atone in 1964 for losing that grand final but did not get the opportunity to do so. At the end of 1963, he was transferred by the Education Department to Stawell Technical School to become Principal. He coached the local team but missed being involved at the VFL level. In 1967 he was transferred back to Melbourne as Principal of Swinburne Technical School, which happily was close to Glenferrie Oval. It was virtually a forgone conclusion that he would again be appointed as Hawthorn's coach. Kennedy would continue to combine his love of teaching with his love of football, and when he was appointed to the Teachers' Tribunal in 1970, a position that forbade him from taking paid outside work, he continued to coach Hawthorn in an unpaid capacity. With Dulcie's support he continued to study, and to his Bachelor of Arts he added a Master of Education and a Diploma in Education Administration from Monash University.

Kennedy came back to a club that was very different from what it had been when he first arrived in 1950. Hawthorn as a club was strong and secure, even though the long-term future of Glenferrie Oval as a League venue had become problematic; Ferguson's plan to build a new stand over the railway line (similar to the one at Dublin's Lansdowne Road stadium) fell through. With a recent premiership to its credit and a strong, stable administration, Hawthorn was by now an integral part of the VFL. The Hawks had missed the finals each year in which Kennedy had been away, even slipping to wooden spooner in 1965. But the club was in a transition period with a number of players from the early 1960s coming to the end of their careers. The administration was determined not to let the hard-won gains of the past ten years slip away, and the club was in the process of recruiting vigorously from its local area and from other states.

The prize recruit of 1967 was Peter Hudson, a full-forward from Tasmania, who had been one of the outstanding players in the 1966 Carnival. Virtually every VFL club chased him and it was a reflection of Hawthorn's determination to recruit well that he finally chose to sign with the Hawks. He was not a great mark and was a fairly slow runner; but he had the freakish ability to read where the ball would go as a player further up the ground was dropping it onto his boot, and then to fool opponents into thinking he was going to run in another direction. As a result, Hudson often marked the ball on his chest with no-one else around him. That required a level of judgement and instinct that few players in the history of the game have had. If opponents did manage to stay close to him, he had the strength to keep them at bay. Leigh Matthews remembered that Hawthorn players only had to kick to a position where Hudson could put his body between the ball and his opponent 'and he would get it nine times out of ten'. After a quiet first year, Hudson proved to be a sensation, kicking 125 goals in 1968, 120 in 1969, and 146 in 1970.

The other event of 1967 that was to Hawthorn's advantage was the introduction of country zoning. The zones allocated to each club were drawn at random and Hawthorn drew the Mornington Peninsula and West Gippsland. This zone not only had a large population — three times that of the Western District zone drawn by Collingwood — but was also home to young talent such as Peter Knights, Leigh Matthews, Kelvin Moore and Michael Tuck.

In an attempt to stay one step ahead of the competition, Kennedy had Brendan Edwards develop a training program to improve the fitness of each player by 20 per cent. A training camp was developed on land donated by a Hawthorn supporter by the Yarra River at Bulleen. Two mornings a week, players were expected to complete an obstacle course that involved running, carrying weights (such as sandbags and bricks), crawling through pipes, and rope climbs across the river. Players signed in when starting and finishing the course, and then headed off to work. It used to take the team's most athletic players about an hour to do the course, while the older or slower players usually took around 90 minutes. Kennedy himself also completed the course twice a week, but he did so after running the five-odd kilometres from his house in Camberwell. He loved running and stayed in shape over the Christmas break; on the early nights of pre-season training, he used to push hard to finish among the early place-getters in the endurance runs so that he could ease off as the season unfolded and the players got fitter. The Hawks also spent time at Percy Cerutty's training camp at Portsea, and Edwards's own gym and fitness centre. Don Scott remembers that the players became so fit that training sessions during the season consisted of a gradual warm-up, followed by only half an hour of intensive, non-stop activity.

By 1971 the Hawks were at their peak and lost only three games out of 24. This team was far from attractive to watch; however, Kennedy's instruction that most of the players crowd around centre bounces left the forward line open for Hudson. Although Hawthorn had some star players — Hudson had another brilliant season and, during the grand final, equalled Bob Pratt's record of 150 goals; Peter Crimmins and Matthews were one of the great roving combinations in football history; Scott was a determined ruckman; and Moore and Knights were outstanding defenders — depth, consistency and power were its major assets. The Hawks triumphed narrowly in two rugged finals games against St Kilda. Kennedy and Allan Jeans were very much kindred spirits and neither of them complained about the physical nature of those games. The Saints led by 20 points at three-quarter-time in the grand final, and Kennedy's message to his players was simple: 'we've been the best side all year — surely we're not going to let it slip on this one day?' The Hawks' desperation in that last quarter was that of a team committed to playing the game in the way their coach wanted them to.

Kennedy was aged only 43 when he coached Hawthorn to its second premiership, but his conservative manner and appearance, his focus on discipline, and the distance he maintained between himself and the players made him seem like a product of another time. 'I can't really remember John teaching me anything about football as a game,' Leigh Matthews once said in an interview. 'John taught about life and competition.' That was the strength of Kennedy's coaching, but at the same time the lack of emphasis he placed on the skills of the game built a weakness into his team. 'One of my many shortcomings,' he says, 'was that I didn't pay enough attention to the skill aspect.' Kennedy used to marvel at the skill of Carlton players in kicking the ball to their team-mates' advantage, but his method of countering the skills of opposition players continued to centre on pressure and getting numbers to the ball. That reflected his personal values about the ability of people who show courage and perseverance to overcome obstacles. Furthermore, his disinclination to get to know his players, his own thick skin that caused him never to take criticism personally, and his policy of never criticising players publicly meant that it never occurred to him that some of his players might take offence at some of the comments he made to them behind closed doors. To some extent, the problem was overcome by the ability of his captain, David Parkin, to communicate and liaise with the players. After Parkin retired as a player in 1973, Crimmins's bubbly personality and his habit of taking young players under his wing helped him as captain to keep team spirit up. But the Hawks remained vulnerable to skilled teams that were able to match their endeavour. In Ron Barassi's seven years as coach of Carlton, the Blues lost only one game at Glenferrie Oval (by four points in 1966). By 1973, Barassi had moved to North Melbourne and, under his coaching, the Kangaroos would become Hawthorn's main rival for the rest of the decade.

During the 1974 season Peter Crimmins developed testicular cancer. After surgery and radiotherapy he attempted to get back to full fitness, but managed only seven games in 1975. In his final game, which he played after learning that the cancer had spread to his lungs, he still collected 20 kicks. When the grand final team was being picked, Crimmins, who as captain was a member of the selection committee, was desperate to play but thought that he could only do so for a short time coming off the bench. It was, as Scott put it, a 'horrific' selection meeting: Ferguson insisted that Crimmins's health would be harmed if he played, but Kennedy thought that the skipper's example might give the team a lift by having him come on at a crucial time. Everyone in the meeting suspected, correctly as it turned out, that it was Crimmins's last chance to play football and realise his dream of leading Hawthorn to a premiership. Kennedy says that he 'didn't have the guts' to insist that Crimmins play. Crimmins listened to the game at home in bed.

North Melbourne won the game, and their first premiership, by 55 points. Hawthorn trailed at every change and it seems unlikely that Crimmins's presence would have made a difference to the result. For Kennedy, the defeat was particularly galling as it was apparent that the North players' desire to win, and thus become part of football history, was greater than that of the Hawthorn players. At the first team meeting of 1976, Kennedy told the players that many Hawthorn supporters had said to him that they did not think that the players had tried hard enough in the grand final. 'I don't believe it, but that's what they're saying,' he said. 'And the way we played I can't blame them.' Throughout the season, Kennedy referred several times to what had happened in 1975 and the players shared his determination to win the flag and to defeat North. When Ron Barassi accused Kennedy of waging a vendetta against his club, Kennedy agreed but added, 'except I don't think vendetta is a strong enough word'.

Crimmins's health deteriorated further during the 1976 season, and by grand final day he was close to death. In the rooms before the game, Kennedy read out a telegram that Crimmins had sent to the team and then added, 'there are a lot of reasons why you have to win today. Most of all, though, win it for the little feller'. Hawthorn defeated North by 30 points, but the result was never in doubt and the margin would have been much greater had the Hawks kicked more accurately for goal. That night a group of Hawthorn players went to Crimmins's home and delighted him by bringing along the premiership cup. Visitors found him to be happy, positive and optimistic. Kennedy called in to see him on the Monday. Peter Crimmins died the following morning.

'He tells it as it is'

John Kennedy did not know it, but the 1976 grand final would be the last time he coached Hawthorn. He had every intention of continuing coaching, but his personal situation became complicated when one of his sons, Bernard, developed a mental illness and required a high degree of close supervision. Over the summer Kennedy realised that it was no longer practical for him to keep up football commitments that required him to spend long periods away from his family. Few details were released to the public about the reasons for Kennedy's retirement, other than that it was due to the need for him to spend more time with his family. John continued his involvement with Hawthorn and served on the committee and as chairman of selectors. In 1979 he was thrilled when his son John Jr played the first of his 241 games for the Hawks.

David Parkin, who had been Kennedy's assistant coach, took over the senior job and led the Hawks to third in 1977 and a premiership in 1978. Under Allan Jeans, who became coach in 1981, Hawthorn won premierships in 1983, 1986 and 1989 (the Hawks also won the premiership in 1988 when Alan Joyce took over the coaching because Jeans was ill). Both Parkin and Jeans were different types of people from Kennedy and developed different styles of coaching. While Kennedy's game plan was in essence a matter of getting numbers to the ball and kicking it long, Parkin and Jeans were tacticians and they both worked to introduce a higher level of skill into Hawthorn's play. Parkin was adept at communicating with players individually, even providing them with feedback about their play through a written report after each match. Jeans was a master at identifying the skills that individual players needed to work on and he developed training drills that helped players to make appropriate decisions under match pressure. But Parkin and Jeans never lost their admiration for Kennedy as a leader and mentor, and the values he embodied and imparted. 'My modest contribution,' Kennedy recalled, 'was to establish a tradition of having players who would go in and *get the ball*, at all costs.' That tradition lived on long after Kennedy left the club. It was in evidence in the 1987 preliminary final, when Hawthorn looked to be in a losing position but kept trying and won the game with a kick after the siren. It also epitomised Hawthorn's play at a crucial stage in the 1988 grand final, when the team swept the ball from the half-back line to score a goal. At no stage was a Hawthorn player in control of the ball, but the team kept moving it forward simply by getting numbers to the contest and denying possession of the ball to their opponents.

After he retired, Kennedy was in demand from clubs that had skilled players but needed a coach who could instil mettle into the team. Carlton was just one of the clubs that made him an attractive offer. But not even Collingwood, the team he had supported as a boy, could persuade him to return to coaching. It was therefore a major shock when North Melbourne announced in 1985 that Kennedy had agreed to become their coach. What was not revealed to the public was that the deal had been clinched by the connections of North officials that made it possible for the Kennedys to place Bernie in Aradale, an institution near Ararat, which would provide the care he needed.

Predictably, Kennedy tackled the North job wholeheartedly. The Kangaroos had a crop of promising young players and Kennedy's mission was to supervise the building of a team that would stand up to the rigours of League football. Kennedy's strength of character commanded the respect of the players immediately, and he was able to communicate with them effectively because, as John Longmire puts it, 'he tells it as it is'. In his years of retirement, Kennedy had not mellowed one iota and he refused to put even the youngest players in cotton wool. He took the players on five-day camps at Bacchus Marsh over the Australia Day weekend each year. There they ran 10–15 kilometres with bags of sand on their backs and carried telephone poles in groups for five kilometres, in 40-degree heat. There were no-holds-barred games of soccer and basketball during which players wore a boxing glove on one hand. They hiked and camped for two days with only a steak, egg and sausage each to live on. During the season they trained some nights in bare feet, in inches of mud, because Kennedy wanted to toughen them up. As he did at Hawthorn, Kennedy himself took part in these activities, as far as he was capable.

Kennedy took North Melbourne, which had won only five games the previous season, to the finals in 1985; they also made the finals in 1987. When he retired as coach at the end of 1989, he had laid the foundations for a team that would win two premierships during the 1990s. Kennedy stayed actively involved in the game, serving as chairman of the AFL Commission and chair of the Hall of Fame committee. He remains dismissive of his own contribution to the history of the game, and continues to wear the reverence with which he is held by those who know and love the game with, as football writer Alf Brown once put it, 'an almost shy dignity'.

9

Jack Oatey
(1920–1994)

> Whatever you can think of, someone else has tried it before . . . but couldn't make it work.
>
> JACK OATEY

In the 1930s and 1940s, premierships in South Australia were shared around between the League clubs. Every club recorded at least one grand final victory during these decades, while no team won more than three. The 1950s and the first half of the 1960s, however, belonged to Port Adelaide. The Magpies won ten flags, including six in a row from 1954 to 1959, with all but one of these being coached by Foster Williams. Port's golden era came to an end when Sturt, coached by Jack Oatey, won the 1966 grand final, the first of five consecutive flags. Between 1950 and 1970, the other eight SANFL clubs (two new clubs were admitted in 1964) won only six premierships between them.

The coaching rivalry between Oatey and Williams was the dominant feature of South Australian football in the third quarter of the twentieth century. The two men had much in common. Both were top class rovers: Oatey played 181 games for Norwood, and Williams played 54 games for West Adelaide and 151 for Port Adelaide. Both had coaching careers of extraordinary longevity and success: Oatey coached for 37 years, in 1945–60 and 1962–82, and Williams coached for 27 years, in 1950–58, 1960 and 1962–78. Williams, who also coached South Adelaide and West Adelaide, won all his flags with Port: six as captain-coach and three as non-playing coach. Oatey captain-coached Norwood to three flags, was non-playing coach at West Adelaide, and then coached Sturt to seven flags. As coaches they were directly opposed in 81 matches: overall, Williams had slightly the better of things, winning 42 of these games. In grand finals, the score was three each. In 1981, the SANFL introduced the Jack Oatey Medal for the best player in the grand final and the Fos Williams Medal for South Australia's best player in interstate games.

Everyone knew Fos. When he died in 2001, after a long battle with a rare illness caused by low blood pressure, the grief was widespread and sincere. The former players and opponents who spoke at his funeral of a principled family man only confirmed what every football fan knew of Fos Williams. There was nothing mysterious about him. A man of great intelligence and determination, Williams not only combined a full-time job and working in a senior position in the post office with playing and coaching at League level, but also completed an economics degree part-time at the University of Adelaide. Port players used to hand over their modest annual bonuses to Fos for him to invest on their behalf in the share market. He maintained an interest in history — especially military history — and psychology. Although opposition clubs and their fans hated Port for its success and the way it played the game, there was always a level of respect reserved for Fos Williams as a leader. No-one ever used the words 'arrogant', 'sarcastic' or 'immodest' in describing their perceptions of him. As Michelangelo Rucci wrote:

> Williams has an enduring image of a man with no façade — what you see is what you get and it is a pleasant introduction that never sours with time. There is no-one who can record when Williams has spoken ill of anyone, unless he was eyeballing a player with a serious assessment of his game.

As a player and a leader, Williams was a worthy successor at Port Adelaide to Bob Quinn. 'He never had the skills of Bobby Quinn, but he had the heart of a lion,' was how Len Fitzgerald remembered him. He was intense and focussed but, above all, honest. As Geof Motley, his vice-captain for many years, puts it, 'you could register his honesty in his addresses. What he said came from here [pointing to his heart], not here [pointing to his head], and that was easily recognised by all players'. Fos's passion for the game would have been obvious to anyone who watched one of his teams play, because his barking of orders and comments, either from out on the ground or from the coach's box, was unrelenting and almost impossible not to hear. This passion was passed on to his three sons, each of whom played over a hundred games for the Magpies. At the time of Fos's death, Mark Williams was coaching Port Adelaide in the AFL and Stephen Williams was coaching the Port Adelaide Magpies in the SANFL. (Mark's twin brother Anthony was tragically killed in a building accident in 1988.) Fos had earlier written a creed, or what amounted to a mission statement, of his principles and values, which remains on display at Alberton Oval. The creed states, in part: 'we concede there can be honour in defeat, but to each of us, honourable defeat of our club and guernsey can come only after human endeavour on the playing field is completely exhausted'. It embodied all that is good about sport, as did its author.

There was no subtlety about the way Williams expected his team to play. He demanded that his team use what he described as a 'minimum approach to goal with maximum body power'. Players were required to get to contests in numbers, win the ball and kick it towards goal, where another contest for the ball would take place. As Keith Butler wrote of Port Adelaide in *The Advertiser* after the 1963 grand final: 'Devoid of frills, the manner of its victory was typical — dedication, relentless pressure, discipline, fitness, big-man mobility, and a willingness to take risks to get the ball and kick it as far as possible'. Len Fitzgerald remembers that 'like Bobby Quinn, he [Williams] led by example. The ball had to be won by a Port Adelaide player and if you didn't follow his example you'd be in strife'. Motley observes that:

> We were very hard at it and the umpire was there to deal with it if it wasn't within the rules. Foster had a basic principle of the shortest distance between two points. The more people you had

> around the ball the more chance you had of getting it. We used to attack anyone who lacked what we called 'football courage' because we thought it was more important to get hurt than let your side down.

Port's direct physical style was typical of the way the game was played in Victoria at the time. Williams's coaching philosophy was similar to that both of John Kennedy and Norm Smith. Like Kennedy, he trained his players hard, and on Sunday mornings as well as the traditional Tuesday and Thursday nights. Williams could tell which players needed extra work by running his eye over them to check their body shape and definition. Brian Cunningham remembers that when he joined Port in 1971, Fos participated in all the endurance running and sprinting sessions, even though the coach was approaching fifty years of age. Anyone who failed to beat Fos home in a run or sprint would have to repeat the exercise. There were also times at training where the entire playing squad would compete for one ball, with no teams and no scoring. Players were simply expected to win the ball, kick it somewhere, and then chase it and try to win it again. Like Norm Smith, Williams loved talking football with players and officials, including those of rival clubs. Off the field, he knew his players and their families personally and cared about their welfare. Bob Skilton, who came across Fos through interstate and practice matches, remembers that, 'although he was hard driving, after the game there was the other side to him — the thinking, softer side that wasn't quite as evident during a game'. Although he never touched alcohol, Fos was in his element at after-match functions. 'He would relax a bit but he wouldn't stop talking about the game,' Motley recalls. 'I don't believe he ever turned off.'

Jack Oatey, by contrast, was a more complex figure. Because he coached over such a long period, and was an innovator from the start, his coaching technique and the game he wanted his teams to play was modified several times. Just as the thin young rover who played for Norwood was a very different figure from the somewhat portly Oatey who waddled onto the oval when he was coach of Sturt, his coaching style evolved from keeping possession through short kicking to a method built around handball and precise long kicking into space, rather than to a contest. In an era when successful coaches emphasised fitness and physical pressure, Oatey's style was truly revolutionary. As Mike Coward, a journalist with *The Advertiser* put it, 'Oatey has succeeded with a philosophy which fundamentally contradicts all that is fashionable and considered essential for success in modern football'. For Oatey, football was not just a game of skill and speed, but also one that could be played successfully by a team that paid little attention to tackling, bumping and spoiling its opponents. 'I'm a great believer that the skill factor is the dominant factor,' he said at the end of his coaching career. Winning was something 'that comes automatically after you've looked after the skill factor'. Accordingly, training at Sturt was always light and held only on Tuesday and Thursday nights. Tackling drills, competitive work and sprints were never used; the players became fit by doing sessions of circle work and drills to practise kicking and handball.

When it finally became apparent that this method could be used to beat Port Adelaide, Oatey tended not to talk about his tactics to people outside Sturt. He loved the game and enjoyed talking football with ordinary supporters, but rarely did so with opposition coaches or players, and never with anyone from Port Adelaide. Members of the press who sought a story about him or an interview with him were invariably disappointed. Oatey's penchant for secrecy in discussing tactics and confidentiality in his dealings with people meant that his relationship with the media was generally non-existent. He would only let his guard down and talk openly in situations in which he felt comfortable with the person he was talking to. Oatey died in 1994; sadly, there is no Oatey creed, no series of newspaper articles written by or with him, no notes or diaries, and no autobiography to provide insight into his way of thinking. Few people got to know Jack Oatey well and, talking to some of those who did, it is difficult to avoid the conclusion that even in his conversations with those who were closest to him Jack played his cards close to his chest. Many of the clues to the origins of Oatey's unusual philosophy about football have to be inferred from what is known about key events and circumstances in his life.

Country boy

Oatey was born in Semaphore, a suburb of Port Adelaide, but his roots were in the country. The Oatey family had been among the first residents of the Yorke Peninsula town of Maitland when it was settled in the 1870s. Ted and Agnes Oatey moved to Adelaide and Ted played League football for Port Adelaide and West Torrens. After their son Jack was born in 1920, they lived in Adelaide for a further seven years before moving back to Maitland to run the family's butcher shop. Maitland was a small town of less than 800 inhabitants, and it was rare for people who lived there to encounter a face that they could not put a name to. During the Great Depression, times were tough for South Australian farmers and money in the Maitland community was in short supply. There were four children in the Oatey family — Joan, Jack, Beryl and Bill — and, although Jack enjoyed school and developed a love of history, his parents could not afford to continue his education. He left school at the age of 14 to start a printing apprenticeship. Agnes Oatey remembered that 'Jack grew up in the Depression, and learnt what life is really about. We never got anything easy. The whole family knew what hard work was. And that's what put them in good stead for later in life'. For Jack himself, the circumstances of his childhood and youth taught him that 'whatever you do, do it to the best of your ability; work hard at it and you will get your reward somewhere along the way'.

Jack inherited his father's love of football. Ted Oatey was captain-coach of Maitland, and Jack first played for the senior team when he was 14. His other sporting interest was cycling and, when he was playing football at the Maitland showground, he also competed in the cycling events that were held during the half-time break. Such displays of energy and stamina were remarkable because, before his day of sport started, Jack would have to work from 7.40 am to 1.40 pm. The local football club folded temporarily in 1937 and Jack joined Port Victoria. After work each Tuesday and Thursday, and after lunch each Saturday, Jack would cycle the 25 kilometres to Port Victoria to train and play.

Four League clubs approached him, and in 1939 his father took him to Alberton Oval to play in a trial (practice) game. Port wanted to sign him but he refused when he learned that the club expected him to go back and play for another year in the country. Opinions are divided about the lasting influence this might have had on Oatey as a coach. On one hand, some observers have suggested that as a coach Oatey was motivated by a desire for vengeance against Port Adelaide for rejecting him when he tried out as a player. On the other hand, Robert Oatey is convinced that his father's failure to sign with Port Adelaide is a red herring and that Jack bore no personal animosity towards the Magpies. They were simply the team to beat and it was for that reason that Jack Oatey savoured victories over them. There are several pieces of evidence that support Robert's contention. After coaching Sturt to victory in the 1966 grand final, Jack went into the Port Adelaide rooms and told the players that 'we all feel the prouder because you are the trendsetters of SA league football'. There are plenty of photos of Jack Oatey and Fos Williams together that suggest mutual respect, rather than a vendetta, between the two men and their clubs.

Jack returned to Port Victoria and won the competition's best and fairest trophy in 1939. At the end of the season, Jack was selected to represent the Yorke Peninsula League in a match played at Adelaide Oval as a curtain-raiser to an SANFL semifinal. Norwood officials watched him closely and invited him to train with their club. They found him an apprenticeship with a local printing firm owned by the McCallum family, who were prominent members of the club. At McCallum's he met Mary Player, who was a member of the secretarial staff. They married in 1941 and would have two children: Robert, born in 1942, and Peter, born in 1946, became fine players in their own right.

Oatey won Norwood's best and fairest in 1940, his first season of League football. In the following season he repeated that achievement, and also played in a premiership match and was runner-up in the Magarey Medal. During 1941 he joined the AIF and was posted in Darwin, where he remained for 18 months. In 1944 he was stationed in Melbourne at a warrant officers' school. During the winter, Jack trained at Collingwood and played a handful of games for South Melbourne. When he returned to Adelaide in 1945, Oatey was asked to become playing coach of Norwood. He was aged only 24. The war had cut three years from his playing career but he was in good shape physically and mentally and had many years of football left in him.

In 1990, journalist Gordon Schwartz asked Oatey who his heroes were. He nominated two: Sir Donald Bradman and Sir Walter Lindrum. These would have been unsurprising choices for any Australian of Oatey's age. Through single-minded pursuit of excellence in sports they loved to play — cricket and billiards — Bradman and Lindrum became icons of Australian society during the gloomy years of the Great Depression.

Bradman in particular, whose first-class cricket career coincided with Oatey's transition from sports-mad schoolboy to League coach, had several personal characteristics that Oatey could identify with. As young men who had left their family homes to pursue sporting careers, both Bradman and Oatey tended to keep to themselves and did little socialising with team-mates. When Oatey ran 12 to 15 laps of Norwood Oval before and after work every day in the summer of 1939–40 to prepare himself for League football, he did so alone. Like Bradman, Oatey hated losing in any type of contest. This did not diminish the love they had for the games they played, and on the field both wore a perpetual smile that some opponents misinterpreted as smugness. As Roland Perry wrote of Bradman, 'until they knew him and his manner, some took that country boy grin as gloating'.

Bradman and Oatey both preferred privacy to publicity. Bradman was uncomfortable with his rapid rise to fame and, 'as a result, and understandably, his character seemed to have developed what some have called an uncertain volatility; in turn, and often unpredictably, he could be brusque or courteous with the press, disciplinarian or considerate to his own players, mutinous or respectfully obedient to the authorities'. Oatey certainly recognised some of those contradictions in his own personality and, while in Bradman's case 'age and a happy marriage smoothed over the rougher edges and allowed the old-fashioned rural courtesy of his background to break through the shell of acquired suspicion', Oatey remained highly selective about whom he would open up to. On the national and international stages, of course, Bradman was a star who commanded far more public attention than Oatey did. In Adelaide, however, football was the biggest game in town, and Oatey, who rarely set foot out of Adelaide except on football trips (during the years in which he was coaching, he and Mary took only one holiday, to Surfers Paradise) had to deal with the media spotlight for over forty years. He generally did so by letting the actions of his teams to speak for him. He later said that he regretted being 'unable to express my feeling for the game outside the confines of the teams I coached'.

Oatey was happy to talk to some people in the media — such as Lawrie Jervis, who he knew through his work as manager of Adelaide Typographers (a trade subsidiary of News Limited) and became a friend, Merv Agars, and Schwartz — but with others he admitted that 'there have been some personality clashes'. Mike Coward could recall several occasions when as a young journalist he 'felt crushed by Oatey's terseness, [and his] deliberately disagreeable attitude or arrogance', but did find that Jack mellowed somewhat towards the end of his coaching career. Oatey did have a small number of 'secret friends' with whom he could talk his problems out during late-night phone calls. 'There have been one or two people in the background always, people no-one will ever know, whom I have relied on, have used as a backstop to talk about all kinds of things.' Despite their obvious affinity, Oatey never sought to confide in Bradman, however. Bradman enjoyed Australian Rules football and lived not far from Oatey, but the two never met.

The great paradox about Jack Oatey is that, while he kept most of the football world at arm's length, he maintained an ability to communicate superbly with the people he worked with directly. As Daryl Hicks put it, 'you had to prove that you were genuine before you cracked the façade'. 'Sandy' Nelson commented that 'if Jack trusted you as a person, he would open up and talk, literally, for *hours*'. At his football clubs and at his typesetting firm, Oatey took the time to get to know his players and workers, to listen to them with empathy and, if needed, offer clear, constructive advice. Even in his fifth decade of coaching, Oatey retained an ability to get through to young people. Under his leadership, Sturt Football Club became a place where people of different races, religions and social backgrounds mixed with confidence and good humour. Although he kept his home life private and largely free of football visitors, Oatey kept the lines of communications open by regularly calling in to see people during the course of a working day to ask how they were going. If a serious issue needed to be discussed, Jack would arrange to have a chat at a secluded location, often under a tree along the banks of the Torrens River, close to his West Terrace printing firm. By the time he was coaching Sturt, Oatey had developed a way of dealing with players' problems and getting the best out of them, but this was never revealed to the media. Jack never discussed the details of his personal issues with players with anyone — not even his own family. This meant that the media's perception of him, and, as a result, that of the vast majority of the football public, was at odds with that of people who knew him personally. As Robert Oatey puts it, 'people in the media portrayed him as distant and cold, whereas to the players he was quite the opposite — warm and honest, everything you were looking for in a person'.

In Robert's opinion, it was his father's country upbringing that led him to get to know everyone he worked with personally — either at his football club or at his business —and to *always* address them by name. He never forgot anyone's name and would address people either with formality (he used to call his runner 'Mr Runner') or by their first name or nickname, but never simply as 'mate'. He had a quaint turn of phrase that also reflected his rural origins. For example, he used to tell Sturt people that Paul Bagshaw, who was club captain for many years, 'could drop kick a pea up a fowl's bottom from 70 yards, and not ruffle a feather'. On more than one occasion later in his life, Jack was overheard talking about football to plants in his garden and to the grass on an oval. Robert also thinks that there were important parts of Jack's character that derived from his army days: his emphasis on teamwork; his belief in the importance of discipline; the value he placed on dealing confidentially with people on a one-to-one basis; his obsession with not discussing things with 'the enemy'; and the value he placed on the privacy of the family unit. He used to tell his teams that, if a situation in a match called for physical contact, this had to be done 'with decorum' and 'within the rules of war'. These were core values that Oatey appears to have developed before he became a coach, and which he retained for the rest of his life.

The time he spent in Melbourne exposed him to a range of potential influences that may have shaped his ideas about handball and team play: Jock McHale; William 'Bull' Adams, Oatey's coach at South Melbourne, who had previously impressed Norm Smith with his ideas about teamwork when he was coach of Melbourne seconds; and Jack Sheedy, his roving partner at South Melbourne, who was a master of the use of handball to bring others into the game. Oatey also found that, in the VFL, players like him were protected and brought into the game by big, powerful ruckmen, such as his South Melbourne team-mates, Jack Graham and Jack 'Basher' Williams. From that point on, Oatey maintained a belief in the importance of a team being built around a strong ruck unit. Bob McCaskill tried at North Melbourne and later at Hawthorn to develop a style of playing that was remarkably similar to that which Oatey later perfected at Sturt; however, there is no record of him and Oatey having met.

Oatey's ideas about football were probably derived from several sources. His success owed less to him being an innovative football thinker than it did to his ability to develop ways of getting his team to play according to a particular method. As Jack once told his son Robert, 'whatever you can think of, someone else has tried it before ... but couldn't make it work'. Over the course of a long career, Jack Oatey came to the view that the success of any team was the result of the ability of their coach to manipulate what the players did, as individuals and as a team. When Oatey began coaching, he believed in the football axiom that players make the coach, but in time he became convinced that ultimately it was the coach who made the team. No doubt some people would have found Oatey's thinking on the primary importance of the coach as being egotistical and self-important, but it stemmed from his view of sport 'as a tactical manoeuvre'. At home, Jack used to read cheap detective novels. When teased by Robert about the quality of his reading material, Jack's response was that he was fascinated by 'all the little strategies and tricks' used by the characters in them.

No second prize

Under Oatey's leadership, Norwood won flags in 1946, 1948 and 1950. Oatey himself, who won two more club best and fairests during this period, played with what Jeff Pash called 'jaunty confidence and aggressive cunning'. Pash wrote that Oatey could read the game so well that he 'came out of trouble at a flat walk' and then disposed of the ball quickly 'with an amazing short-range punt such as I have not seen from that day to this.' On the field Oatey was dynamic, forever talking to his players and pointing out the errors they made, as well as antagonising the opposition. 'Jack and I didn't get off on the right foot', recalled Len Fitzgerald. 'He had a great habit of mouthing off — he used to swear at people.' Fitzgerald's response to that was to give Oatey a backhander that 'kept him quiet for about ten minutes', and he was just one of many opponents whom Oatey provoked into giving away free kicks and, in some cases, getting reported. Hartley Bagshaw, who played for Sturt during this period, had been so unimpressed with Oatey's behaviour as a player that he was wary about his son playing for Sturt when Oatey was the coach.

After winning the flag in 1950, Norwood faced the challenge presented by the rise of Fos Williams's Port Adelaide. When Williams took over as captain-coach in 1950, Port had only three players with more than 100 games' experience. But the club had plenty of promising young players, such as John Abley, who was recruited from Hawthorn after being transferred in his job to Adelaide, Dave Boyd, Roger Clift, Harold McDonald, Dick 'The Rock' Russell, Ted Whelan and Lloyd Zucker. For Fos, who simply did not know what to say when he made his first address to the players, the club had great potential and 'it was just a matter of getting everyone to work in one direction'. In 1951 Port went through the season with only one loss and duly won the premiership. Williams was helped by a stable administration that recruited well, and a productive local area that yielded players like John Cahill, Neville 'Chic' Hayes and

Geof Motley. Throughout the 1950s and 1960s, Port lost many great players, but kept replacing them with more great players. Thus, when Williams retired as a player at the end of 1958, Port replaced him with a young lad recruited from Mt Gambier, Jeff Potter, who himself turned out to be a champion rover. Although the Port players were paid next to nothing, the club's friendly atmosphere and the success it enjoyed made it a place where recruits wanted to be and which established players did not want to leave.

As coach of Norwood, Oatey's response to Port Adelaide's success was to maintain strict discipline and encourage his players to use short kicks to bypass the opposition's packs. He took Norwood to grand finals in 1952 and 1955 but they were never in the hunt in either game. In the 1952 grand final, Oatey's last game as a player, Norwood was trounced by 108 points by North Adelaide and, in the 1955 grand final, Port was far too good, winning by 63 points.

Oatey hated to see people anywhere drinking to excess and, in his enforcement of standards of discipline at his own club on this and other matters, there was, as Coward wrote, 'a brusqueness about his approach to personal relationships which grated on some of his contemporaries'. During the 1956 season, when Norwood finished a disappointing fourth, it transpired that several players had become unhappy with Oatey's coaching methods. Oatey was also convinced that he did not have the complete support of the committee. He felt that he could not continue as Norwood coach under those circumstances, and shortly after his resignation he was signed to coach West Adelaide.

When Oatey became coach of West Adelaide, he took over a working-class club that Jeff Pash described as 'the brilliant, harum-scarum urchins of SA football'. 'Norwood have a stately dignity,' Pash wrote, but 'Westies' struck him as being 'some vast, squabbling, easy-come, easy-go boarding house'. After winning the 1947 flag, West lurched into a period of instability during which Fos Williams was let go to Port, Bernie Smith was cleared to Geelong, and several other star players left the club. By the mid-1950s, however, another fine group of players was being assembled which included a young ruckman, Neil Kerley. The team finished runners-up in 1954 and 1956, losing to Port by only 3 and 16 points respectively. Oatey had plenty of raw materials to work with. Oatey's strategy at West Adelaide was to develop a game based on short kicking, to 'short-circuit', as he put it, Port's strength and willingness to get numbers to the ball. He reasoned that unless the ball was kept moving in this way it would tend to be kicked to the big packs in which Port players tended to cluster. Over time, Oatey also introduced more handball to his game by training the players to think of it as a method of retaining possession, rather than as a defensive measure that players would use only when they were tackled and unable to kick the ball.

By 1958, Oatey seemed to have been able to make this formula work. West defeated Port twice in the minor round that season and, before the teams met each other in the grand final, Jervis wrote:

> There comes a time in every champion's life when the longer he reigns, the closer must loom the inevitable defeat. For the first time in years, the ageing champion, Port Adelaide, will not start favourite, against the younger, faster and very confident challenger, West Adelaide.

During the third quarter, West looked a certain winner when it opened up a 24-point lead. But, as Keith Butler wrote, 'instead of going in for the kill, it over-indulged in half-distance kicking, spilled easy marks and fell into handball errors when within goal range'. John Marriott, also writing in *The Advertiser*, observed that 'suddenly, perhaps through inexperience, West defenders, in particular, became lax and experimented with ineffectual handball and short passing'. These mistakes allowed Port to kick two late goals that reduced the deficit to 10 points. Port was still in trouble because in the last quarter it would be kicking into a strong wind. But in his last game as a player, Williams made an inspirational speech at three-quarter-time, asking his players not to give up hope of winning a premiership because they were behind and kicking against the wind. The team responded and, with 90 seconds to play, Port was clinging to a three-point lead. A West Adelaide shot for goal seemed to be going through but at the last second the ball was blown off-line by the wind and it hit the post. With only 47 seconds remaining, West Adelaide's Ken McGregor marked at around 45 metres from goal, on an angle. Instead of shooting for goal, McGregor passed to his captain, Colin Brown. Unfortunately, Brown was limping with an injured ankle and his shot for goal from about 40 metres failed to make the distance. From a ball-up near the goal line, Fos Williams grabbed the ball and kicked it out of bounds as the siren sounded.

The 1958 grand final was a contest between two very different styles of playing and coaching: one emphasised hard running and tackling, getting numbers to the ball and long kicking; the other was a skilled, possession game based on handball and short kicking. Victory that day, when the opposition was in the box seat, was probably the finest achievement of Williams's football career, while for Oatey the loss would have been heartbreaking. Although the margin between winning and losing was very narrow, the result seemed to confirm that Williams's method was more suited to the pressure of finals games than Oatey's was. On one hand, Williams's men knew that even if they fumbled the ball, team-mates would be close by to protect them and help them out; when they got the ball and kicked it, they knew that even a miskick would send the ball a long distance from the opposition goal. On the other hand, Oatey's men were vulnerable when they made the type of judgement and skill errors that West players made at key moments in the 1958 grand final. This seemed to be confirmed the following season when West again lost a close grand final to Port by 10 points. Keith Butler's verdict was that 'West had chances to win, but too often indulged in foolish short passing and unintelligent handball, even within kicking distance of goal'. In wet conditions the West players often fumbled and overran the ball, while 'against this the physically stronger Port matched a long-kicking, hard-tackling game which carried less margin of error'.

Surprisingly, Port Adelaide did not appoint Williams as non-playing coach after his retirement as a player. Apparently, the club wanted a coach who could be on the field and lead by example. Geof Motley was promoted to captain-coach, and he took Port to the 1959 flag. Fos stayed around the club and took over the coaching when Motley was busy training for and playing interstate football. He had his university studies, his job and a young family to help raise. Williams missed coaching full-time, however, and in 1960 he coached South Adelaide, although he failed to improve the performance of the League's weakest club. The 1960 season was also a tough one for Oatey. West Adelaide was eliminated in the first semifinal when they were beaten comprehensively by Norwood. When North Adelaide won the flag that year, Port's great run of six consecutive flags had come to an end. It seemed as if Oatey had got all that he could out of West Adelaide and he resigned at the end of the season.

Complete control

Jack Oatey had no direct involvement in the game in 1961 and spent the football season standing on 'the mound' (in the outer) watching his son Robert, who was beginning his League career with Norwood. After 16 years of coaching, it was a chance for Jack to reflect on the hard-won lessons of five grand final defeats. It is not clear whether Oatey at that time had any intention of coaching again. When he was approached at the end of the season about coaching Sturt, his response was an emphatic 'no'.

Sturt was by no means a big club, and its recent playing record had been mediocre. The club had won five premierships but none since 1940. In 1961, under the coaching of Glynn Williams (one of Fos's younger brothers), the Double Blues had finished last. Unley Oval, the club's base, was a tight, narrow reserve surrounded by densely built-up suburban housing. The facilities were basic: there were two small grandstands, built in 1901 and 1924, and no off-street parking. At the southern end of the oval, there was only a metre or two of space between the oval fence and the Sturt Bowling Club. Sturt's location gave it a large area of potential support drawn from Adelaide's southern and south-eastern suburbs, but its recruiting district had been reduced in size when new boundaries were drawn up in 1921, when Glenelg entered the League, and in 1929 and 1958 when more territory was given to South Adelaide.

Change, however, was afoot. In 1959, Ray Kutcher was invited to become chairman of the club. Kutcher, who had played for West Torrens and had been a member of its 1953 premiership side, began assembling a team of vice-presidents who would put money into the club. They were drawn from senior positions in business and government authorities, such as the Electricity Trust of South Australia where Kutcher worked. Plans were drawn up to buy some of the houses adjacent to Unley Oval to provide space for the construction of a social club. Kutcher lobbied the SANFL to redraw the boundaries of Sturt's recruiting territory; when this was unsuccessful, he and his vice-presidents began a major recruiting campaign in country districts and interstate, where recruiting was open to all clubs. Recruiting officer, Alan 'Fountain' Fenn, scoured country newspapers in search of reports of promising players; he kept voluminous records and, once a player had been identified as a recruiting target, pursued his or his parents' signature with remarkable persistence.

Kutcher and his team needed a top quality coach to blend its new recruits and established players into a winning team. When Glynn Williams failed to achieve success, the club identified Oatey as its first choice to replace him. Sturt pursued Oatey relentlessly: every time Oatey declared that he was not interested in the job, Kutcher adjusted his sales pitch and used different members of his team of vice-presidents to sell the club and where it was planning to go. When Oatey finally accepted, he insisted that the appointment be on a year-to-year basis. The vice-presidents paid Oatey's salary from personal funds: officially, Oatey received no payment from the Sturt Football Club for coaching the team.

Jack Oatey came to dominate the Sturt Football Club. Both on the field and off, the Double Blues became the embodiment of Oatey's philosophies about how people should be treated and how football should be played. 'Bo' Morton, who had captain-coached Sturt's last premiership in 1940 and saw Oatey at work in his capacity as one of Kutcher's vice-presidents, put it well when he observed that Oatey 'patiently moulded players to his will and inexorably chips his way into the very lives of all who surround him'. This was done through a mixture of honest, good quality management and fox-like cunning. While Oatey had confidence in Kutcher's ability to run the financial and administrative side of the club, he still had 'spies' on each of the subcommittees that considered these matters to tell him what was going on. Oatey's staff, including the chairman of selectors, club doctor, trainers and the runner, was hand-picked by him and he made it clear at the outset that no-one else — not even the chairman or vice-presidents — was to have any say in what the players were doing on the training track or on the field.

The club's recruiting staff used to tell young lads that they were being given a chance 'to play under Jack Oatey, the best coach in the League'. This was an important selling point in an era when players received only modest match payments. Over time, Oatey became directly involved in recruiting by visiting the parents of prospective recruits, not only to give them his personal guarantee that their boy would be looked after, but also to enable him to make a judgement about the stability of the player's family background, which he believed was an important influence on the quality of a footballer. The families with whom country recruits were billeted in Adelaide were selected personally by Oatey. He had little time for players whom he thought 'couldn't play'. When Malcolm Greenslade had his first training run he ran past Jack and attempted a drop kick, a kick that was still in common use then. Greenslade stubbed his toe instead of executing the kick properly and heard Oatey mutter, 'what's he doing here?' Greenslade soon redeemed himself and became a star full-forward, but Oatey was rarely wrong in his judgement of whether a player had the potential to play at the standard required. For example, Bruce Jarratt had been discarded by the club and was playing suburban football when Oatey rang him and asked if he would like to have another try at playing at League level. When Jarratt said yes, Oatey told him 'well, I think you can'. Under Oatey's coaching, Jarratt played at full-back in four premiership sides. At the same time, Oatey never shirked the unpleasant job of telling players that they were not quite good enough to wear the Sturt guernsey.

Training followed a set routine, from 4 pm to 6 pm every Tuesday and Thursday. Pre-season training didn't last long and in all training sessions there was a marked absence of running work and drills involving physical contact. Sessions would begin with goal kicking practice, followed by circle work and then a variety of skill training exercises. At all times, the emphasis was on developing the ability of players to control the ball through accurate disposal by hand or foot. When young players arrived at the club, Oatey sometimes had to take them aside and show them the right techniques for various types of kicks and handballs. Though the routine of training hardly ever varied, Oatey still managed to keep things interesting. 'He was like a ringmaster,' says John Halbert. He controlled all activities and chuckled when a task had been done well. One of his, and the players', favourite exercises was to set up a target made out of a 44-gallon drum for the players to aim stab kicks at. Oatey used to put his head through the target and challenge the players to 'hit me', which they often did. During circle work, Oatey would stand near the centre of the ground and if he called out a player's name that player was required to change direction and pass the ball to him as quickly as possible. One night, Oatey called out 'Brenton', looking at Brenton Miels. Unfortunately, Brenton Adcock also had a ball at that time and drove a stab kick to Oatey. Jack never saw it coming and the force of it spun him around and separated his shoulder. At finals time, his team was happy to 'put on a show' for the crowd that had gathered. Training was an activity that the Sturt players enjoyed; 'people wanted to be there', was how Greenslade remembered it.

To prevent players splintering into cliques, and to prevent Sturt from becoming more of a social club than a football club, Oatey had his runner, Dave Edwards, organise all social gatherings, which included card nights and trips to the movies as well as the usual after-match get-together. At these functions Oatey would keep a low profile; he usually sat in a corner with Edwards, nursing a beer, but kept an accurate count in his head of how much everyone else had drunk. End-of-year trips were organised and supervised by Oatey. The extent of Oatey's dominion at Sturt aroused little, if any, resentment or opposition at the club. He and Kutcher and the vice-presidents got on well with each other. Having weeded out any potential troublemakers and surrounded himself with people who met his own standards of ability and character, Oatey was able to avoid any major personality clashes. The atmosphere at the club was positive and good-humoured. On a flight during one end-of-season trip, some senior players told a young Paul Bagshaw, who was not yet of legal drinking age, to walk past

Oatey with a can of beer in his hand. Oatey was flabbergasted. 'Look at that!' he told Dave Edwards, who was sitting next to him. 'He's only 16 years old, he's been on a plane for half an hour and he's drinking beer. I've got to put a stop to this.' Oatey stood up and then realised that the players had broken up with laughter.

It seems that Oatey had learnt from his experience at Norwood that, while it was important to maintain discipline, it was counter-productive to dictate to players what they should do. At Sturt, Jack worked more subtly by listening to people and then suggesting other ways in which things might be done. Bruce Jarratt thought that 'he was the most positive person I've met in terms of getting you around to his way of thinking'. He often sought to involve his players and staff — even the sprigger (boot studder) — by asking them in front of the entire team what they thought about a particular match situation. As Keith Chessell observed, Oatey always knew the answer to these questions, but he was skilled in getting people to think that it was *their* answer and that their thoughts were of great importance to the team. With the exception of a few rules — for example, racially based comments were forbidden at all times and, as a result, Sturt's Aboriginal players, Roger Rigney and Michael Graham, were treated with respect — Oatey preferred to avoid telling people what to do.

Keith Chessell says that Oatey was a father figure to every player at the club. In Chessell's case, his respect for Oatey was reinforced by the concern the coach showed for him when he decided to enter Bible College. On the banks of the Torrens, Oatey discussed with Chessell issues such as the quality of food and sleeping quarters at the college. Oatey hoped that Chessell could combine his Bible studies with playing football, and offered him the club's support. A less sincere person might have tried to persuade Chessell that he would have been better off concentrating on football, but Oatey made no attempt to influence his decision. Oatey did not wait for players to approach him if they had a problem. He talked to all of his players regularly, as he did with his employees, and if he believed that there was a problem he did not hesitate to take action. At Sturt, his preferred method of helping a player who was down on form or showed signs that something was troubling him was to take him on a very slow jog after training, up and down the centre of the oval with the training lights switched off. What was said never went beyond Oatey and the player. Daryl Hicks remembers the 15-minute jog that he was taken on during the worst form slump of his career. For five minutes, Oatey talked about Hicks's career, and then the coach spent another five minutes going through every error that Hicks had made on the field that season. Oatey then cited a series of statistics that he used to support the contention that if Hicks 'could find Greenslade three times next week, we would win'. 'I went off the track having got the message, but also knowing that I was the most important player in the team.'

Hicks had an opportunity to see first-hand the importance that Oatey placed on knowing his players personally when he worked as Oatey's assistant coach. Oatey drove Hicks home one night after training. Hicks had grown up on a dairy farm, and while driving Jack asked him about his father's cows and how well they were producing. When they got to Daryl's house they sat in the car and kept talking. Jack asked about Daryl's wife and children, whom he knew by name. As Hicks said goodnight and got out of the car, Oatey leaned across and said, 'That's what you call coaching'.

Although the players to a man liked Jack, and he himself had the highest regard for 'my charges', Oatey knew when to step back and give the players space to live their lives. 'You can't make good judgements if you live in people's pockets,' he used to tell Robert. Jack chose to keep a distance between himself and others at the club and, although he put in long hours at both his job and at coaching, he also set aside time to be with his family. The result was that even at Sturt, where he spent the happiest years of his football career, Oatey made few close friends. He probably did not relate as well to women as he did to men, but he knew each player's family members personally, made a point of thanking the players' wives and girlfriends at the annual general meeting, and tried to limit the demands that football made on the players' family lives. Fortunately, Mary Oatey enjoyed watching football and she also had her sons' careers at Norwood to follow.

There was a level of respect for Oatey at the Sturt Football Club that was in evidence every time he spoke to a group of people. At large gatherings, such as the annual general meeting held at the Unley Town Hall, Oatey would speak without the aid of a microphone and, if there was any murmuring from the audience, he could silence it by simply lowering the volume of his voice. Because the players respected him, he could use coaching methods that were psychological in nature. He never swore at his players and hardly ever had to shout to get their attention. A glare was enough to let someone know that he had done the wrong thing. 'Sometimes you'd play really badly and he wouldn't say anything,' Bagshaw recalled. 'Sometimes we'd play extremely well and he'd just say "go out and do it again".' For Chessell, one of the secrets of Oatey's success in motivating people was that 'he made you believe that he had confidence in you; you would have a go if Jack believed that something could be done'.

The Oatey game plan at Sturt, as John Halbert summarises it, centred on four basic principles: first, never kick to where a player is — kick the ball to space; second, never kick to a contest between players — kick the ball to space; third, find the body of a team-mate, with a reflex handball; and, last, when the ball is kicked to space, a team-mate will be there to take possession.

This method of playing the game differed in two ways from that outlined in Len Smith's golden rules. First, Oatey never attempted to simplify these rules by making them available to his players in written form. Second, Oatey gave no instructions about what to do if the opposition had the ball or if the ball was in dispute. It was almost as if Oatey was prepared to concede possession to the opposition and wait for them to lose it. He used to tell his players that, if Sturt got only 40 per cent of the play, it would still win because of its superior disposal. This approach left Sturt open to the accusation that its players were 'soft', but the team did have players who could put physical pressure on the opposition (especially Halbert and ruck-rover John Murphy), while the rest of the team showed its mettle in big-game situations.

Sturt players moved the ball quickly into space, keeping the ball away from packs, with a variety of disposal techniques. In handballing, players used 'backplay' to find a team-mate who was on the defensive side of a pack, or 'checkside play' to find one at the side.

The players honed these skills during training drills that Oatey devised. The team's most accurate kicks, Bagshaw and Chessell, who played as ruck-rovers, were also encouraged to kick the ball sideways to switch the direction of play and enable others to find space more easily. Bagshaw's view is that everything about Sturt's game worked around checkside play and backplay. It allowed them to keep moving the ball to where team-mates would be in a position to attack, using either short or long kicks.

For many Sturt players, and other football observers, Bagshaw was the cornerstone of the team. He could take a towering high mark, dispose of the ball exquisitely on either side of his body or, having taken possession near the centre of the ground, drive a long drop-kick goal; Oatey considered him to be the best footballer he had seen. Oatey always regarded Bagshaw as the 'starter motor' rather than the 'engine' of his team. After a piece of play by Bagshaw had lifted morale or brought others into the game, Oatey expected the rest of the team to see that it was now their turn to contribute. Sturt never needed Bagshaw to accumulate large numbers of possessions to win matches. He was part of a strong ruck unit that included a fine tap ruckman, Tony 'Doc' Clarkson, Chessell and Murphy as ruck-rovers, and rovers such as Rigney, Roger Dunn, Peter Endersbee and Michael Nunan. The rest of the team was made up of reliable specialists, such as defenders Adcock, Jarrett and Nelson and wingman Tony Burgan, and others who were highly versatile. Bagshaw and Hicks could be played as loose men on the back line; Halbert could play at centre half-forward or in the centre; Rick Schoff was equally at home at centre half-forward as he was at centre half-back and could also play in the centre. Sturt's attacks were usually directed to a fast leading full-forward, with this role being played first by Malcolm 'Emmy' Jones, then Greenslade, then Ken Whelan and, later, Rick Davies. Oatey also developed plays to suit the individual characteristics of players. For example, Clarkson's lanky frame was not suited to heavy body contact, so he and Oatey developed a method of checkside ruck play in which Clarkson would approach his opponent at right angles and tap the ball in the direction of an unguarded Sturt player.

John Tilbrook was a very fast, strong half-forward flanker who could kick enormous screw punts (torpedoes). Oatey instructed his players to kick the ball over his head so that he could turn and run onto the ball and be heading in the direction of goal.

Everything about Sturt's play — from avoiding physical contests for the ball to moving the ball with teamwork and skilful disposal — was the reverse of Port Adelaide's aggressive, long-kicking style. While Sturt sought to move the ball into space, Port closed down the available space and always moved the ball directly towards goal. During his early years at Sturt, Oatey was plagued by self-doubt about whether his unique style could in fact be used to beat Port. Williams returned to Port as non-playing coach in 1962, and in his first game against Sturt his team won 22.23 to 4.3. Port then won 11 of its next 12 games against the Double Blues. In 1964 South Adelaide won the premiership by beating Port at its own game. As Merv Agars wrote in *The Advertiser*, 'the fierce desire of the South players to be first to the ball, their willingness to take physical risks to get to it and their dogged refusal to allow opponents easy kicks were the big factors in South's win'. This seemed to confirm, once again, that Oatey's methods were not the way to beat Port Adelaide.

Oatey remained positive and confident when speaking to his players, but he was a bundle of nerves once play got under way. During a game he would play obsessively with a handful of pebbles — rather as Humphrey Bogart did in the movie *The Caine Mutiny* — and hurl them to the ground when things went wrong. From the bench, Oatey was capable of proclaiming that a given player was 'hopeless', and then 'a champion', in the space of a few seconds. Sitting next to him, Edwards remembers being kicked and elbowed as Oatey followed the play, and being physically pushed out of the dugout when he had to take out a message. When he was under pressure and results were not going his way, Jack used to spend hours pottering around his backyard. Hicks remembers overhearing him talking to the watermelons he grew, telling them: 'I am right. I am the only one who knows. All the others are wrong'.

Sturt made the grand final in 1965 and, although Port lead by 35 points at three-quarter-time, the Double Blues came home strongly, losing by only three points. In the last few minutes Halbert, Adcock and Hicks had simple shots for goal but failed to score. A shot by Clarkson hit the post. Oatey remembered the club dinner that night as being the saddest moment in his football career. As the players and officials sat around, Oatey brooded and, according to some observers, almost decided that his game plan was wrong. But when he rose to speak to the players, Oatey was calm. 'We're now ready to win one,' he told them.

Fos Williams was in no doubt that Sturt had emerged as a difficult opponent. 'Step by step, Jack Oatey was building a team and a game plan that would beat us,' he recalled. 'The danger would come as soon as his players at Sturt believed it.' The Sturt players of that era are unanimous in believing that the turning point in their rivalry with Port came on 16 July 1966 at Alberton Oval. Before an almost capacity crowd of 18 000, Chessell had marked close to goal when the siren sounded, with Sturt trailing by four points. (The story has been told many times that, as Chessell was lining up to kick for goal, Schoff called out: 'Rowdy, if you kick this, I'll buy a Bible from you'. In fact, Chessell says that Schoff offered to buy a Bible in the rooms after the game. The next Tuesday at training, Chessell arrived with a Bible wrapped in brown paper, which Schoff paid him for.) Once Chessell's kick wobbled through for a goal, the Sturt players had gained the confidence they needed for future big games against Port. Of the next 14 matches between the two clubs, Sturt lost only three. In the 1966 grand final, Sturt doubled Port's score, 16.16 to 8.8, Chessell recalls, without the slightest trace of arrogance, that from that point on, 'the harder Port tried, the easier it was to beat them'. Some Port players tried bad language to unsettle their opponents, but this had no effect. When the Magpies tried to set up play using handball, they often made costly mistakes.

Port Adelaide had been badly affected by injuries during the 1967 season but, in the grand final that year, the Magpies showed tremendous determination to lead Sturt by nine points halfway through the last quarter. But as Keith Butler wrote, 'a glorious mark by Bagshaw and his subsequent 60-yard goal was the stimulus Sturt needed. It lifted and took the game away from a leg-weary Port'. Sturt drew away in time-on to win by 11 points. The margin in the 1968 grand final was a comfortable 27 points, and Butler wrote that:

> Bagshaw, who plays with an almost contemptuous ease, was, apart from one or two attempts to finesse, the most devastating player in the game. His overhead marking was sound, his ground work quick and strong and his handball, in either attack or defence, polished.

The 1969 grand final, in which Sturt beat Glenelg by 65 points, was notable for the dominance of Sturt's ruck unit:

> Bagshaw was dominant, particularly in the first half, with his strong marking, great handball and foot passing. Chessell repeatedly got the ball free of packs to set up drives.

It was a closer game the following year when a spirited Glenelg got to within a goal early in the last quarter, before a burst of three goals by Tilbrook put the result beyond doubt. Sturt's rovers, Rigney and Endersbee, were brilliant, while Bagshaw, 'seldom forced to commit himself to do anything hasty or foolish, showed superb ball control with both foot and hand'.

Once Sturt's run of five consecutive flags came to an end, the rest of Oatey's coaching career was almost an anticlimax. Sturt still won flags in 1974 and 1976 and should have won in 1978. The Double Blues kept winning premierships because the club was able to replace the champions of 1966–70 who had retired or moved on. Graham, Whelan and Robbert Klomp became new star players. The ruck division remained strong because of Bagshaw's consistency and longevity, and the emergence of Rick Davies, who became one of South Australia's greatest players. The 1974 grand final, the first played at Football Park, was a tight, low-scoring game, but Sturt eventually prevailed over Glenelg by 15 points. Robert Oatey, nearing the end of a superb playing career, had transferred to Sturt after being sacked as captain-coach of Norwood, and played in a premiership team coached by his father. Port Adelaide, now coached by John Cahill, was a short-priced favourite in 1976 but, when Port was kicking with a strong wind in the first quarter, Davies repelled attack after attack with his brilliant marking. The Magpies never recovered from this bad start, and Sturt took control as Davies played one of the great individual games in football history. 'From the outset,' wrote Schwartz in *The Advertiser*, 'the Sturt ruckman provided gilt-edged openings at the bounces, marked superbly all over the ground and found team-mates with unerring foot and handpasses.' His match statistics read: 21 kicks, 21 handballs and 15 marks. In 1978, Sturt let the grand final slip through poor kicking for goal, but Norwood's one-point victory will always be remembered for a mysterious umpiring decision that gave the Redlegs the winning goal. Another of the match's controversial incidents was a Norwood player running into the Sturt dugout, apparently in an attempt to unsettle Oatey.

A new grandstand was opened at Sturt in 1980 and the club honoured Oatey by naming it after him. But Oatey's final years at Sturt were difficult for him. Injuries and the loss of Klomp, who had joined Carlton, saw the team slip to ninth in 1979. Although things improved in 1980, with the team finishing third, a number of retirements and the move by Davies to Hawthorn at the end of the season weakened the club's playing strength dramatically. Oatey had planned to retire at the end of 1980, with his assistant coach John Halbert taking over. But when Halbert took the coaching job at Glenelg in 1979, Oatey felt let down by his former protégé. Because Oatey saw himself not just as the patriarch of the Sturt Football Club, but also as 'the coach who made the team', he was hurt by the declining quality of his playing staff and by players he had nurtured choosing to leave the club. As Chessell puts it, 'he had an ego that needed to be supported by excellence. He took great strength from having those people around him and to lose them was to lose part of his own ego'.

By now Oatey was suffering badly from arthritis and both his hips had been replaced. He could barely move on the training track and needed Mary's help at home to lift his legs. After one interview he got up slowly from his lounge chair, saying 'Come on leg. Move. Come on. Come on'. Oatey had earned the right to leave football on his own terms. He announced that the 1982 season would be his last as a coach. On training nights during that season he could be heard talking to the grass at Unley Oval, saying 'Hullo grass, I won't be seeing you next year'. In truth, he was no longer physically up to the job, but his mind remained sharp and he was able to pass on his wisdom about football and life to a new group of Sturt players that included Peter Motley, a son of Geof. After a defeat in the first semi-final that ended Sturt's season, Jack addressed his players, telling them that 'there will be other years, but unfortunately, it will be without me'. He cut his formal ties with the club, but found it difficult to stay away completely. In later years, people standing in front of the Jack Oatey Stand on training nights occasionally spotted him watching from a small gate on the outer side of Unley Oval.

Southern accent

Jack Oatey developed a method of countering the Port Adelaide game and imparted it to a Sturt team which he had played a key role in building. Oatey's method of teamwork enabled players to find space and move the ball to each other when confronted with physical pressure. This method centred on skilful disposal that required vision, judgement and precise execution. Although Len Smith had advocated the use of such skills as a means of keeping possession, they were used very rarely in Victoria. 'Checkside play', 'backplay' and kicking to space gave South Australian football a character that distinguished it from its Victorian counterpart. As was the case with the game's terminology (South Australian players 'stand' their opponent and ruckmen compete for 'bounce-downs') and equipment (lace-up guernseys and behind posts that are painted red), these methods of play were uniquely South Australian.

By the late 1970s, Jack Oatey and Fos Williams were the venerable men of South Australian football, still guiding League clubs with tried-and-true coaching methods that Oatey had not deviated from since his early days at Sturt, and Williams had been using since he had first played for Port Adelaide. The two men respected each other, but their coaching philosophies and game plans seemed as compatible as oil and water. Nevertheless, several of their former players who had become coaches had already started to take these ideas in new directions, in ways that the old masters were probably not capable of. In Oatey's last year as a coach, four of his former players were coaching League clubs: Halbert (Glenelg), Hicks (Central District), Kerley (West Adelaide) and Nunan (North Adelaide). John Cahill was a disciple of Williams. 'I could always trust Johnnie to show what I was looking for,' Williams wrote. After losing the 1976 grand final, Cahill introduced a running game to his Port Adelaide teams, with more emphasis on handball, while sacrificing nothing in tackling or attack on the ball. Cahill later wrote:

> The two coaches I have admired most have been Jack Oatey and Fos Williams. To play against Oatey and Sturt was always to play against a talented and disciplined team. The one factor that always stood out was the unselfish teamplay of the club. As a coach I have tried to take a leaf out of Oatey's book. I hope I'm half as successful.

Cahill led Port to the flag in 1977, and then followed up with three more flags in the next four years, before moving to the VFL to coach Collingwood. After returning to Port, he led a new generation of players to a further six flags in eight years, thus equalling Oatey's record of ten premierships, before becoming the first coach of Port Adelaide's AFL team.

By the end of the twentieth century, many of Oatey's ideas, such as those about kicking to space and checkside play (now generally referred to as 'switching play') had become standard practice at most AFL clubs. Williams's ideas about the importance of discipline and pressure have never gone out of fashion. The two styles complement each other and together they go a long way towards what football has become in the modern era and what it is likely to become in the future. The blend of the two styles can be seen in the play of many of the scores of South Australians playing in the AFL. For example, Essendon's Sean Wellman developed his defensive style by reading the play well and invariably making correct decisions about leaving his man to make space for himself, and bringing others into play through accurate disposal by hand or foot. Adelaide's Ben Hart and Carlton's Andrew McKay are two other players with the vision and disposal skills that characterised Oatey's champion Sturt teams. None of these players would shirk a physical issue and they would always run straight at the ball. When Port Adelaide, coached by Mark Williams, won its first AFL premiership in 2004, it did so with a team that ran and tackled hard, carried no passengers, and made use of exquisite kicking — long and short — and handball skills. One can imagine Jack Oatey and Fos Williams watching that team play, both of them nodding and smiling in approval.

Part 4

Nationwide

Barry Round (1950–)

Tim Watson (1961–)

Jason Akermanis (1977–)

WHEN FOOTBALL PARK, the headquarters of the SANFL, was opened in 1974, it was testimony to the popularity of Australian Rules in South Australia. The stadium was constructed by the SANFL after it was unable to negotiate an agreement with the South Australian Cricket Association to build a new stand for football members at the Adelaide Oval. Built on an area of former swampland, Football Park was poorly served by public transport and lacked the charm of the Adelaide Oval, but its potential as a major football venue was obvious. At least 75 000 people turned up for the 1976 grand final (the equivalent, per capita, of a crowd of 225 000 in Melbourne) when the stadium was little more than a bowl of concrete terracing. As further improvements were made to its facilities, Football Park became a modern, comfortable stadium and its popularity with fans made it a highly valuable economic asset to the SANFL. The funds it generated provided dividends to the clubs and funded a junior development program that taught young people basic skills and encouraged them to take a continuing interest in the game.

The SANFL was the most prosperous league in Australia outside the VFL. Every Saturday afternoon during the football season, clubs with long and proud histories battled each other in rivalries that kept their tribes of supporters enthralled. Although the players were not paid much, they remained loyal to their clubs and few left to play in the VFL. Like every other metropolitan and country league in Australia, the SANFL was protected by distance: football in the early 1970s was still a game that most people watched in person, and fans found it difficult to follow the fortunes of teams that played in other parts of the country.

During the 1970s, the distance protection that local leagues enjoyed started to break down. Television coverage of the VFL was boosted by the introduction of colour TV in 1975, and by *The Winners*, a one-hour highlights program broadcast nationally by the ABC. For Victorians living outside their home state, *The Winners*, as John Harms put it, 'was like a letter from home'. The show exposed kids from other states to a high-standard competition that they could follow as well as their local team. The VFL was also becoming more attractive to interstate footballers because of the increasing amounts of money that clubs were prepared to pay to recruit players.

This aggressive recruiting had started during the 1960s, and the trend continued after the Coulter Law was abolished and country zoning was introduced. Clubs with zones that were not highly productive began to look outside Victoria for potential players. Interstate recruiting, and a short-lived rule that made all players with at least ten years' service at one VFL club free agents, added to inflationary pressures on player salaries in general. At a time of rising inflation, player payments rose much faster than average weekly earnings and the costs of running a football club increased faster than the growth of revenue from gate money, membership fees and sponsorship. A small group of clubs that recruited effectively and were well coached and administered were consistently successful, while their rivals struggled to lift themselves up the ladder. Only four clubs — Carlton, Hawthorn, North Melbourne and Richmond — won premierships between 1967 and 1983; economist Ross Booth has calculated that between 1979 and 1982, when Carlton won three premierships, the competition was more uneven than at any time in its history. After the League's transfer rules were declared by a court ruling in 1983 to be a restraint of trade, players became free agents when their contracts expired and the resulting competition between clubs to attract and retain players drove wages up further. A year later, half of the League's clubs were effectively bankrupt.

Australian Rules football had entered a period of crisis so severe that action had to be taken to ensure the survival of its major competition, the VFL. South Melbourne was one club that was heavily in debt and its main source of revenue, the Lake Oval, was shabby and run-down. Fitzroy, another club that had struggled to attract new fans after World War II, had splurged on players with borrowed money. Clubs as well supported as Richmond and St Kilda owed millions of dollars and their long-term future seemed problematic. Even Collingwood was in financial difficulties. The crisis extended well beyond the VFL, however. Interstate and VFA clubs lost many of their best players to the VFL and found their costs escalating. Economic and demographic stagnation in many rural and regional areas made it difficult for country football clubs to make ends meet and for some to field teams. Every club, from the VFL to the bush, was operating in a regional market with limited spectator and corporate support. Distance had once protected football clubs; now, it threatened to punish them. Before the mid-1970s, clubs that struggled on the field were merely underachieving; by the 1980s, such clubs were under pressure to stay in business and retain their own identity.

The traditional heartlands of Australian Rules — the centres of manufacturing in Melbourne, Adelaide and Perth, the old mining towns and the wheat belt — were growing more slowly. An increasingly globalised and deregulated economy, that was less protected by tariffs, created new job opportunities in services and a growing proportion of this work was located in the metropolitan areas of Sydney and Brisbane. Sydney had become Australia's most populous city during the 1890s and maintained its lead over Melbourne at every census. Brisbane was still virtually a big country town in the 1960s, but transport and other infrastructure improvements led to a boom in office and residential construction that created a sprawling urban mass extending north of Brisbane to the Sunshine Coast, and south to the Gold Coast. With a population of 2.2 million in 2000, Brisbane was home to as many people as lived in Melbourne in 1966. The potential of Australian Rules in the Sydney and Brisbane markets, and much of their hinterlands, was largely untapped. Rugby League was the traditional game and this was reflected in its blanket media coverage. The local Australian Rules leagues were considered by most sports fans and the media to be of minor importance.

The VFL had been looking for ways to expand the competition into the northern states for some time. League clubs had played exhibition matches in Sydney and Brisbane as early as the 1930s, and AFC carnivals had been held in both cities. The VFL president, Allen Aylett, regarded the sponsorship, marketing and TV rights that would accrue from linking up to the Sydney market as crucial to the future of the game. The League began scheduling matches in Sydney in 1979 and, in the following year, a League report recommended that a team be based permanently in the city. In 1982, South Melbourne decided that it could not survive unless it relocated to Sydney.

In 1983, three representatives of the VFL flew to America to gather information about how professional sports organised their competitions. In New York, they met Pete Rozelle, who had been the Commissioner of the NFL since 1959. Rozelle had transformed gridiron football from a minor sport into a huge business; he told the VFL representatives how a national competition, kept even by a player draft and with games played on perfect surfaces in modern stadiums, generated billions of dollars in TV rights, which were then shared among the member teams. In return for a share of the value of the NFL brand, member teams signed licensing agreements to abide by the League's constitution. They also met a senior executive of the NBA, who explained how a salary cap controlled team expenditure. By the end of the year, the VFL clubs had agreed to create an independent commission which would have responsibility for making decisions about the future of the game. This required the clubs (and their members) to give up some of their autonomy, and reduced their power to act in their own interests rather than those of football in general. After decades of conservative and largely *ad hoc* decision making, League football began to reinvent itself.

The restructured VFL, later renamed the Australian Football League, was modelled on the organisational principles of American sports leagues. Its cornerstone was a national competition with teams in Sydney and Brisbane, and eventually two in each of the football strongholds of Adelaide and Perth. By 2004, Adelaide, Brisbane, Port Adelaide and West Coast had all won AFL premierships. A national draft replaced country zoning and a salary cap regulated clubs' spending on player wages. The result was an even competition — between 1990 and 2004, nine clubs won at least one AFL premiership, while only three teams did not play in a grand final — that was attractive to spectators. Games were played on several days of the week — some of them at night. Ground-sharing became the norm, and matches involving the biggest Melbourne clubs were played at the MCG where a massive new southern stand was built with cooperation between the AFL and the MCC. Average attendances at AFL games rose from 21 000 in 1987, the first year of the national competition, to 35 000 ten years later. By the time Ross Oakley retired in 1996 after a ten-year stint as Chairman of the Commission, AFL football was a high-rating national television product that generated lucrative broadcast rights and sponsorship deals, and, in turn, salaries that allowed players to become full-time professionals.

So much about the game had changed, and much of it for the better. Ten times more people watched games on TV than in person. A dedicated football fan could watch most of each weekend's games on free-to-air TV, and all games, multiple times, on pay TV. A fan who watched games in person was likely to do so from a seat, often undercover, in a clean, modern stadium with amenities that encouraged people to take their families along. Muddy grounds and, at Melbourne's Docklands Stadium, wet weather became things of the past. Potential players were more likely to be drawn from a national under-18 competition that extended across Victoria, New South Wales and Tasmania, where training facilities and coaching were of a high standard, than from suburban or bush leagues. Clubs and the AFL Players' Association developed policies and employed specialist staff to monitor the welfare of players and encourage them to finish their education. The image that the game presented to prospective players (and their parents) was improved by video reporting and a blood rule. The ability of Michael Long to articulate why racial abuse was so hurtful to Aboriginals prompted the AFL to introduce a code of conduct with a racial vilification rule. In an era when AFL matches nearly always involve at least one Aboriginal player on each side, the football community seems at peace with itself over the issue.

The concentration of revenue, high salaries and media attention on a single league does have several downsides. The amount of money that players can earn and the broadcasting of all matches nationally means that, in the future, it is unlikely that a player would choose to carve out a stellar career while being watched only rarely outside his own state, as champions such as Barrie Robran and Stephen Michael did. While football fans in general are the beneficiaries of this, it has weakened the links between clubs and their traditional communities. A drafted player is increasingly unlikely to play for a club close to where he grew up. When a talented young player joins the national under-18 competition, his absence reduces the standard of play in his local or junior team and league. Although the AFL sees promotion of the game at the grassroots level as fundamental to the long-term success of the code, and allocates a proportion of its revenue to clinics and equipment for schools and junior leagues, many metropolitan and country leagues struggle to retain teenagers when it is time for them to move up to senior football. The SANFL, the WAFL and the VFA (now renamed the VFL) have lost much of their traditional support and now function to a considerable extent as reserve-grade competitions for AFL clubs. Media scrutiny has highlighted the off-field behaviour of AFL players who, rightly, are seen as role models for young people. Historically, footballers have been underpaid for the sacrifices they have made; part of the price of rectifying this has been the modern player's loss of basic privacy.

The careers of three great players illustrate football's transformation. Barry Round, Tim Watson and Jason Akermanis all grew up in country Victoria with ambitions to eventually play in Melbourne. Round and Watson started in the VFL when it was still a metropolitan competition and when most games were played on windswept suburban ovals. Round's team, South Melbourne, relocated to Sydney and he and his team-mates struggled to cope with playing in a city where Australian Rules was only a minor sport. Watson's career coincided with the reinvention of Essendon as one of Melbourne's most powerful and popular clubs. When Brisbane drafted Akermanis, it took one of the most significant early steps in building a team that would spearhead the successful growth of Australian Rules in the rugby-dominated Brisbane market. Each became a recognisable face of his club, and the game, through increasing TV coverage: Round with his easygoing capacity for hard work, Watson with his athleticism and power on the field and his modesty off it, and Akermanis with his flair and his willingness to use the media to promote the game.

10

Barry Round

(1950–)

> We were made to feel like a naughty kid who had been kicked out of home.
>
> BARRY ROUND

When Barry Round started playing junior football at Nilma, a small town outside Warragul, his home ground was a cow paddock which a farmer had allowed the local club to use in winter. The under-16s played first thing on Saturday mornings and Barry remembers that 'the odd cow pat would still be a bit fresh and we'd be trying not to fall over and land in the cow shit'. The changing rooms were made of corrugated iron and had dirt floors. There were no showers. Twenty years later, Round had become the public face of the VFL's push into the Sydney market after his club, South Melbourne, which was then broke and close to going out of existence, relocated there. At the official launch outside the Sydney Opera House, Round and another player were photographed lifting a model dressed in a Swans jumper onto their shoulders. After the first game, he and the players attended a garden party at Lady Fairfax's house at Potts Point, where there was champagne, caviar, and a swimming pool filled with red and white balloons. When the Swans became Australian Rules' first privately owned football club, Round and the players went to a party at the home of the new owner, Dr Geoffrey Edelston. 'It was about a kilometre from the front gate to where the house started,' Barry recalled. After years of not knowing whether their next pay cheque would be on time, they walked in past a fleet of Edelston's luxury cars, which had number plates with wording like 'Sexy', 'Spunky' and 'Groovy'.

It was a long journey from Gippsland's cow paddocks to Sydney mansions, but through it all Barry Round remained essentially unchanged; that was the key to his broad appeal to football fans. It is doubtful whether a more universally popular person has played the game. In a VFL career that spanned 17 seasons, 328 day games and 36 night and representative games, his easy, down-to-earth manner, his sense of fair play and his total commitment to his team embodied everything that followers of the game admired. He played in an era in which, at many clubs, ruckwork — arguably the most important job in the game — was in the hands of men who were highly eccentric, in their behaviour (like 'Crackers' Keenan), their physique (Mick Nolan, 'The Galloping Gasometer'), or both ('Percy' Jones). To all appearances these were easygoing characters but they were also fine exponents of their craft. Round's eccentricity was his kicking, which was awkward and far from reliable, and after taking a mark he would usually look to give a handball to a running team-mate. He was more than able to hold his own against the game's leading tap ruckmen, and also against tougher players such as Carl Ditterich, Don Scott and Neil Balme, who tested the courage of their opponents. The attitude of Round and his fellow ruckmen was that:

> If someone elbowed you in the face at a boundary throw-in or at a centre bounce, there'd be another throw-in in another 10 or 15 seconds. If the umpire saw a bloke with a cut eyebrow, he knew at the next throw-in or the next quarter there'd be the evener-up and he'd look at you and nod and say 'fair enough, now get back to playing footy' and that was the law of the jungle.

During the game, players might sledge or belt each other mercilessly, but after the game there was always the 'fifth quarter', as Round calls it, when they would get together and bury the hatchet over a few beers. In the early years of the Sydney venture, Round was one of the good reasons for watching the Swans' games on a Sunday afternoon, even if you supported another club. Whenever the Swans won at the SCG, Round's triumphal salute, with his body almost drained by 100 minutes of exertion, brought the most enthusiastic response from the crowds that lined the race to cheer the players off.

As Round's career was coming to an end, the Sydney Football Club was heading into uncharted waters as a privately owned club controlled by a marketing company called Powerplay. The chief executive of Powerplay, Bob Pritchard, was of the view that football clubs were under the mistaken impression that 'the game is the almighty thing'. In the advertising and presentation of its product, Powerplay placed as much, if not more, emphasis on pre-game and half-time shows as it did on the matches themselves. There were publicity stunts and cheerleaders, and theme music played after every Sydney goal. The players knew that the club had to be marketed to establish itself in a new location, but they were uncomfortable with the flashy image that their club was projecting. 'I just thought it was all a wank really,' Barry admitted. Even though he was club captain, Barry says that while Powerplay was doing its marketing and its associated companies were negotiating deals for TV broadcast rights, 'I just decided I wasn't going to concern myself with it. I'd just try to get a kick and win a game of footy'.

After Powerplay was bought out in 1987, having lost millions of dollars, the Swans lurched from one crisis to another. It was not until 1993, when the club hit rock bottom, that the AFL provided financial assistance and set in place an administrative structure to provide the appropriate level of stability and support to the coach and players. This made it possible for people, like Barry Round, who loved the game to get on with the job of getting a kick and winning matches. It was as if the game's administrators had finally realised that it was the actions of people like Barry Round, rather than marketing gimmicks, that would bring crowds to football games and that providing support for such people was indispensable to the success of the national competition.

Almost famous

Barry Round was born in Albury in 1950. His parents split up when he was aged around four or five and his mother moved with him and his younger sister to Nilma, where her mother lived. Barry was 16 and still at school when he played for Nilma seniors in the Ellinbank Football League. The following season he transferred to Warragul which played in a much stronger and rougher competition, the Latrobe Valley Football League. He was a big lad who played in the ruck, although no-one had ever taught him anything about how to play the position. Playing for Warragul pitted him against timber cutters and farmers and, although he saw 'a few king hits' being dished out, he coped with the physical side of the game and his enthusiasm remained undiminished.

Round would have signed for Richmond in 1967 had the introduction of country zoning not prevented him from doing so. He was visited by Graeme Richmond, who offered him no financial incentives — just the opportunity to be a part of a successful club. The Round family was a guest of the Richmond Football Club during the 1967 finals series. Barry was taken into the rooms before the grand final, met some of the players and then watched them win the flag. In retrospect, Round was the big man that the Tigers were looking for to replace Neville Crowe, who was about to retire. For Round, becoming tied to Footscray prevented him from joining a club that would play in several grand finals in the following years. 'It didn't bother me too much,' he recalls. 'I just wanted to have a crack at League footy.' When he joined Footscray in 1969, the move from the country to the city caused little disruption to his personal life. He was doing a carpentry apprenticeship and it was a straightforward matter to transfer that to a Melbourne location. Barry's mother had remarried and his stepfather had been transferred in his job to Melbourne and the family had moved with him.

Barry played a few reserves' games for Footscray in 1968, but it was not until he arrived at the start of pre-season training that he met the Bulldogs' senior coach, a suntanned man 'who just about broke four of my fingers when I shook his hand'. The legendary Ted Whitten had captain-coached the club in all but two seasons since 1957. Round joined Footscray at a critical time in the club's history. The Bulldogs had been in decline since winning the flag in 1954. Recruiting was hampered by a lack of finance and the club's image as a bunch of battlers. Under Whitten's coaching, Footscray had developed a fast, team-oriented game centred on the use of the flick pass, which took the club to runner-up in 1961. But internal divisions began surfacing between the football club and its coterie group (the Kennel Masters), the Footscray Cricket Club and the Footscray City Council. Whitten was replaced as coach in 1966 and thought seriously about going to Richmond. Although he resumed the coaching role two years later, further trouble lay ahead.

Footscray had high hopes for Barry Round. The club gave him the number 14 worn by their recently retired champion ruckman, John Schultz, and selected him in the opening round of 1969. This was Whitten's three hundredth League game and Round made an immediate impact, grabbing the ball from a boundary throw-in the forward pocket and snapping a goal with his first kick in League football. He played every game that season, mostly in the forward pocket as a backup to another promising ruckman, Gary Dempsey. Round averaged 30 goals a season in his first four years and seemed set for a long VFL career.

But things did not go smoothly at the Western Oval in the 1970s. At the start of the 1970 season, Whitten was told by the committee that its offer to him to coach was conditional on him retiring as a player once he had played the four games he needed to break Dick Reynolds's VFL record of 320 games. Whitten was hurt deeply by this and, although he was aged 36, many within the club felt that he should have been able to continue playing as long as his form warranted. Round's view was that Whitten 'was still worth his place in the side and in hindsight they should've let him keep playing because he made everyone walk tall and he could help umpire the game'.

Whitten's role as a protector of his team-mates, which Round euphemistically describes as 'giving assistance where required', meant that he would have been of value on the field to his young players. 'We were all in awe of him and so were the opposition to a certain degree', was how Barry remembered Ted.

Whitten was sacked at the end of 1971 and the Bulldogs appointed Bob Rose as coach. Rose's coaching credentials were impeccable and he was, as Round put it, 'a fantastic fellow'. But in his time at Footscray, he endured two tragedies which made the coaching job difficult — his son Robert was left a quadriplegic after a car crash, and an accident during a game left one of his players, Neil Sachse, with a damaged spinal cord. The Bulldogs made the finals in 1974 but Collingwood trounced them. Round remembers that:

> We played our final before we got to the ground. After the last game we all went down to Phillip Island for a bit of team bonding and I think we all thought it was an end of season trip rather than preparation for the week after.

The team's partying and then dismal exit from the finals was proof, if any was needed, of the negative football culture that then existed at Footscray. The club had some talented young players — in addition to Round and Dempsey, it had key forwards Bernie Quinlan and Kelvin Templeton, and rover Geoff Jennings — and was capable of competing with the better teams. Inconsistency consigned the team to middle-of-the-road status, however. By the mid-1970s the club was again in financial difficulties and at one stage the players threatened to go on strike. As the writers of the club history, *Unleashed*, observed, 'morale was ravaged further by administration considered to be so poor as to border on self-destruction'.

Clearly the club needed to make changes. Bill Goggin was appointed coach at the end of 1975, and over the summer break the chairman of selectors took Round aside and told him that, as the club would be having a clear-out of players, it would be in his best interests to look for another club. Barry was annoyed at the club's decision as he had played 20 games in 1975, but got on with talking to other clubs. He seemed likely to go to Geelong, but did not like the idea of having to drive several times a week up and down the Geelong Highway, and he also spoke to Melbourne and Collingwood. He eventually signed with South Melbourne which was in search of a first ruckman.

If anything, South Melbourne's future looked shakier than that of Footscray. South was heavily in debt and the Lake Oval was what estate agents would call a renovator's delight. After the club won only two games in 1975, a new administration took over. The new president, Craig Kimberley, provided a $100 000 sponsorship from his highly successful jeans company and Ian Stewart was appointed as coach. The perfectionism Stewart displayed as a player extended to his coaching; this and his insistence on hard training could rub some people up the wrong way. Brian Roberts and Peter Bedford were two valuable players who left the club after falling out with Stewart. Although Round found Stewart to be a 'Jekyll and Hyde' temperamentally, he got on well with the new coach. Having left Footscray, where 'you could go along week after week and amass numbers of games without really going anywhere', Barry was keen to impress his new club. Stewart played him as a centre half-forward who did the ruckwork on the forward line. The coach fostered a 'them and us' mentality among the players, built around the club's image as the poor relation of the League, that took them to the finals in 1977. Stewart was appointed coach of Carlton in 1978 but, after a disastrous period during which he alienated the players in a matter of weeks, he returned to coach South from 1979 to 1981.

South Melbourne was slipping further into a financial mire. The club was now heavily in debt and had to sell players to pay the bills. On a few occasions the players were paid only because of the generosity of Kimberley, who dipped into his own pocket. Membership was falling and the League had informed the club that the Lake Oval was no longer up to standard as a senior venue and that no money would be allocated to it from the League's ground improvement fund. To anyone who looked at South Melbourne's account books, the conclusion was inescapable that the club could not survive much longer in its own right. If the club was to continue, the only alternatives seemed to be a merger with another club (St Kilda, also in financial trouble, was the obvious choice) or relocation to Sydney. In July 1981, South Melbourne applied to the League for permission to play half its matches in 1982 in Sydney.

The issue tore the club apart. The committee, coach and all but a few of the players saw the move as inevitable. As Round said later:

> In a perfect world it would have been great to stay at South Melbourne. But now when you look at the national competition, and whether we would have been able to keep trading as one of the poor relations in Melbourne, a la Fitzroy, I'm sure we would have been one of the most vulnerable, if not the most vulnerable. It's probably ensured that the red and whites of the Swans are still part of it, and I doubt we would have been if we'd stayed in Melbourne.

Most of the South's dwindling number of supporters were bitter over the committee's actions and strongly opposed to them. Even the run-through (made by the cheer squad for the players to enter through) for the final game of 1981 at the Lake Oval was black. Round was awarded three Brownlow votes that day but, although it transpired that those votes won him the Medal (in which he tied with his old friend Bernie Quinlan), even that success was not enough to lift the poisonous atmosphere at the club. At the end of the season, a reform group called 'Keep South At South' won control of the club at an extraordinary general meeting. Although Stewart was in favour of the move, he had announced that he would be resigning as coach; former captain Ricky Quade had agreed to take on the coaching job on the condition that the relocation went ahead. Before the general meeting, Quade and his family were harassed by a rogue element among South Melbourne supporters. Round was not a target for such a level of abuse, but he did receive 'some silly phone calls' and he avoided South supporters whenever he could. The players were called one by one to meet the new board and be told that the club would be staying in Melbourne. They were led in through one door and out through another to prevent them talking as a group. The players went on strike and did pre-season training away from the club for three months. Other League clubs were circling, waiting to sign up the Swans' best players. Round signed a contract to play with Footscray again if the Swans folded. He remembers that:

> I didn't know where we were going. Morale was pretty low and blokes were saying, 'That's it. I'm out.' . . . There were blokes going off in different directions everywhere saying, 'Well, if there's not going to be a club I better look after myself, and I might sign with this club or I might sign with that club,' and some were going to retire. It was terrible.

While it was common knowledge that the club had been mismanaged for years and was in serious financial difficulties, the new administration was shocked to discover that the club in fact had only a small reserve of cash and a debt of around $600 000. 'We knew immediately that we couldn't overcome that,' recalled the 'Keep South At South' chairman, John Keogh. Eventually another board was formed, Quade was re-appointed as coach and, with the aid of a $400 000 grant from the League's ground improvement fund, South Melbourne began preparing to play its home games in Sydney in 1982.

Prime time

The last years at the Lake Oval had been difficult, but the Sydney Swans, as they became known officially, had seen nothing yet. The sports coverage in the Sydney media was focussed almost exclusively on Rugby League and reporters were largely indifferent to the former Melbourne club and the code it played. Sponsorship and other forms of revenue were hard to secure and the money that the VFL had loaned the club was soon used up. 'I don't think the League had any idea how tough a market it would be,' Barry says. Meanwhile, the bills kept piling up. By 1983 the club's annual revenue was $2.5 million, but a further $1.2 million was owed in payments to the players and staff and to other creditors.

The players felt the effects of the situation in several ways. As Barry points out, the players thought they were being neglected by the VFL and this made them feel 'like a naughty kid who had been kicked out of home'. The SCG's no. 2 oval, where the club trained, had no lights and was bumpy because it was used as a car park when the SCG was in use. One night they trained when there were cars on the oval. Barry recalls that after the club asked its landlord, the SCG Trust, to provide some lights, 'they nailed up a bit of timber with four spotlights and that was it. It gave us light with a radius of 30 metres'. The training rooms had only the barest of facilities and the players had to bring their own weights. The nonpayment of players and staff was a more serious issue. Several had moved up to Sydney, away from potential support networks of family and friends, and had families to feed. One player told the *Herald Sun*'s Trevor Grant that his and another player's wife would pool their food when the cupboard was almost bare. Although Barry says that morale among the players was 'pretty good', many of the players and their families were under stress. Barry and his wife and two children were living in a beautiful house on the Georges River, with rent subsidised by the club, but there were still difficulties in the marriage during this period. This led to a physical confrontation between Round and Ricky Quade in the middle of 1984, which destabilised the club further. Quade resigned from the coaching job and Round was dropped from the senior team. Round refused to play in the reserves and announced his retirement, but eventually he was reinstated in the senior team.

In the circumstances, the players did remarkably well on the field. In 1982 the Swans won the night premiership and were in the running for a finals berth until the last two weeks of the season. They did have some excellent players who came from the old Melbourne metropolitan zone: Steven Wright, the Morwood brothers, David Rhys-Jones and, later, Warwick Capper. The Swans got into a travel routine quickly while the other League clubs tended to be unsettled by their annual visit to Sydney, which Round says some players regarded as a holiday from wintery Melbourne. After all they had been through, the Swans wanted credibility as a football team, both for their professional pride and to secure their economic future. As Round observes, they took the night premiership so seriously because they saw the competition, which carried a prize purse of $105 000, 'as a chance to get paid'.

At the end of the 1985 season, Round was approaching 36 years of age. He was still in good shape and carried no injuries. Throughout his career, his work as a carpenter and his love of running and swimming had kept him fit. On 10-kilometre runs at training, he was in his element and usually finished in the leading group. He was proud of the fact that he played his three hundredth game during his sixteenth season, which meant that he averaged close to 20 games per season. His philosophy was that, after a few beers or a barbeque, it was important to get back to work straight away 'to balance up the scales'. As a result, he always turned up to pre-season training in peak condition and maintained his fitness during the year. This and good fortune with injuries were the keys to his longevity, but by now he knew that his time as a League footballer was just about up. Being beaten soundly by Essendon's champion Simon Madden in the final game of 1985 was enough for him to make up his mind. No-one at the Swans asked him to retire but he did so at the end of that season. Barry still wanted to play football at the highest level he could and, because he had moved back to his Melbourne home, which had been rented out during his time in Sydney, he did not consider seriously any of the offers made to him by country clubs. Because of the proximity of the South Melbourne and Port Melbourne districts, many Swans players had played VFA football at Port when their League careers were over. Before Port Melbourne contacted Round, however, he received a phone call from Terry Wheeler, a former Footscray team-mate who was coaching Williamstown. Over a few beers, Wheeler and the club president, Tony Hanneberry, explained that they thought the club needed only a few more good players to win the premiership. Williamstown had lost a close grand final to an excellent Sandringham team in 1985, and Wheeler's view was that what his team needed most was an experienced centre half-forward. Hanneberry had for years watched his club recruit, as he put it, 'washed-up' ex-VFL players without having much success on the field; when he was elected president, one of his platforms was that 'as long as I'm president we won't recruit anyone aged over 30'. In Round's case, however, he was prepared to make an exception.

In many ways, the move to Williamstown took Round's career almost full circle. The Williamstown area was not yet the hot property market it would become, and Barry liked the village feel of the place. With its location away from major through roads and its strong sense of community, it seemed to Barry to be more like a country town than a suburb, and he was happy to buy a house and move there. After the turmoil of South Melbourne and the flash of Sydney, he was delighted to be at a grassroots club that was well-administered and ambitious for success. Williamstown is one of football's oldest clubs, having joined the VFA in 1884. It had been the dominant power in that competition during the 1950s, when it won five premierships in six years, but in the 1970s and early 1980s it had fallen on hard times and its financial position was insecure. At the start of the 1980s, the Seagulls were playing in the VFA's second division. Although the Point Gellibrand Oval had only the most basic facilities (apart from a stately white grandstand built in 1930, the ground's amenities were comparable to those of most country football clubs), Hanneberry and his administration organised fundraising activities and sponsorships. The club had a convivial social atmosphere. Few big name players were recruited; apart from Wheeler and Round, most of the Williamstown players were from local areas such as Spotswood and Altona and had not played at a higher level than League under-19s. Round was paid much the same as the other senior players. 'I wasn't playing for the money,' he says. 'I just wanted a kick I suppose.' As a result, 1986 was the most enjoyable year that Barry had had in football. To someone who simply loved playing, this was the equivalent of smelling the roses.

Williamstown faced Coburg in the grand final that year. Led by captain-coach, Phil Cleary, Coburg had been the outstanding team all season and were hot favourites. Cleary, who later became an independent member of federal Parliament, was an inspirational leader whose conspicuous presence always seemed to antagonise the opposition. Barry found Cleary to be 'a good bloke' at the after-match get-togethers, but thought he was 'an annoying little pest' on the field. The game was close until the third quarter, when Cleary was reported for what Round, who was not directly involved in the incident, recalls as 'a bit of push and shove'. Under VFA rules, Cleary was sent from the field for 15 minutes, and in that time Williamstown took control of the game. Round was moved from centre half-forward to the ruck and by three-quarter-time the Seagulls had a lead of 45 points. Coburg came back in the last quarter but, when the siren sounded, Barry's team was 13 points in front. Barry remembers that he and Wheeler were chaired off the ground after the game by a crowd of supporters. Someone called out to Barry that winning a premiership was a wonderful note on which to bow out as a footballer. 'Bow out?' he shouted back. 'I'm just starting to enjoy it.'

Terry Wheeler became coach of Footscray at the end of 1988, and Williamstown appointed Round as his replacement. Barry had no real ambitions to coach, but the club did not want to risk changing its winning formula by bringing in an outsider to do the job. The Seagulls were runners-up in 1988 and 1989 to Coburg. At three-quarter-time in the 1990 grand final, played against Springvale at Princes Park, they were staring at a third consecutive grand final defeat. They trailed by 28 points and Barry admits that, at the time, he didn't think his team could win. Springvale was playing confidently and Williamstown's star player, Ian Rickman, a burly forward who had not quite made the grade at Footscray, was being kept quiet. Round simply asked that his players 'chip away and see how it goes'.

What followed was a dramatic last quarter. Williamstown was 34 points down within a few minutes, and at the 23-minute mark the deficit was still 16 points. Rickman then goaled twice within minutes, the second being a drop punt that travelled at least 60 metres. With only a couple of minutes left to play, Bill Swan, an experienced centreman who had crossed from Port Melbourne, marked about 50 metres from goal. Swan had never kicked a 50-metre goal in his life, so Round ran back to the goal square hoping he could take a match-winning mark. Swan timed his kick perfectly and the ball sailed over Round's head for a goal.

The 1990 premiership was a playing, as well as coaching, triumph for Round. He won the Norm Goss Medal, awarded to the best player on the ground. As *The Age* reported, 'Round rucked tirelessly all day and consistently won the ball out of the centre during the Seagulls' late charge'. Though he was now 40 years of age, he was still more than worth his place and saw no reason to give up the game. After the match he told the press, 'If the liver and the kidneys can survive a couple of months of celebrating, I think I'll put the boots on again next year'.

Round's VFA career, in which he played 110 games and around a dozen VFA representative games, took his senior career total to 486 games. He would almost have certainly reached the 500-game mark but for a nagging knee injury that made running difficult. After seven rounds of the 1991 season he stopped playing and had arthroscopic surgery, but was unable to get the knee right and resume playing. He stayed on as non-playing coach and took Williamstown to runner-up in 1992. After his last year of coaching, 1993, he joined the Williamstown club board. He was ruck coach at Williamstown and Geelong for a time, but his job as a sales representative often took him to the country, causing him to miss training nights. His final game of football was in 1999; he returned to his home town to play one game with Warragul when the club was short of players and struggling to survive. He was 49 years of age.

Part of a great football family. Ethel Smith with her sons Norm (left) and Len just before they faced each other as opposition coaches for the first time in 1958

Len Smith with his grandsons Stephen (left) and Wayne Harmes

A clash between Fitzroy and Melbourne in 1958 was called the Battle of the Brothers — Len Smith (third from left), the Lions' coach, and next to him the Demons' coach, Norm Smith. On either side of the Smith brothers are the Lions and Demons who were selected for the state team — from left: Kevin Murray and Owen Abrahams (Fitzroy) and John Beckwith, Laurie Mithen, Ron Barassi, Don Williams and Bob Johnson (Melbourne).

© Newspix/Michael Dodge

John Kennedy (left) and Leigh Matthews with the portrait for the Hawthorn Football Club Hall of Fame inductee night, 2003

Hawthorn's John Kennedy leaps over Jack Garrick of South Melbourne

Mutual respect: Jack Oatey (left) and Fos Williams during the early years of a coaching rivalry that lasted for almost 30 years

© Newspix

As his coaching career drew to a close in the early 1980s, Jack Oatey still regarded football as a 'tactical manoeuvre'.

© Newspix

© Newspix

(ABOVE)
Barry Round in action for South Melbourne, in one of the last games played at Lake Oval.

(LEFT)
Round (left) and his friend Bernie Quinlan with the Brownlow Medals they won together in 1981

© Newspix

Tim Watson, whom Martin Flanagan wrote played as if he had 'swivel joints and shock absorbers in his ankles'

© Getty Images/ALLSPORT/Hamish Blair

A rare moment of triumph in Tim's unhappy spell as coach of St Kilda. Barry Hall is the player on the left.

© Newspix/David Kapernick

© Getty Images/Hamish Blair

(ABOVE)
Brisbane Lions 'Fab Four': (from left) Lappin, Akermanis, Black and Voss. Yeah, yeah, yeah, *yeah!*

(RIGHT)
Jason Akermanis performs his trademark handstand after winning his first premiership in 2001.

11

Tim Watson
(1961–)

> From 15 to 22 football consumed me and there was a time when I thought 'Crikey'. I can't remember being 15, 16, 17 or 18 because I never did anything other kids that age did.
>
> TIM WATSON

There was no doubt about it; Bob Watson could play football. He once kicked 20 goals in a match at Phillip Island and, in the early 1960s, Bob Davis was forever trying to get him to try out at Geelong. The Cats' coach had launched a major recruiting drive and, although Davis and his club secretary were prepared to compete with other League clubs by offering cash to prospective players, they found that recruiting was a hit-and-miss process. Some players wanted more money than Geelong was prepared to pay, others did not want to leave their parents' farm, while only 'some, very few I must admit, just could not wait to put pen to paper'. Bob Watson's answer to Davis was always the same: he was running a business driving trucks with his brother, Alan, at Dimboola, a small town just north-west of Horsham in Victoria's wheat belt, and was simply unable to find the time to play and train at League level. Like countless other country footballers, Watson chose to concentrate on making a living in his home town, rather than gamble on trying to forge a League career, where the prospects of success were uncertain and the financial rewards were modest.

Bob Watson's rejection of the opportunity to test his football skills at the elite level could not have contrasted more sharply with the attitude of his nephew, Tim. 'I can't recall a time when it wasn't what I wanted to do,' Tim once wrote. 'Like all my mates at primary school, and then high school, we all had the ambition that that's what we were going to do.' He was zoned to Essendon and, after playing in a schoolboys' carnival in December 1976, received a letter from the club inviting him to Melbourne to watch a practice match. By that time he 'was desperate to get there and it was going to be hard for my parents to keep me at home because of the desire I had to play VFL football'. When three Essendon officials visited the Watson house to discuss when he might move to Melbourne, Tim already had his bag packed. He got into the car and went back to Melbourne with them that night. He was aged 15.

Tim Watson was born in 1961, and grew up in an era when the amount of money in League football increased significantly. But the prospect of making money out of football played little, if any, part in Tim's decision to move to Melbourne. He was from a football household, and a small town where football was an important part of community life, and grew up at a time when technological change was making it easier for country people to keep in touch with what was happening in the VFL. On Saturdays during the football season, Alan Watson, Tim's father, played for local teams and his family — his wife, daughter and four sons — went along to watch him. The Watsons then went home and switched on the television to follow the fortunes of Richmond, the team they all barracked for, which was then enjoying its glory years under Tommy Hafey. On Sundays there was a further treat, Channel Seven's *World of Sport*, which featured Tiger legend Jack Dyer and his verbal sparring partner, former Collingwood captain Lou Richards. Tim recalls that 'each Sunday, we would sit down over mum's lamb roast to watch Jack and Lou go head-to-head'. Like his older brothers, Mark and Larry, and his younger brother, Rick, Tim was fanatical about football. He 'devoured' Dyer's autobiography, *Captain Blood*, and knew the history of the Richmond Football Club 'back-to- front'. He wore a Richmond jumper or tracksuit everywhere and he and Rick 'would play games in the backyard and take it in turns being Royce Hart and Kevin Sheedy'. The family home was across the road from Dimboola Primary School, and the boys often kicked a football on the oval there until dark. Keith Bromage, who had played for Collingwood in the 1950s, lived in the same street as the Watsons. Bromage recalled that when Tim was aged only seven he 'showed he had the ability to play League football. Even then he could kick 20 or 30 yards and hit you straight on the chest'.

Tim did not see Dimboola as a place that he needed to escape from. Like most country towns, it was an open community where kids played together without much need for adult supervision. In such places, the fears and insecurities that children had as they were growing up could be blanketed by an environment in which there were never enough hours in the day to do things. Tim loved the freedom of country life, where he and his friends 'could always find something to do'. They roamed the town on bikes, swam in the Wimmera River and raced objects down open gutters after storms. On weekends, the Watsons would drive out to their grandma's farm where, during mouse plagues, the kids would belt the animals with cricket bats. The Watson boys all did paper rounds at various times, which put spending money in their pockets and helped to nurture their independence. Tim's parents acknowledged his self-reliance, and at the age of 14 he was allowed to take the train to Melbourne on his own to spend a day watching Test cricket at the MCG. Tim recalls that while growing up 'you were subjected to alcohol and other things, but you always had a choice about what you wanted to do'. With a population of just under two thousand, Dimboola offered facilities for football, cricket, tennis, basketball and athletics. The Watsons used them all, and also held running races in the primary school grounds and had a high-jump bar set up in their backyard.

> We had rules and discipline in terms of our family life, but there was a great feeling of freedom about doing what you wanted to do. Our parents weren't worried about what we were doing, because anything we were doing was a healthy pursuit to do with sport.

Tim's parents had links to the Wimmera that went back two generations to when land in the area was made available in the 1870s to people who wanted to farm it. His mother Edna's paternal grandfather was born in England and after marrying in 1883 took up land in the Wimmera and fathered nine children, all of whom were born in Kiata, Dimboola or Nhill. Edna's maternal grandparents, one born near Ararat and the other near Nhill, had six children, all born in Nhill or Dimboola. Edna's mother was born in Dimboola in 1913. Alan Watson's side of the family lived mostly in Horsham. His paternal great-great-grandfather, Andrew Watson, was born in England and arrived in Melbourne at the height of the gold rush. Andrew's son later took up land at Burrumbeet, west of Ballarat and, after his third child, Archibald (Alan Watson's grandfather), was born in 1879, the family moved to Horsham. Alan's maternal great-grandfather also arrived from England during the 1850s and then moved to Skipton after his marriage. Alan's grandparents had nine children, all of them born in Horsham.

Alan and Edna were involved in the Uniting Church and its social life, and sent their children to Sunday school. They supported their children's sporting interests wholeheartedly, driving them to Melbourne to watch football and cricket, and to the football games they played throughout the Wimmera in towns such as Warracknabeal and Kaniva, which were well over an hour away. When Tim was trying out for the Victorian junior team, his parents drove him to Melbourne, along with another promising boy, Glenn Hawker, whose parents drove him from Kaniva to the Watsons' house.

Alan and Edna's support of their children's sporting activities and Tim's sense of independence are probably the reasons why Tim was 'only mildly' punished for two acts of disobedience in his early teen years. By the time he was aged 13, Tim, who was tall and solidly built for his age, was training with Dimboola seniors. Nevertheless, his parents were apprehensive about him playing alongside men and instructed him to play only under-age football for the time being. One night when his parents were away, Tim not only played for a Horsham team in a lightning premiership match, but also hitchhiked thirty-odd kilometres to do so and hitchhiked back home the same night. Tim's parents were in Queensland later the same season when he caught the bus to watch his brother Mark, who was then aged 17, play for Dimboola at Stawell. Tim and Mark ignored their parents' instructions and Tim played in the seconds, and sat on the bench when the senior team was one short, coming onto the ground in the last quarter. These incidents reflected the awkward situation that Alan and Edna were in. By encouraging a precocious son to play at the highest level that his ability warranted, they were exposing him to the risk of physical harm. Furthermore, Tim's progress as a footballer made it more likely that he would want to leave home at a very young age to live in Melbourne. Tim's brother Larry had joined Essendon in 1975, but he was aged 17 at the time. In the end, the Watsons knew that it was not feasible to keep Tim at home any longer, and trusted their judgement that he was mature enough to cope with the change.

In Melbourne, Essendon took care of Tim's housing and schooling arrangements: the club arranged for Tim to board with a committee member for three months and, at Tim's request, he was enrolled at Essendon High School. He was not greatly interested in school and finished only Year 11. He had played at Windy Hill once in a schoolboys' match, but he knew virtually nothing about the Essendon Football Club and its history. When the club acknowledged Tim's potential by giving him number 32, formerly worn by Barry Davis, one of the club's greatest ever players, 'I didn't even understand the significance of that, and I was disappointed that I was given a high number'. But there was no doubting the single-mindedness of his desire to succeed as a League footballer. Although he was now in the company of men, some of whom drank and smoked, he was never tempted to do anything that he thought might have jeopardised his football career. 'I had a singular focus that if I wanted to be a VFL player, then I couldn't do it if I drank or smoked,' he recalls. 'I pretty much had that attitude right through my football days.' Tim was still over two months short of his sixteenth birthday when, after five matches in the reserves, he made his senior debut. His first game, against Richmond at Waverley, ended in a draw. He was invited to appear on *World of Sport* the following day, and was shown around the studio by Bob Davis. Tim recalls being introduced to a group of football people including Ron Barassi, who was then coaching North Melbourne:

> You would not meet a better bloke than Ron today, humble and generous with his time, but back then he bristled with arrogance. The pimply kid from Dimboola got a cursory acknowledgement. And then, as though I did not exist, he remarked about what a joke it was to be playing a 15-year-old kid in VFL footy. He also made the observation that kids who played early never went on to do anything in footy and he quoted a couple of names that meant nothing to me. His comments stuck and never left me. I had arrived to receive a couple of freebies and see close up some men with whom I had shared our lounge for all my childhood years and I left with a reason to want to be great and prove someone wrong.

The Dick Reynolds spirit

The Essendon of Albert Thurgood's day — the club known as the 'Same Olds', the enclave of private school old boys who played at the East Melbourne Cricket Ground — was a very different football club by the 1930s. After the Railways Department announced that it needed the land on which the East Melbourne ground was located, the club established a base in the suburb of Essendon itself in 1922. Moving to Windy Hill enabled the Bombers, as the club became known because of the proximity of the ground to Essendon Airport, to establish a strong supporter base in Melbourne's rapidly growing north-western suburbs. While Essendon itself remained a leafy, genteel suburb, the semirural character of the area changed after World War I as its vacant blocks became covered with Californian bungalows. Melbourne's post-World War II suburban expansion, which saw jobs and housing created on the flatter ground towards Essendon Airport, at places such as Niddrie, Glenroy and Airport West, also enlarged the catchment area of the Bombers' growing and increasingly working-class fan base. Windy Hill itself seemed to reflect the transition that the club had gone through. Though well served by trains and trams, it was one of the League's most basic grounds. Big crowds after World War II taxed the facilities in the bluestone-terraced outer, which reeked of beer and drew criticism from spectators and the press for its unhygienic conditions. The playing arena had a pronounced slope, like the floor of an old house in need of restumping. By the 1950s, the football club was sufficiently fed up with the Essendon Council's lack of investment in upgrading facilities for spectators that it seriously considered moving to play at the showgrounds.

One thing about the Essendon Football Club that did not change was its 'conservative' ethos, and image, as Robert Pascoe puts it, as 'a club of wowsers who saw football as a means of teaching young men — especially Protestant men — the virtues of self-control'. Players visited local schools to warn students about the dangers of smoking and drinking, and the club itself was proud of the fact that it spent more on soft drinks than it did on beer. No-one epitomised this approach to the game more than Dick Reynolds. Reynolds, who passed away in 2002, is regarded at Essendon with an awe that is matched by no other figure in the club's history, or possibly by any figure at any other football club. Reynolds's love and respect for football, as he believed the game should be played, his passion for the Essendon Football Club, and his insistence on 'the highest standards of personal behaviour', were instilled quietly and by example into the teams he coached. Watson met Reynolds for the first time in the rooms after an Essendon game. Without any fanfare, the legend introduced himself and chatted to the rookie. 'The thing that struck me the most on that very first day, and it's a word that you hear again and again and again when people talk about Dick, was what a total gentleman he was.' As Tim met the other greats of the club informally, he found them to be similarly humble. Ken Fraser, then working as an assistant coach, was 'almost shy'. Barry Davis, who became coach in 1978, had ended his playing career at North Melbourne and captained the club to its first premiership, but while at North he had refused to wear the logo of the club sponsor, a brewing company, on his guernsey as a matter of principle.

'King Richard' was aged 23 when he won the first of his three Brownlow Medals and, with skill and judgement that were unaffected by pressure situations, he often played a lone hand in teams that were short of quality players. Essendon's playing fortunes had declined after winning the 1922 and 1923 flags with its 'mosquito fleet' teams (that included six players no taller than 5 foot 6 inches), and between 1927 and 1939 the club did not finish higher than fifth on the ladder. That changed in 1939 when Reynolds became captain-coach and led a new generation of predominantly local talent to nine of the next eleven grand finals, winning four flags. This was the Bombers' golden era. The club could easily have won six consecutive premierships from 1946: the Dons won in 1946, lost in 1947 by a point, and drew the 1948 grand final before losing the replay. Essendon won two consecutive flags after full-forward John Coleman burst onto the League scene in 1949, but Coleman's controversial suspension on the eve of the finals almost certainly cost his team the 1951 title. As a coach, Reynolds retained a gentlemanly demeanour and positive outlook, never shouting at or criticising his players and refusing to move them to another position if they were not playing well. It was an approach that brought the best out of players who were of similar disposition, such as Bill Hutchison, John Coleman and, later, Jack Clarke. Reynolds was replaced as coach at the end of 1960, but his standards continued to be maintained by clean-cut players from the local area who had leadership skills, such as Fraser and Davis.

The Reynolds football philosophy was, of course, admirable. But, in the cutthroat world of the VFL, there was downside to the lasting influence it had on the Essendon Football Club. The period after Coleman's retirement in 1954, due to a knee injury at the age of only 25, coincided with the rise of Norm Smith's Melbourne. While Essendon's strong suit was its pace and skill, Melbourne's greater size and strength gave it a crucial advantage in finals matches. Runners-up to the Demons in 1957 and 1959, Essendon was at times dubbed 'The Gliders' by the press. Throughout the 1960s and 1970s, Essendon's playing fortunes lurched from one brief upturn to another. Coleman took over from Reynolds as coach and he was able to develop a greater level of determination in Essendon's game, which took the club to the 1962 and 1965 premierships. By the late 1960s, however, Essendon was again struggling to keep pace with the game's trendsetters — Carlton under Ron Barassi and Richmond under Tommy Hafey. There was a brief revival at the end of the decade under Jack Clarke's quiet, methodical coaching (which was influenced heavily by Len Smith), but by the early 1970s, John Kennedy's Hawthorn had set new standards of fitness and aggression. The 1970s was, as club historian Michael Maplestone writes, 'a period of mediocrity' during which 'the resilience of Essendon supporters was put to the test'. After finishing eleventh in 1970 and 1971, the Dons responded by appointing Collingwood's Des Tuddenham as captain-coach in 1972, and his young team, playing a tougher brand of football, made the finals that season and the next. Tuddenham was sacked at the end of 1975 after a couple of disappointing seasons during which the team failed to improve. Bill Stephen, an experienced former Fitzroy coach, and his captain, champion ruckman Graham Moss, acted as mentors to a talented group of recruits from the club's country and metropolitan zones, but Moss's return to Western Australia after winning the Brownlow Medal in 1976 was a major setback to the club.

When Watson went to Essendon in 1977, the club was developing a list of promising young players who, it was hoped, would form the nucleus of a successful side in the future. This was the team that the press dubbed the 'Baby Bombers'. Tim knew two of the Wimmera recruits well: Merv Neagle, who was also from Dimboola, and Glenn Hawker, a passenger in the Watson's car on trips to junior football trials in Melbourne. Roger Merrett had played against Tim in primary school football 'and used to frighten the hell out of us'. Shane Heard was from Horsham. Paul Van der Haar and Neil Clarke were products of the metropolitan zone, centred on Ringwood. Of these players, only Heard had reached twenty years of age at the start of the 1977 season. Furthermore, Simon Madden (aged 19) and Garry Foulds (aged 20) were regular senior players with over two seasons of experience. Van der Haar made an immediate impact in 1977, his first league season. His electrifying leap, combined with strength and mobility, made him a similar player to Hawthorn's Peter Knights and these two blondes would have several classic duels over the years. Madden was already developing a reputation as a champion ruckman. Neagle, with his hardness at the ball, and Hawker, with his superb disposal skills, were promising midfielders. When South Melbourne cleared Terry Daniher and his younger brother Neale (whom the Swans had never seen play) to Essendon in exchange for Neville Fields, the Bombers were handed two potential key position players. Temperamentally, the brothers were like chalk and cheese — Terry was laid back and outgoing while Neale was quiet and studious — but they shared a capacity to play leadership roles in the future. Watson recalls that when Neale started pre-season training 'he was such a mature 18-year-old, who looked like he'd been playing for ten years'.

As for Watson himself, his game went from strength to strength. He was never an outstanding kick like, say, Nathan Buckley — in one game in 1979 he scored seven goals, but during one part of the game he managed only three behinds from four shots close to goal — and he was never a high-marking player, like Trevor Barker. When he got the ball he ran with it in a straight line, but he was not a 'bash and crash' type of player who tore through packs, like Leigh Matthews. As Martin Flanagan observed, what was remarkable about Watson was his ability to run in a straight line and then be able to move to another line as if he had 'swivel joints and shock absorbers in his ankles. It is the angles linking the lines that make him so alarmingly different'. Watson was more than just a gifted athlete: as team-mate Mark Harvey observed, 'he was always running with a purpose and finished up with the football. It is something that doesn't come naturally to a lot of footballers'. Early in his career, Watson was, in the view of a writer in *The Age*, 'a frustrating player to watch. He would perform with most extraordinary moments of flair, ripping through an opposition, and then disappear'. His game soon developed the consistency that characterises champion players.

Under Barry Davis's coaching, the Bombers made the finals in 1979 and, although the team's performance declined slightly in 1980, Watson had an outstanding season, winning Essendon's best and fairest. 'We were probably too young, too light, and worried too much about the fairness of the game, rather than the hardness of the game,' Tim recalled. Essendon's youth was a weakness that some other clubs exploited through aggression. By the end of 1979, the team was worn out and several players were carrying injuries; they were beaten by 81 points in the elimination final. Watson recalled that the week before, when Richmond 'smashed us' by over ten goals at Windy Hill, the Tigers 'were so much bigger, so much more physical than we were'. Richmond's Barry Richardson recalled that 'there is no doubt that when we played Essendon we thought they were soft . . . They were an amateur club playing professional football'.

Barry Davis resigned at the end of the 1980 season; the club was looking for a full-time coach to complete the building of a premiership team, but Davis was unwilling to give up his work as a physical education lecturer. The club's appointment of Kevin Sheedy as Davis's replacement was something of a surprise. Sheedy had finished playing with Richmond less than two years earlier, while the other leading applicants, Allan Jeans and John Nicholls, had previously coached League premiership teams. As a player, Sheedy was not blessed greatly with natural talent, and early in his career his progress was held back by his lack of pace and his inability to kick the ball long. Through hard work and a ruthless approach on the field, Sheedy built a 251-game career that included being part of three premiership teams. Now, Sheedy impressed the Essendon coaching subcommittee with his youth, his ambition, and his ability, honed through a year of media work, to think laterally about football. When the players turned up for pre-season training, the new coach surprised them with several unorthodox procedures: they were weighed and given their own football to keep and practise with at every opportunity; they kicked footballs at training that night, rather than after several weeks of endurance running. The players were trained hard, five nights a week. Watson, who had idolised Sheedy as a boy, noticed the immediate impact that Sheedy had on the club:

> When Kevin Sheedy arrived there was a noticeable difference about Essendon. It's very hard to put your finger on and say this is what it was, but you just felt that something was going to happen. He shook the place like a tornado.

As the 1981 season approached, Essendon played Carlton in a practice match at Skinner Reserve, a huge, barren oval that was the home ground of VFA club Sunshine. 'It was a God-forsaken place,' Tim says, and the oval, baked in the February sun, was hard and rough. The Blues at that time were notoriously complacent about practice games, but the Bombers were fit and enthusiastic after Sheedy's pre-season program. 'Carlton probably turned up and treated it as a practice game. We turned up, and because of how intense Kevin was, treated it as a mini-grand final.' Tim did not play in the game as he was recovering from a broken ankle, but in the rooms afterwards he could sense the excitement among the Essendon players and administrators after the Bombers won the game: 'You just felt it was the beginning of something major'.

Injuries to key players hit the Bombers hard in the early rounds of 1981, and after six matches the team had won only one game. The Bombers then won their next 15 League games. They confirmed their progress by winning the night competition, which at that time was played on Tuesdays during the season proper. At a cold and boggy VFL Park, Essendon defeated Carlton in a match that will always be remembered for a piece of play by Tim Watson. Gathering a loose ball at half-forward, in front of a fallen pack of players between him and the goals, Watson instinctively tucked the ball under his arm, hurdled the pack, and then kicked a goal. Essendon had trailed in the first half, and Watson's third-quarter goal was the turning point of the match. As the home-and-away rounds drew to a close, the Bombers were almost irresistible. In round 20, they seemed to be in a hopeless position against Carlton at Princes Park when the Blues extended their lead to 26 points with about ten minutes to play, but three goals in time-on by Neale Daniher gave his team a one-point win. Essendon was a hot favourite for the flag, but their season started to unravel when Neale Daniher seriously injured his knee the following week. A last-round loss pushed Essendon into the elimination final, where it was narrowly defeated by Fitzroy.

The 1982 season was similar in many ways to the previous one: an early season slump as injuries took their toll (Neale Daniher had been appointed captain but he did not play at all that season, and problems with his reconstructed knee kept him out of the side until 1985); a long winning sequence; loss of crucial games towards the end of the season; and narrow elimination in the first week of the finals. After winning the elimination final in 1983, the Bombers won their next two finals and moved into the grand final. Watson was Essendon's outstanding player in that finals series, but early in the grand final he was concussed after an incident with Hawthorn's Colin Robertson. The result — a humiliating 83-point defeat — only seemed to confirm Essendon's reputation as a club that could not stand up to finals pressure. Tim remembers very little of the game, and nothing of the collision with Robertson. He was in hospital when Sheedy spoke at the club dinner that night. Infuriated by the light-hearted mood at the gathering, which was to a large extent the result of the reserves' players celebrating the premiership they had won, Sheedy 'warned that some of the afternoon's losing grand final team had probably played their last game for the Bombers'. Indeed, three senior players never played for Essendon again. Tim reflects that 'we were a very fair club' and that Sheedy 'probably saw that fairness as a weakness. He had to weed out an attitude of us being a club that accepted being second'.

Over the next twelve months, the players carried with them what Watson calls 'a built-up anger' about the grand final debacle. 'That was the fuel we all had inside us.' Sheedy hardly mentioned the previous season again, but worked at strengthening his list, replacing players who lacked discipline and a killer instinct and, with the help of his recruiting department, headed by Noel Judkins, enlisted new players with resilience and versatility. In the previous two seasons, Western Australian Bill Duckworth and South Australian Paul Weston arrived as ready-made players, rover Darren 'Daisy' Williams was persuaded to rejoin the club after playing three seasons of suburban football, and a boy from the local area, Mark 'Bomber' Thompson, worked his way into the seniors. In 1984, Leon Baker, a much-travelled 27-year-old centreman, was signed after being spotted by Judkins playing in Perth, and Mark Harvey, another local product, claimed a place in the senior team. Sheedy had by now built a team of tough, strong players who also had talent and flair. They played Hawthorn again in the grand final and, although the Hawks got off to a flying start, the Bombers stayed in touch and during the third quarter 'were running hard, on top of the ground'. The Hawks still led by 23 points at the last change, but Watson recalls that 'I don't think that anyone who went into the huddle at three-quarter time thought we were going to lose the game'. The Bomber players were excited and Sheedy reinforced that feeling by pointing out that the Hawks were tiring. Within seconds of the game restarting, Baker brought the Bombers to life by roving the ball off a pack and kicking a goal. Daisy Williams kept the momentum going by getting the ball out of the centre, capitalising on Simon Madden's ruckwork. The boys from the Wimmera — Neagle, Heard, Hawker and Watson — kept running and sending the ball forward. The coach moved Weston from defence to centre half-forward with telling effect. Duckworth played an outstanding four-quarter game that won him the Norm Smith Medal.

The Dons had hit the front, after a stunning blind turn and goal by Baker, when defender Kevin Walsh was 'coathangered' by a stray elbow from Hawthorn's Robert DiPierdomenico and knocked unconscious. Other teams might have become unsettled by such an incident, but the Bombers remained totally focussed on the game. At the time, a bitter rivalry had built up between the two clubs. Niggling and, at times, violence were characteristics of matches between them. Off the field, Tim says, 'we had nothing to do with Hawthorn; they had *nothing* to do with us'. Sheedy fanned the rivalry by cultivating the 'them and us' attitude that he had learnt at Richmond. He referred to the Hawthorn players as private school boys and his own team as one that was blue-collar and tradesman-like. When Kevin Walsh hit the turf, his team-mates were used to such things in games against Hawthorn and simply got on with the game. Watson recalls looking at the scoreboard soon after the incident and realising that the game was beyond Hawthorn's reach:

> You get to a point in a game when you actually start to enjoy it, because you know you're going to win, and the other side knows they're going to lose. That's when you really start to do the damage. I reckon they knew they were going to lose; we knew we were going to win. Even though you're tired, you get this third wind and you feel like you're running on air.

Indeed, Tim seemed to be floating when he kicked two late goals on the run from around 30 metres out.

After the game, the rooms were packed with players' families, Essendon coterie members and former Essendon players. Tim remembers seeing Dick Reynolds hugging everyone in sight:

> His face was lit up like Luna Park. He could have been out there playing himself, he was so excited. Essendon, this great club that had always been so successful under his stewardship, had gone 19 years without a flag, but this victory ended the drought. I think he felt that there had been some sort of restoration. He was probably the man that understood the history of this club better than anyone — certainly better than anyone in the rooms that day in 1984. He felt that after being in the wilderness for almost two decades, the club he loved was back where it belonged, and the pleasure that gave him was obvious.

The Bombers set about winning the 1985 premiership in a businesslike way. After they did, there was more of a sense of satisfaction and pride in a job well done than the boisterous excitement of the previous season. In the grand final, Hawthorn's straight kicking and the brilliance of Dermott Brereton, who finished with eight goals, kept it in touch for almost three quarters, but it was only a matter of time before the Dons powered away. This was a team of such strength, consistency and talent that it deserves to be ranked with the finest the game has produced. Madden's ruckwork was again magnificent and he was a worthy winner of the Norm Smith Medal. But Watson was not far behind, gathering the contested ball and disposing of it at great speed and under extreme pressure. His decision making was impeccable, his stamina seemingly limitless. As Martin Flanagan wrote in *The Age*:

> Whenever Hawthorn looked as if it might get on terms, Watson was the player who tilted the balance of the match. He was never far from the action and in the final quarter he led an Essendon onslaught on goal which was wild, instinctual, utterly disciplined.

Watson was one of many Essendon players whose careers reached a peak that day, and for whom the 1985 grand final was a showcase for their talents.

As a coach, Kevin Sheedy's greatest achievement was to add new dimensions to Essendon's playing style, while retaining the tradition of 'closeness' between players, coaches and officials that the club had developed under Reynolds. Sheedy imbued hardness in Essendon without suppressing the flair of his players, and developed a ruthless attitude without weakening the stability that the club had developed in previous times. After all, Sheedy had supported Essendon as a boy and watched them play every week, even though he lived south of the Yarra. He had no need, and not the slightest desire, to sever Reynolds's influence on the club; after Reynolds retired to live on the Gold Coast, Sheedy made a point of visiting him once a year to chat about football over a cup of tea. His knowledge of and respect for the club's history, his willingness to listen to others, and a determination to help his players become better people, and not just better footballers, snuffed out any criticism of him being an 'outsider'. Sheedy nurtured an Essendon culture that in the 1980s was embraced by leaders such as Watson, Madden, Thompson and the Daniher brothers who passed it on through the standards they expected from younger players. In the 1990s and early 2000s, the custodians of this culture included James Hird and Matthew Lloyd. That culture is the football philosophy of Dick Reynolds, with elements of professionalism added to give it the strength needed to cope with modern football. As Watson later wrote:

> Essendon's greats have all been stamped from the same mould — good solid citizens, dedicated, wholesome — and through that chain of succession, Dick Reynolds's influence is still being felt today. [His] spirit has pervaded the entire culture of the place. I believe that every time someone pulls on an Essendon jumper, he carries onto the field a little bit of the Dick Reynolds spirit.

'Tim, is this how you want it all to end?'

Tim was aged only 24 when he collected his 1985 premiership medal. Although in football terms he was approaching the veteran stage, having played 191 League games, the early start he had made to his career meant that he was still a young man. After 1985, Tim found it increasingly difficult to live a life that was dictated by the routines and commitments required of a League footballer. As a youth, Tim had shown a high level of self-discipline in looking after himself, but in many ways that was easy for him because he had already decided that playing elite level football was what he wanted to do with his life, and because he was spending much of his time with older men who were similarly ambitious and competitive. As he acquired more responsibilities, the demands on his time became more pressing. In 1983 he had married Susie Lynch, whom he had met through one of his team-mates and two years later their first child, Jobe, was born. Three more children, all girls, were born in the next five years. Susie and her parents shouldered much of the load of looking after the kids, but Tim was simply not at home as often as he would have liked. To supplement his football income, Tim started a landscaping business with another team-mate; they later sold that business and bought another hiring and supplying indoor plants. Over time, he found it difficult to juggle his family, work and football responsibilities. He told a reporter in 1990 that 'from 15 to 22 football consumed me and there was a time when I thought 'Crikey'. I can't remember being 15, 16, 17 or 18 because I never did anything other kids that age did'. At the time, he reflects, 'I was getting to the point where I was resenting the intrusion that football was making on the rest of my life'. More than a decade later, Watson reflected on a similar situation faced by his former team-mate, James Hird, who was battling to recover from injury while working to establish a career outside of football and spend quality time with his young family. Watson's conclusion was that Essendon 'will need to give him some space; failure to do so may result in the premature end to a magnificent career'.

Tim now thinks that, in some ways, it may have been 'a blessing in disguise' that a knee injury in 1986 forced him to take a break from the game. In round 3 of that season, he was running backwards with the flight of the ball when his leg clipped Footscray's Doug Hawkins and the whiplash effect tore the anterior cruciate ligament in his knee. Watson's recovery after having the knee repaired was slow and painful. Recurring pain and swelling made him feel sick and he lost a lot of weight. A further operation was required in 1987 to remove polyps from the knee. It took hard work — mainly a routine of cycling — to strengthen the muscles around his knee, and it was not until the final round of 1987 that he was fit enough to return to the seniors.

Watson's injury, and those to other key players (Van der Haar and Williams both suffered broken legs), had a significant impact on Essendon's playing fortunes. In an attempt to cover these losses, Sheedy traded two premiership players, Peter Bradbury and Stephen Carey, who were popular with their team-mates and Essendon supporters, for Geoff Raines and Mike Richardson, who had been playing at Collingwood. Watson recalls that there was a perception at the club, 'which may or may not have been correct', that Raines and Richardson had left Collingwood after refusing to take pay cuts, and this 'created an air of mistrust' among Essendon players. 'It wasn't a very happy place in 1986 and I think it took us a while to rebuild as a group after that.'

Sheedy attracted a good deal of criticism over the sacking of Bradbury and Carey, some of it from within Essendon. He survived a tight vote by the Essendon board to replace him and, thereafter, became somewhat less of a hard-driving coach. He kept his message fresh by thinking constantly about the game, by delegating effectively to specialist fitness advisers, nutritionists and sports psychologists, and by giving increasing responsibility to his panel of assistant coaches. The recruiting department continued to be highly effective in an era when drafting became the most important method of recruiting. At Sheedy's instruction, Essendon began drafting increasing numbers of Aboriginal players, a policy that brought Michael Long, Gavin Wanganeen and Derek Kickett to the club. Returning to full fitness in 1988, Tim played some of the best football of his career. He won the club's best and fairest awards in 1988 and 1989, and was appointed captain of a team that was gradually adding quality players to its line-up.

The Bombers made the grand final in 1990, but the club's finals campaign was, in Tim's words, 'a major balls-up'. Several players were unfit, including Watson who was carrying an ankle injury. Early in the finals series, Collingwood and West Coast drew and their game had to be replayed. Watson is of the view that this was to

Essendon's disadvantage, as most of its players needed a run rather than an extra week's rest. Although Essendon won the preliminary final, its performance was lacklustre and training the following week was devoid of energy and sparkle. 'We were mentally and physically jaded as a group,' Tim recalls. Their opponents, Collingwood, were building to a peak and were on a mission to end their club's long premiership drought. A brawl at quarter-time resulted in Collingwood's best player, Gavin Brown, taking no further part in the match because of concussion, but the Magpies refocussed on playing a disciplined, defensive game that Essendon had no answer to.

During the 1991 season, Tim Watson turned thirty; by the end of the year he had spent more than half his life as an Essendon footballer. Niggling injuries, which made it more difficult to prepare for a game each week, were starting to take their toll. He had already had one wrist reconstructed, and his other wrist also needed surgery. For several seasons he had been battling a hamstring tendon problem. When he and his manager met with the club president at the end of the year to discuss a two- or three-year extension to his contract, Tim decided to put his cards on the table. He told them that he lacked the necessary motivation to do another pre-season, and that he really should be thinking about retiring. Tim agreed to think things over for a week or so and, while Sheedy suggested that he could take some time off, Tim's mind was made up that he needed a complete break from the game.

Tim stayed involved with football, spending the 1992 season as a 'boundary rider' on Channel Seven's match broadcasts. West Coast drafted him at the start of the season, but at that stage he had no intention of playing again. After St Kilda's coach, Ken Sheldon, approached him about joining as an assistant coach and, possibly, as a player, Tim started thinking seriously about making a comeback. He was drafted by Essendon in 1993; from 1992, Essendon was playing its home games at the MCG and was developing a playing list of promising young talent. It was an exciting time to be back at Essendon.

Watson's return to AFL football also coincided with the period in which Aboriginal players became less inclined to accept racial abuse as a normal part of the game. Tim's team-mate, Michael Long, bravely made himself the spokesperson for those who were demanding an end to racism in football; Long's ability to articulate why racial abuse was so hurtful to Aboriginals demonstrated that the practice was incompatible with the image of fair play that the League was trying to develop. Dimboola was home to lots of Aboriginal families — there had been a mission not far from the town — and, although Tim admits that he knew little of their culture, he played sport and went to school with them without giving a second thought to their skin colour. In the VFL, however, Tim encountered a level of racial abuse that 'was more common from certain clubs that other clubs', and which he found hard to take. 'I heard some appalling things on the football field that made me feel sick, that players had spoken like that to another human being.' By 1995, the activism of Long and a group of Aboriginal players encouraged the AFL to introduce a racial vilification rule; this included provision for fines and suspensions for players and clubs that breached the rule. This had an educative as well as a deterrent effect. Tim's view was that 'football's done a lot of great things, and the role models that have appeared in football who have actually made a stand have forced people to examine their own views on other races and cultures'.

At the start of the 1993 season, most football experts, including Kevin Sheedy himself, thought that the best Essendon could hope for was to sneak into the finals. The team seemed to be a couple of seasons away from being a genuine premiership contender, but the youngsters developed and improved more quickly than anyone expected. Watson had not done any pre-season training and 'had no money in the bank' with his fitness. He played all season in the forward pocket, but his experience, and that of Thompson and Harvey, was invaluable to the rest of the team.

At half-time in the preliminary final, Essendon trailed Adelaide by 42 points and the season seemed to be drawing to a close. Only a couple of Essendon players had not been moved from their original positions. In the rooms, 'Bomber' Thompson, the captain, spoke forcefully of his anger at the way that they were playing. Sheedy was calmer, pointing out to the players that they would be judged as footballers by how they performed in big games. As he walked among them, Sheedy reached Watson and said:

> Tim, is this how you want it all to end? Tim, do you want your whole career to end like this? This might be the last match in your last season, your last 60 minutes of football . . . Do you want to look back on your career and know that it ended in defeat, that you never played in one last Grand Final that you should have been in?

Sheedy then put the players back into their original positions and asked them to take risks. They responded magnificently, and close to siren time they were hanging on to a five-point lead. Tim was exhausted when he picked up the ball near the boundary line, just forward of the wing. One of Essendon's team rules was that everyone had to play defensively when holding a lead near the end of a close game. Instead of keeping the ball close to the boundary, Tim instinctively swung onto his left foot, cut back inside and kicked the ball, not very well, towards centre half-forward. 'The moment I did that, and it was a pretty scrubby kick, I thought, "Oh shit, I've done the wrong thing". I really charged after it because I was trying to rectify an error.' He ran to where the ball was, managed to win possession of it, and kicked a 50-metre goal to seal the game.

During grand final week, Watson could detect 'this underlying eagerness for players to explode, and when the match started it was soon obvious that Carlton would be struggling to match Essendon's pace and vigour. Tim spent part of the game sitting on the bench and marvelled at the energetic play of his team-mates. Wanganeen, who had won the Brownlow Medal that season, gave a brilliant performance in the back pocket, as did Long, who won the Norm Smith Medal.

Watson's season and his playing career 'petered out' in 1994. After doing a full pre-season, he suffered a corked thigh that bled badly, then a hamstring injury, and then torn ankle ligaments. He did manage to pass the 300-game mark, however, and qualified for AFL life membership. The decision to retire at the end of the season was an easy one that caused him little stress: he had retired once already and had received offers to work in the media.

At the end of 1998, Watson received a phone call from St Kilda's president asking him if he would be interested in taking on the senior coaching job. The Saints had made the grand final in 1997, but had several players who were now past their best and there was a noticeable absence of young talent at the club. Tim now feels that he underestimated the size of the job he had taken on, and that he should have 'shaken up the joint' more after he arrived. During the 2000 season, when the Saints won only two-and-a-half games, Tim lost confidence in his own ability to lead the team and make appropriate coaching decisions. He insists that the decision to resign was his alone. 'To announce that I'd resigned, when in fact I'd been sacked by the club, would be just about the most distasteful thing for me to do.'

Life gave Tim Watson a sport — Australian Rules football — that he loved and could play at the highest level. He gave, and continues to give, plenty back in return. Through football, the boy who was disinterested in school has learnt new skills and matured into an articulate and respected thinker who has reached a wide audience through his media work. This has ranged from light-hearted TV skits — such as his demonstration of a knee reconstruction, using pieces of rope, a staple gun and a bottle of tomato sauce — to serious pieces in the print media on issues ranging from the state of grassroots football to the demands that professional sport places on young players. This work is characterised by humility, wisdom, respect for others and a concern for the greater good of the game and the society in which it operates. Tim Watson was one player who made the game thrilling to watch; in retirement he remains involved as the generous, thoughtful person that football deserves.

12

Jason Akermanis

(1977–)

> There's no doubt that our club has come the furthest of any club in history to win a premiership.
>
> JASON AKERMANIS

'There's a saying about clay and porcelain,' Jason Akermanis says. 'Clay, under extreme heat and over a long period, turns into porcelain. But it never goes back to clay.' Until the mid-1990s, a trip to play in Brisbane held few fears for most AFL clubs, while a home game against the Bears was a chance to boost a club's percentage. Within another ten years, the Brisbane Lions — as they were called after Brisbane merged with Fitzroy — had won three consecutive premierships in 2001–02–03 and were widely regarded as the greatest team of all time. Once the Lions had learnt to cope with the pressure of big games, the youthfulness and depth of their list gave them the opportunity to build an extended period of success. The body strength and sheer talent of the typical Lions player gave other team-mates confidence and tended to intimidate the opposition. 'Because we've won three premierships,' Akermanis reflects, 'our reputation is like porcelain, but we'll never go back to clay.'

The metaphor that Akermanis uses to describe his football club could easily be applied to own career. 'When I was young I was a bit of a ratbag,' he admits. When he entered AFL football at the age of seventeen, he was like a lump of clay: a rough, raw boy with highly promising skills. From a kid who might easily have fallen by the wayside, as a footballer and as a person, he matured like a piece of exquisite porcelain. Few players in the game are as fast as he is; to see him gather the ball anywhere within 70 metres of goal and then race into a scoring position like a heat-seeking missile is one of the most thrilling sights in modern football. He rarely misses these shots, whether using his left or right foot, directly in front or on the boundary line, in the clear or under pressure. Although at times his play is spectacular, there is a workmanlike quality about his game in general that allows him to bring team-mates into the play. There is not a trace of selfishness or laziness in his game. When *The Australian*'s Matt Price wrote after the 2001 grand final that 'the Lions are part bully, part brilliance; perfectly epitomised by Brownlow Medallist and acrobatic tough nut Jason Akermanis', he was making the simple point that Akermanis was a typical, rather than an exceptional Lions player. Akermanis is part of a team rather than the star around which the rest of the team orbits. Despite his Brownlow Medal, it would be a mistake to call Akermanis a saint on the field: he has been suspended three times and admits that he responds in kind to taggers who use physical pressure to try to keep him out of the game. Nevertheless, both on and off the field, Akermanis is rarely provoked into anger and it is almost impossible to imagine him doing anything that could be regarded as thuggish. Marriage, he says, has helped him 'find a path' in life. Impeccably groomed, yet without pretension, Akermanis enjoys being involved in a range of charity and community work. On and off the field, he carries himself as a person who understands that football has a soul and that those who play the game have a duty to honour and preserve its best traditions.

All this should make Jason Akermanis one of the most admired players of his generation. Indeed, Lions fans adore him ('everyone's favourite footballer', as one writer in Brisbane's *Courier-Mail* put it), and a great number of football followers in general enjoy watching him play. However, he has his critics in sections of the media, and at away games there are sometimes boos when he gets the ball. As Richard Hinds once wrote in *The Age* after watching a match from the stands at the Gabba, 'It would be educational, you think, for Lions supporters to learn that in the game's southern heartland, Akermanis is considered by some to be an arrogant crackpot'. But to call Akermanis 'arrogant' would be unfair, for several reasons. As Akermanis himself puts it, 'I think if someone doesn't have great communication skills but has enormous self-belief, it gets confused often with arrogance'. The label of arrogance is never applied to people such as, say, Luke Darcy or James Hird, who are just as self-confident as Akermanis is, but are more articulate. In Akermanis's earlier media work, ideas came out of his head faster than his ability to structure a sentence, but over time his remarks have become more cogent. The comments that Akermanis makes as a TV show panellist, radio show host and newspaper columnist, and in interviews with the media are at times forthright, but only rarely about himself. He will speak about issues related to young people growing up, about the playing conditions at AFL grounds, about the role of taggers in football, and about his club, his coach and his team-mates, but hardly ever touch on his own personal achievements. Clearly, Akermanis has no desire to be self-effacing — as his dyed blonde hair and black goatee attest — but he never attempts to big-note himself or belittle others. He does admit that he will occasionally make public statements about upcoming opponents to put pressure on them and to motivate himself. His humour, often directed at team-mates, is too silly to be hurtful. His statements are never offensive, or at odds with the values of society. There are no histrionics about his play: he performs his trademark handstand — something he started doing on impulse — only after a game and in response to the demands of the crowd.

Jason's quirky blend of honesty and flamboyance guarantees him a high profile in today's AFL. Most players prefer to keep a low profile, but Akermanis is one of a small group of highly public stars whose words and actions are monitored closely by the media for possible nationwide transmission. At times, Akermanis seems to draw criticism simply because of his ability to grab a headline, rather than what he has said. Jason is dismissive of such critics: 'I have the confidence and belief in what I am doing now. If some people have an opinion or observation about me and they don't like what I do, then who has the problem? Is it me or them?' Akermanis simply enjoys promoting the game that he loves and educating people about its finer points, in a state where it has traditionally struggled to attract media attention. The emergence of the Brisbane Lions as Aussie Rules' champion team has enabled the code to break the stranglehold that Rugby League has traditionally held in Queensland at the elite and grassroots level. As the *Courier-Mail*'s Darren Cartwright wrote, 'it was not long ago in Queensland that schoolkids were ridiculed for turning up for class with an Aussie Rules ball under their arm. And Auskick, the AFL's introductory coaching program for seven to 12-year-olds, was harder to sell to Queensland parents than time share'. By the time the Lions had racked up the third of their premierships, Australian Rules was being played in 579 Queensland primary schools (compared with 255 in 1998) and 100 independent schools (compared with 15 in 1991). For Akermanis, whose hostility to Rugby League stemmed from being bullied at high school because of his preference for Aussie Rules, the improved media profile of the game was 'good for the club and good for footy in Queensland more than anything, because I've seen the other side, the almost ugly side ... I've seen the attitude of the people here, and seen it change'. His role in football's northern expansion has been significant, both through his efforts on the field and his media work, which has a candour that many observers have found refreshing. As one writer in the *Sunday Age* put it, 'Jason Akermanis is a real one-off ... He's the only guy involved in football who gives a completely straight, unexpurgated and remarkably detailed answer on team tactics and match-ups when he's asked a straight question'. For journalist Matt Deighton, Akermanis 'is a breath of fresh air into today's homogenised, sterilised, media trained sporting environment. The game is richer for having the likes of Aker, who freely speaks his mind, without fear of the consequences'.

'Nothing was going right'

'Akermanis' is a Latvian name, but Jason Akermanis has not a trace of Latvian ancestry. Shona Carswell, who was born in Brisbane in 1956, was aged around twenty and married to a man named John Akermanis when she joined her brother, Russell, and his wife, Julie, on a working holiday around Australia. They got as far as Mildura, where they decided to stay after making good money picking fruit. They found jobs at the same firm, Shona working as a secretary and Russell as a mechanic. Shona began a relationship with one of the other mechanics and together they had two children: Jason, born in 1977, and Rory, in 1979. Jason met his father 'once or twice', but had no contact with or support from him. Shona brought the boys up while working at a variety of secretarial jobs. 'We weren't *poor,*' Jason recalls, 'but we weren't well off and we couldn't afford things when we knew we needed to get something new.'

In many ways, Jason had a difficult childhood and youth. He was unable to concentrate on most tasks for any length of time, and did only just enough at school to get by. Although he never got into any serious strife, he had a way of attracting trouble, often unintentionally. His habit of speaking out of turn was mistaken by some teachers for insolence and he was in trouble 'all the time — mainly for talking'. He had a sense of humour but few other kids appreciated it. He tended to say what he was thinking rather than keep it to himself, and this, together with his cheeky grin and ginger hair, invited bullying. At high school in Brisbane, 'there were a couple of Kiwis and they used to beat me up and kick me, and they spat on me once'. He was a loner from an early age: his first junior football coach recalled that Jason was 'not appreciated' by his team-mates and that 'sometimes you'd see Jason by himself'. When Jason reached puberty, his moods started to swing and there were times when he felt depressive and flat for no apparent reason. During a period of about five months, Jason was unable to sleep for more than about three hours a night. He did not tell anyone about these mood swings and attempted to use humour to cover up how he was feeling. When he was aged around 14, he was nearly killed in a rollerblading accident when he hit his head on the corner of a brick pillar. Not one of his school mates came to visit him in hospital.

Jason's restlessness, his impulsive interrupting and talking, and his poorly developed social skills were indicators of hyperactivity. This was diagnosed when he was aged about five, and Shona's doctor advised her to encourage her son to become involved in sport. As soon as she thought that Jason was old enough — around seven — she took him to join South Mildura's under 11s, a team coached by Gordon Casey, a former Footscray player who was a teacher at the local primary school. 'Mr C,' as Jason still refers to him, had a huge influence on Jason as a footballer, teaching him the fundamentals of the game and then insisting that he (and the other boys) practise the skill of kicking with both feet. The Akermanises grew up in a humble neighborhood in the eastern part of Mildura where lots of Aboriginal families lived. Jason used to spend hours kicking a full-sized football in the street with two Aboriginal boys who were neighbours. Mildura's Mediterranean climate suited him perfectly, and he remembers long summer evenings waterskiing on the Murray River and riding a BMX bike, which sowed the seeds of his enduring love of motor sports. He spent his days 'just being a kid', doing Little Athletics, and playing cricket in the summer and footy in the winter. Because her son was devoted to sport, and did not engage in antisocial or destructive behaviour, 'Mum was never worried about me. She always felt I had purpose'.

When Jason was aged about nine, Shona returned to Brisbane with her sons to be closer to her family. Jason was not distressed at having to move, but it did mean that he had to leave a home town in which Aussie Rules was the dominant winter sport; in Brisbane, it was a marginal sport played mostly at club level. Rugby League and Rugby Union dominated school sport, and Akermanis was not afraid to display his indifference to the two codes by bringing a Sherrin footy to school to kick on his own. He played junior football at the Mayne Football Club but, after his rollerblading accident, doctors ordered him not to play any contact sport for at least a year. For twelve months, Jason kicked his footy on his own in a park but devoted his competitive energies to athletics. His and Rory's achievements in athletics led to offers of scholarships to go to Nudgee College, a Catholic school that offered financial help to children from low-income backgrounds who showed promise at sport. Jason was like a fish out of water at Nudgee: he was not a Catholic — 'I hardly knew anything about what they were talking about' — and he refused to become a part of the school's rugby culture. 'People joke that Nudgee is a Rugby camp with classrooms,' writes John Harms, but Akermanis carried his footy with him at all times and played soccer, a game that suited his ability to read the play and pass the ball into gaps with either foot. He still got into trouble at various times for talking out of turn in class, which led to threats that he would be expelled, but in his final year of school he worked hard and was dux in Recreational Studies and second in Small Business.

When Akermanis returned to playing football in 1993, it was against the advice of his doctor, but he felt that the risk of receiving another heavy blow to the head during a match was slight. (The roller-blading accident remains the only time in his life that he has been knocked unconscious.) He graduated from the Mayne under 19s to the senior team, and in the middle of the season represented Queensland in the Australian under-17s (Teal Cup) carnival. He then did pre-season training with the Bears, who had pencilled him in as a possible home-state priority draft pick. At the Teal Cup in 1994, he was Queensland's outstanding player and won All-Australian selection. During that season, the Bears gave the Akermanises a family season ticket, and Jason decided that he would like to play for the team after watching them at the Gabba. He had been to see some games at Carrara, the Bears' original home ground on the Gold Coast, but 'I was always there supporting the other team. They [the Bears] were *hopeless*'.

When Brisbane joined the VFL's expanded competition in 1987, along with the West Coast Eagles, the Bears had no ground to play on and were virtually ignored by the Brisbane media. As Garry Linnell wrote in his book *Football Ltd*, this shaky beginning forced the Bears, like the Sydney Swans, 'into a shotgun marriage with big business'. The game's second experiment with a privately owned club was every bit as disastrous as it had been with the Edelsten/Powerplay-owned Swans. The Bears' chairman, Paul Cronin, and financial benefactor, Christopher Skase, knew virtually nothing about running a football club and they gave inadequate support to coach Peter Knights and the administrative staff. As the start of the 1987 season approached, the VFL agreed to Skase's request that the club set up a base for one year at Carrara, a huge oval that lacked the facilities for elite level football. Goalposts were about the only features that Carrara had in common with other League grounds. The club had advertising hoardings everywhere, but there were practically no amenities for spectators. Fine wines and lavishly catered meals, flown in from Melbourne, were served to sponsors and their clients in temporary entertainment facilities, but there was no gymnasium for the players. Once established at Carrara, Skase refused to move the club to Brisbane, threatening to walk away from the club and its debts if he was forced to do so. As Linnell observes, 'Brisbane was a fabricated club living in prefabricated surrounds and trying desperately to buy itself a soul and a tradition'. Through Skase and Cronin, club sponsors were allowed to influence team selection by demanding that some players never be dropped from the senior team and insisting that others be sacked, as Knights was during the 1989 season. Knights had been given a squad made up of a few high-priced recruits, some experienced players whose best football was behind them, and a bunch of triers who had not made the grade at other League clubs. Some of the senior players, notably Roger Merrett, made fine mentors, but local talent like Marcus Ashcroft, a boy from Surfers Paradise who would eventually play over 300 games for the club, faced enormous obstacles in building a career under such circumstances.

By the time Reuben Pelerman took over as club owner, after Skase's corporate empire had collapsed, the Brisbane club had become a financial black hole that required major restructuring to survive. This work began in 1991 when ownership of the club was transferred to a membership-based structure and the club played four home games at the Gabba. The club negotiated a permanent move to the Gabba, which would take place in 1993 after a major redevelopment of the ramshackle old cricket ground. For the first time, the club appointed a coach who had previous experience at a senior level. Robert Walls had learnt to play League football at Carlton, where he made his debut as a 16-year-old under the hard-driving coaching of Ron Barassi. Walls, who responded so enthusiastically to Barassi's coaching that his team-mates dubbed him 'teacher's pet', built a stellar playing career at a club that demanded success in big, high-pressure games against rivals such as Richmond and Collingwood. As a coach at Fitzroy and Carlton, Walls built a reputation as a tactician, but when he arrived at Brisbane there were more fundamental issues to address. He immediately set about dismantling the flashy culture that had developed under the Bears' private ownership and began building a playing list by promoting young talent. When Walls arrived at the club, he recalled that:

> You had all these older players coming up, the $300-a-head lunches when Skase was here, and all that sort of crap. People thought, it's not a football club, it's a plaything for a rich man. We more or less decided then and there that any young player who showed a lot of enthusiasm and was a chance, we must give them senior games. We actually said to the players 'You're in for the next five weeks regardless of how you play, as long as your enthusiasm is there during training and in games'.

In one match in 1992, fourteen Bears players had played fewer than 22 AFL games each. Walls's philosophy that the club's future lay with kids left the team vulnerable to fearful thrashings — such as the night at Carrara when Geelong kicked 37.17, a VFL/AFL record score — but players such as Ashcroft, Shaun Hart and Darryl White still made steady progress during these hard times. The Bears targeted young talent in the 1992 and 1993 drafts, picking up Michael Voss as a zone selection, and Nigel Lappin, Justin Leppitsch and Chris Scott from Victoria. One draft pick was traded for Alastair Lynch, a strong, experienced key forward from Fitzroy.

In 1995, the year that the Bears drafted Jason Akermanis, the club gave historian Ross Fitzgerald completely free access to observe how it operated on a day-to-day basis. Fitzgerald wrote that Akermanis got off to a bad start with Walls on the first night of pre-season training by forgetting to bring his football, rolling an ankle that he had not had strapped (even today, Akermanis only straps his ankles for matches) and by refusing to get into a swimming pool ('I'll do anything to avoid getting into water'). 'He doesn't know how lucky he is to be alive,' Walls told Fitzgerald. For Walls, Akermanis's attitude was symptomatic of a general lack of discipline and intensity among players from Queensland, something he was determined to remedy:

> Players here just aren't caught up in the hurly-burly and nitty-gritty and gossip and the intrigue of what is going on in AFL footy. So many young Queenslanders on our list frustrate me because they lack the intensity about their football that the typical Victorian kid takes for granted. When they arrive they have no idea about the passionate level of professionalism that is required to succeed. They are going to have times when they think I'm a real bastard because I'm going to push them and flog them, and that's what they have to get through.

Akermanis's side of the story is that he was then only seventeen, still at school, and still developing physically. It was not determination he lacked; 'all I needed was to be exposed to the game'. Walls must have seen something in Akermanis that was worth persevering with; like his mentor, Barassi, and Barassi's own mentor, Norm Smith, Walls knew that blunt criticism, delivered with force, could have a positive effect on the game of some players. The trick for the coach was to identify the players who could tolerate such tirades and use them as motivation to prove the coach wrong. Akermanis proved to be determined enough to take such criticism and, as he adapted to Walls's coaching, he found himself becoming more resilient:

> Wallsy was really *tough*; real old school. A bit of a prick, really. Trained you hard, flogged you, tried to wear you down mentally. I think it made us so much tougher. It's completely different today. A lot of the young blokes go to water; give 'em a spray and they go home crying.

Akermanis played in 17 games that season, including the Bears' first finals match. To all appearances, his football career was progressing nicely but, in fact, his world had started to crumble. Late in 1995, his mother was diagnosed with a brain tumour. Shona was sick for eighteen months, and the deterioration in her physical condition and eventual death, were heartbreaking for Jason and caused the depression of his early teenage years to return. 'You can't help thinking that the world owes you something, because it's so cruel,' he said six years after his mother's death. Robert Walls announced midway through 1995 that he would be resigning at the end of the season and Brisbane appointed another experienced coach, John Northey. Jason did not have a good relationship with the new coach. 'I always thought that with John I was on the back foot because he had a pre-conceived idea about me because I was really different from the other guys in a lot of ways.' The weekend after his mother passed away, Jason made himself available to travel with the team to Perth and play in an important match against Fremantle. Although Akermanis kicked two goals in a tight last quarter, his opponent won the ball that resulted in the Dockers' winning goal. If Northey had any sympathy for what Akermanis was going through, he did not communicate it well. After the game, the coach delivered a tirade to the team, and when he looked at Akermanis he roared, 'And you! You wanted to play!' 'I just didn't want to hear that,' Jason recalled; 'I just lost all respect for him then.'

Under Northey, the Bears had a good season in 1996, winning two finals games. Akermanis's view is that, in 1997, the players lost confidence in Northey because they found it hard to come to terms with his complex game plans, which he sometimes changed at quarter-time during matches. The team's performance slumped that year and, although some new players arrived after Brisbane merged with Fitzroy, injuries to key players saw the team slip to last place in 1998. Akermanis and probably a number of other Brisbane players were, by this time, just playing for their personal pride. Jason was still feeling the loss of his mother and a recurring injury to his back affected his form. 'Nothing was going right,' he recalls. 'The world seemed against me.'

At the end of the 1998 season, the Brisbane Lions appointed a new coach, and Jason met him briefly while the Lions were in South Africa for a pre-season exhibition game. On the first day of pre-season training, Jason was sitting in an office at the Gabba. The door was open and the new coach walked past. He recognised Jason belatedly, walked back to the office and shook his hand. Jason remembers that he knew then that 'it's going be different'.

Building the perfect beast

Leigh Matthews had already achieved legendary status in the game as a player and coach. Solidly built and with a wonderful ability to read the play and execute his skills under pressure, Matthews embodied the philosophy that John Kennedy imparted to all Hawthorn players of running straight at the ball, and straight at the opposition if they had it. As a rover and forward pocket, Matthews scored a remarkable 915 goals in 340 senior games, and won his club's best and fairest eight times. 'On the field, he was a silent assassin,' says David Parkin, his former team-mate and coach. 'Off the field, he was his own man who spent little time with his teammates.' He became coach of Collingwood in 1986, and in 1990 led the Magpies to a premiership. After leaving the club in 1995, Matthews worked as a media commentator, and in 1998 the AFL approached him about taking over as coach of the Brisbane Lions.

The League needed a coach with stature who could present a positive image to help strengthen the game in the large, but still untapped, Queensland market. When Matthews dealt with the media, where he himself had worked for three years, he was open and informative. He insisted on assuming ultimate responsibility for the club's football operations, with the assistance of his former Collingwood football manager, Graeme 'Gubby' Allan. Matthews kept only recruiting manager Kinnear Beatson and a few of the existing administrative staff on the books, and appointed completely new coaching, training and medical staff. His support staff would come to include an endurance running coach, a sprinting coach, a tackling coach, a team of physiotherapists, a dietician, and a 'mental skills coach' or sports psychologist.

Training facilities, which had been abysmal at Carrara, were state-of-the-art at the Gabba, and the rebuilt stadium, which would eventually have a capacity of around 44 000, provided superb amenities and potential for revenue raising. The merger with Fitzroy provided a more marketable guernsey and brand ('Kings of the Jungle' suited Brisbane perfectly) and gave the club a base of vocal support at games in Melbourne. Matthews himself resolved to be less moody and ill-tempered, and 'a better man manager' than he had been at Collingwood. On his first day at the Gabba, he met the players as a group and spoke to them for 45 minutes, promising 'to give them the best football structure in the AFL in their joint quest for optimum performance'.

The way that Matthews dealt with Akermanis and helped him to get the best out of himself as a player is a revealing case study of his skills as a manager. Akermanis always thought that his previous coaches, Walls and Northey, decided early on that they had to confront his attitude, which they saw as presenting discipline problems. Matthews made it clear that Akermanis, like everyone else, was starting with a clean slate. In February 1999, Jason bought a motorbike and started riding it to training. At first, he hid the bike because he assumed that Matthews would not approve of him riding it. When Matthews found out, he simply commented: 'I don't care how he gets here, as long as he gets here'. Matthew's physiotherapists fixed the problem with Akermanis's back, while the club's sports psychologist, Phil Jauncey, developed a strategy to help Jason move on after the death of his mother. (Akermanis had to find a photo of Shona and himself, and look at it regularly for a period of time. Jason chose a shot taken when his mother was critically ill. Jauncey then told him to burn the photo; Jason cried all that day, but the experience helped him to get the grief out of his system.)

During the pre-season, Akermanis missed a practice game due to injury and was required to attend a recovery training session the next day. When he turned up, he was ill and trained in sunglasses and, because he looked hung over, Matthews assumed that he had been out drinking the night before. The coach wanted to sack him, but avoided making an error by having 'Gubby' Allan check whether

Akermanis had in fact been ill. During the 1999 season, a fit and motivated Akermanis won the club's best and fairest (tying with Leppitsch), All-Australian selection and the Jim Stynes Medal for Australia's best player in the international series against Ireland. Although Akermanis would continue to be on the receiving end of a reprimand from Matthews from time to time, his improving on-field performances and new level of consistency had Matthews 'off my case for a while'.

During the 1998 season, Jason met Megan Legge, through friends at a nightclub, and they started going out regularly the following year. When Jason proposed to her early in 2000, he did it with typical flair and a total lack of self-consciousness. Jason arranged for a friend who worked at a radio station to phone Megan and tell her she had won a prize and that all she had to do was to go to a certain park bench and collect it. She drove to the park from work and walked to the bench, where she found a parcel. Inside was a picture frame with the message: 'Will you marry me?' Jason then appeared from some bushes carrying a video camera, which was recording the whole thing. He got on one knee and put a ring on her finger. The couple married in 2001.

Being in a stable, loving relationship completed the turnaround in Jason's life. Megan had a Business degree and was completing post-graduate studies in Speech Pathology, and her influence helped Jason to discover a love of learning and of using his life experience to help others. He learned sign language so that he could communicate with Megan's parents, who were both deaf. Later, he took a course in Spanish, and during one end-of-season break he spent time in Japan. He and a group of Lions players started making weekly visits to talk to secondary school students to assist 'Here For Life', an organisation that attempts to deal with teenage depression and anti-social behaviour. 'People forget that the hardest years of their life are from 13 to 17 or 18,' Jason said. 'I don't know how much we help, but if for a brief moment we can make them aware of a few subtle things that might help them then or down the track, then great.' At the footy club, Akermanis also began to assume a leadership role, taking the time to talk with and help the young players who were making their way. 'The older guys will still talk down to me because of the way I was,' he says. 'But the younger guys who've come along in the past couple of years all respect me because of what I've done. So, I always think that's funny.' The humble speech that Jason made, moments after the shock of winning the Brownlow Medal in 2001, was further evidence of his maturity.

Matthews moved Akermanis, who had played most of his football with Brisbane in the back pocket or on the wing, into the midfield. With Michael Voss, Nigel Lappin and Simon Black, Akermanis completed what someone in the media dubbed the 'Fab Four'. (What team in football history has had a group of midfielders that even comes close to matching this quartet?) Like Akermanis, Voss and Lappin had been born in country Victoria (Voss moved to Queensland with his parents when he was aged eleven). Black was born in Mt Isa but was living in Perth when he was drafted. Voss was already an out-and-out champion who had won the Brownlow Medal in 1996; Lappin, one of the kids that Walls had encouraged, was by this time a young veteran. When the 1999 season started, Voss was still only 23, Lappin 22, Akermanis 21 and Black 19. They complemented each other perfectly — Voss with his body strength and long kicking, Lappin with his stamina and ability to read the game, Akermanis with his explosive speed and kicking skills, and Black with his ability to dispose of the ball quickly and accurately when under pressure. Under Matthews's coaching, each of the Fab Four improved as a player; Akermanis won the Brownlow in 2001, as did Black in 2002.

The playing style that Matthews wanted for his team was a simple one that suited the skills and physical characteristics of his players. 'Leigh drills the same thing into you,' Akermanis observes. 'I could run the meetings because you know what he's going to say, but it works.' Matthews's approach remained low-key during the home-and-away rounds: he encouraged the team to 'just play', as Akermanis puts it, and allowed the level of intensity to build only as the finals approached. The side was built around strong players in the key forward roles. For years, Alastair Lynch had suffered from chronic fatigue syndrome but, through careful management of his training and travelling schedule, the medical staff was able to bring this under control and extend his football career. 'Kick it long to Lynchy' was the essence of the Brisbane game plan and, when teenager Jonathan Brown made his debut in 2000, the Lions had another mobile key position player who could provide a target up forward. Matthews had the Lions move the ball quickly and directly to Lynch and Brown, while they were one-out with their opponents. Players were to kick the ball short to a team-mate in space only if extra defenders had dropped back to cover the opposition's key forwards. This still gave the team plenty of scope for creative play, as players were encouraged to run with the ball and move it quickly with handballs or short kicks, or send penetrating kicks into the forward area.

There was no finesse about the Lions' play — just plenty of hard running, willingness to help team-mates and preparedness to take knocks when the ball was in dispute. As Matt Price observed after the 2001 grand final, 'Leigh Matthews has fashioned a team out of his own legendary toughness'. The Lions were willing to run from one side of the ground to another to make space, and run back into defence to close the space available to the opposition. They were not afraid to kick the ball to where there would be a contest for possession because they knew that even their smaller team-mates were strong and marked well, and that all players would have the speed and willingness to get to contests for the ball and pick up crumbs. This was a superbly even team, with every player being strong enough to have a good chance of breaking tackles, or applying and holding onto them. Akermanis and the rest of the Fab Four were supported by a group of running players that included Ashcroft, Shaun Hart, Craig McRae and Luke Power, and the attacking play of defenders such as Chris Johnson (acquired as part of the Fitzroy merger), White, and the Scott twins, Brad and Chris. The club obtained Mal Michael through a trade with Collingwood to give key defensive support to Leppitsch, and he became the final component of a brilliant goal-to-goal line. The ruck division, led by Beau McDonald and Queenslanders Clark Keating and Jamie Charman, simply concentrated on smashing the ball forward for their team-mates to run to. Voss was an inspirational captain, but several other Brisbane players also displayed the characteristics of football leadership: the ability to work hard for the good of the team and the boldness to change the course of games that were not going the team's way. As Akermanis puts it, 'probably the key to our success is that leadership doesn't just come from a couple'.

In 1999, Essendon had been hot favourites to win the premiership until their shock one-point defeat by Carlton in the preliminary final; in 2000, they made amends by losing only one home-and-away game and capping off the season with a convincing, almost contemptuous grand final win over Melbourne. With a core of outstanding key position players, an excellent midfield, and a group of strong, skilful supporting players, this Essendon team was almost as powerful and tough as the club's great premiership sides of 1984 and 1985. As the 2001 season unfolded, Brisbane emerged as the most serious challenger to Essendon's title. Injuries to key players tested Essendon's depth and, at a press conference before the round 10 match against the Bombers, Matthews expressed his confidence by using a line from the Arnold Schwarzenegger movie, *Predator*, 'If it bleeds, we can kill it'.

The Lions won that match and the following fourteen games to claim a spot in the grand final. They had a good run with injuries and their confidence and momentum were building. Walls spoke to Akermanis in 2000 when Jason was representing Australia in the international series against Ireland; he told him that 'one year, you're going to notice its all going your way, and you'll just know'. 'Maybe he isn't such an old prick after all,' Jason remembers thinking after Brisbane won its first flag. Essendon was struggling to put its best team, fully fit, on the field, and Akermanis says that when the Lions watched the preliminary final and saw the Bombers hang on for a narrow win, 'we saw Hawthorn just about run over them, and we couldn't help but think, "these guys don't have the legs". We knew that if we were close at half-time, the game was going to be ours'.

On grand final day, Matthews followed his usual pre-match routine of speaking quietly to the players as a group, and then individually. Just before they ran onto the ground, Matthews simply said, 'I don't know what to say to you guys, but I just know I'm with you'. From that point on, Jason recalls, the Lions 'were ready to play'.

It was a hot, windy day, although cloud cover later took the edge off the heat. Just before quarter-time, Akermanis snapped a brilliant left-foot goal from the pocket to give the Lions a five-point lead. Essendon had the better of things in the second quarter but, as half-time approached, Scott Lucas missed a shot for goal that could have given the Bombers a 25-point lead. A goal from Lynch in the last minute of the half cut Essendon's lead to 14 points. In the rooms, the Lions' mood was positive: 'There's nothing like smelling a victory', was how Akermanis recalled it. Brad Scott, who shut James Hird out of the game with a disciplined performance, recalled that during the break 'the midfield group got together as we always did. There wasn't a lot of talk, but we just looked around, and looked each other in the eye and said "we've got them"'.

The turning point of the game came midway through the third quarter. Essendon was still leading by nine points and the ball was in dispute just in front of the Essendon goal square. Hart, who played magnificently during this quarter, stood his ground and punched the ball towards the boundary line; under extreme pressure, the Lions then worked the ball up to the wing, with eight handballs and a short kick. Eight Brisbane players were involved in this passage of play. Tim Notting then kicked the ball long towards Lynch and Brown and, after a contest for the ball, Brown handballed to Power, who kicked a goal. If anyone wanted to know what it was about the Lions that enabled them to win three consecutive premierships, this sixty seconds of play summed it up perfectly. Two 50-metre goals from Lappin, and further goals to Brown and Martin Pike resulting from long kicks into the forward line, gave the Lions a 16-point advantage at the last break.

Akermanis was a spectator for much of this period of the game. He had been relatively quiet for most of the day and Matthews had taken him off to keep him fresh for the last quarter. Akermanis responded with a quarter of strong running and unselfish play that helped his team sew up the premiership. After giving a handball to Power and watching his team-mate kick a goal, Akermanis remembers thinking 'we've won this'. Jason could easily have finished with four goals: one of his shots was touched on the line and another hit the post. He scored Brisbane's final goal after running on to a kick from Brown. He remembers thinking when the final siren sounded, 'what about that for a journey'.

The 2002 grand final was a completely different type of game. The Lions' opponent, Collingwood, was a rank outsider, but the day was cold and wet and this suited the Magpies perfectly. Within the first five minutes, McDonald dislocated his shoulder, and at quarter-time, Akermanis and Pike had serious groin injuries. Jason had had problems with his fitness that season due to the side effects of acne medication that caused him to gain weight and feel tired and sore. In the grand final, he tore an adductor muscle almost off the bone and, although he had his groin strapped, the pain made sprinting and turning quickly impossible, and he could not kick with his right foot. 'I don't know why I stayed on,' he says. 'I knew I shouldn't have been there.'

The Lions seemed to be getting on top in the second quarter but could not translate this into goals. By the end of the third quarter, Collingwood seemed to be the fitter and fresher team. Lynch goaled from a free kick midway through the last quarter to give the Lions the lead. With a few minutes to go, Brisbane still led by only three points. Akermanis had been running to the back of packs, thinking that this was where the slippery ball would end up. Matthews, who had agreed to a TV station's request to wear a microphone in the coach's box throughout the game, told his runner to 'get out to Aka and tell him to get in front of Lynchy at the marking contests'. The ball was kicked long to Lynch and his opponent in the goal square; it spilled to the front where Akermanis, as instructed, was waiting. Akermanis bent down, picked the ball up and, as he ran away from goal to evade a charging pack, he heard Lynch call out 'Aka, you're clear'. Although, as Akermanis put it later, 'I couldn't kick over a jam tin', Lynch's call gave him a fraction of a second to steady and snap the goal over his shoulder with a left-foot kick.

Despite the sluggishness of Brisbane's grand final performance, the group of players that the club had assembled during the 1990s was, at the time, probably at the peak of its powers. The core of the team was made up of seasoned footballers: Akermanis, for example, would turn 26 before the start of the 2003 season and at that stage he had played 163 AFL games. Thirteen of the 2002 premiership team were older that he was, but the squad showed few signs that it was running out of challenges. Not many of the players were satisfied with their personal performances in the 2002 grand final, and Akermanis's attitude was typical of many of his team-mates. 'I wasn't in great shape in 2001 and didn't contribute as much as I would have liked and last year I tore my groin in the opening minutes which was incredibly frustrating,' he wrote in his *Courier-Mail* column. 'Both times, while victory has been wonderful, I have been left feeling a bit unfulfilled.' Some very good players — Daniel Bradshaw, Charman and Robert Copeland — had been left out of the 2002 grand final side and they wanted to win their places back. There were promising youngsters, such as Richard Hadley, who were determined to break into the team. Winning back-to-back flags was a mighty achievement, but just about everyone at the club had their own reasons for wanting to do better in 2003.

For much of that season, it seemed as if injuries would prevent the Lions from returning to what Michael Voss called 'the big dance' — the grand final. Voss himself had a chronic knee injury; Leppitsch a dislocated shoulder; Brad Scott a broken leg; McDonald an injured knee; and Johnson missed most of the second half of the season with a hamstring injury. Most of the other Lions players, including Akermanis, missed some games because of injury during the season. The Lions won eight of the first ten home-and-away matches but, after losing five of the next seven, the team was in danger of missing the finals altogether. During this mid-season slump, Matthews called a team meeting and for the first time spoke of the opportunity they had to win a hat-trick of premierships. By the time the finals started, the injury crisis had eased somewhat; however, Voss hurt his knee again in the qualifying final, and a loss that night to Collingwood meant that the Lions had to play the preliminary final away from the Gabba. Lappin broke some ribs after a collision with Hart in the preliminary final and, at three-quarter-time, Sydney seemed to have the momentum. After Matthews spoke to the team and headed off the ground, Voss, who had needed pain-killing injections to play, addressed the players and told them not to give up without a fight. The players responded magnificently, no-one more so than Akermanis who had been quiet all night but had kept chasing and tackling, and in the last quarter he made a telling contribution to the Lions' victory.

Akermanis seemed to be rarely out of the media spotlight in 2003. When the issue of which club Wayne Carey would join was being discussed, Akermanis commented that, if Brisbane recruited Carey, it would have to trade players or draft picks to do so and that would be disruptive and weaken 'the fabric of trust' at his club. Jason attracted the headlines with his throwaway line that he would play Rugby Union if Carey came to Brisbane. During contract negotiations with the club, Akermanis, who represented himself, leaked stories to the media that he had received a lucrative offer to play in Sydney. Before the preliminary final, he attempted to needle his upcoming opponent, Jared Crouch, with comments about him on a TV panel show. 'I know he's a lovely fellow,' he said a few months later. 'He just holds on to you . . . I just wanna punch him.'

During grand final week, when the media was allocated a day at the Gabba to interview the players individually, Akermanis did not 'so much face the media scrum as conduct it', as the *Courier-Mail*'s Mike Colman put it. 'Some people would rather have teeth pulled than sit in front of a room full of cameras. Akermanis is so at ease the Lions' PR people can't stop him sneaking into other players' press conferences, interjecting, cracking jokes and generally being Aker.' Akermanis chose that time to announce that he had agreed to a new contract, and that he had fabricated reports of an offer to him from Sydney. 'People may be surprised I chose to make the announcement in grand final week, but I just feel the mind works better when it is clear of any distractions,' Jason wrote in his *Courier-Mail* column. 'On Saturday I am looking forward to playing in a grand final where I can run around like I know I can and hopefully be productive for the group.'

Such public statements put Akermanis and, as some critics argued in the media, his team under extra pressure. A poor game by Akermanis, or a defeat for his team, would have made him a target for derision.

Matthews tried to get that point across to him in countless one-on-one meetings, but Jason remained unperturbed. Before the grand final, the coach simply argued that, if Jason was going to talk so much about the game, he had better 'walk the walk' on the field.

A few days earlier, Jason wrote:

> In 2001, we were confident of our chances against Essendon but in all reality we hadn't really done anything to that point. We were just a talented group of players not sure whether we could go all the way. But having successfully climbed to the top of the mountain, it provided us with an incredible base for our self-confidence, trust and nerves. Collingwood on the other hand haven't reached that point. They have a little bit more doubt in their minds this week. They have some new players and like a lot of people they will not realise what this week entails. There's a ton of hype, media obligations seem endless and no one ever seems to stop talking about the big game. But virtually every player in our squad has been through this twice before and trust me it can make a huge difference.

In short, Akermanis's view was that Collingwood was still like clay, while the Lions were like porcelain. Having seen Collingwood play an excellent finals series, few media experts agreed with him and the Magpies were warm favourites. However, it was apparent from very early in the match that Akermanis had made a realistic assessment. If Collingwood had an edge in pace and youth, Brisbane exploited it ruthlessly by running hard and straight at the ball. If Collingwood had an edge in numbers of fully fit players, Brisbane matched it with their depth and the willingness of injured players to defy pain. Lappin's broken ribs punctured his lung early in the game, but he played on and was a valuable contributor, as was Voss. Collingwood's midfield had closed down its opponents' play in previous finals, but Brisbane had the Fab Four, supported by Hart and the ruckwork of Keating. Black won the Norm Smith Medal, just shading Akermanis who won plenty of the ball on the wing; he could easily have finished with eight goals, instead of five, had he not hurried his work in the first quarter.

Akermanis had an excellent home-and-away season in 2004: statistically, he was the League's leading player that season in setting up goals for others, and his consistency suggested that he had reached peak maturity and performance. After a crushing win in the qualifying final over St Kilda, however, things started to go against Brisbane. The Lions' position on the ladder entitled them to play the preliminary final at the Gabba, but the AFL was contracted to play the game at the MCG. Furthermore, the match was played on Saturday night. This meant that extra travelling was required and gave the Lions one day less recovery time than their grand final opponents. Hart suffered serious facial injuries in a collision with Bradshaw during the preliminary final, and several other Brisbane players picked up injuries during the game. Lynch and McCrae were struggling with hamstring problems, and Brown with a jarred knee. Although Brisbane won the game against an emerging Geelong side, the team that had seemed to be cruising towards a fourth consecutive flag suddenly seemed vulnerable. Throughout grand final week, the Lions exuded confidence — after all, several players had been under injury clouds the year before, and the team had a clear edge in experience over Port Adelaide, its 2004 opponent. Akermanis kept a relatively low profile during the week, although he did say that he thought his team would win. At this grand final, however, Brisbane was bleeding more seriously than in previous years, and it was facing a side that was fit and hungry for success.

The Age's Rohan Connolly summed up the 2004 grand final best when he wrote, 'In the end, the Brisbane Lions handed over the baton of AFL power in much the same fashion as had their predecessor four seasons ago'. In 2001, Akermanis was part of an even, young and enthusiastic team that overran a tiring Essendon; in 2004, it was the Lions who were tired and struggling to keep a fresh and talented challenger at bay. Akermanis kept Brisbane in the game with two goals in the first quarter and, when he kicked a signature left-foot goal from the boundary just before half-time, the Lions seemed to be gaining control. He battled bravely when moved into the centre in the third quarter, and was probably Brisbane's best player on the day, but a couple of uncharacteristic errors marred even his game. In the second quarter, having received a free kick close to goal, he had it reversed after he pushed an opponent in the face and, in the third quarter, the ball fell out of his hands as he was running into a scoring position. Port Adelaide opened up a handy lead by three-quarter-time and went on to win its first AFL premiership in some style.

Watching someone else collect the premiership medals and cup was a new experience for the Lions, but they accepted it with good grace and Port's Mark Williams expressed his pride in having defeated 'the best team *ever*'. Matthews was generous in his praise of Port Adelaide, as was Brad Scott who said that the loss would spur the Lions on as they prepared to challenge for the crown in 2005. The day after the match, Akermanis made some light-hearted but low-key comments to the media about the fisticuffs during the game and apologised for giving away a crucial free kick, but made no predictions about the future.

References

Part 1 The game takes shape

The quotations were taken from:

Paul Daffey 2003, *Beyond the big sticks: country football around Australia*, Lothian Books, Melbourne

John Stanley James 1983, *The Vagabond Papers*, Hyland House, Melbourne (first published 1877–8)

The Adelaide Chronicle

Kalgoorlie Miner.

Chapter 1 Henry Harrison

Harrison's autobiography, edited with an introduction by Anne Mancini and Gillian M. Hibbins, was published in 1987 under the title *Running with the ball: football's foster father*, Lynedoch Publications, Melbourne.

See also:

Geoffrey Blainey 2003, *A game of our own: the origins of Australian football*, Black Inc., Melbourne

Hugh Buggy & Harold Bell 1958, *The Carlton story: a history of the Carlton Football Club*, Eric White Associates, Melbourne

Graeme Davison 2001, 'Gold-rush Melbourne', in Iain McCalman, Alexander Cook & Andrew Reeves (eds), *Gold: forgotten histories and lost objects of Australia*, Cambridge University Press, Cambridge

Martin Flanagan 1998, *The Call*, Allen & Unwin, Sydney

Gillian M. Hibbins 1989, 'The Cambridge connection: the origin of Australian Rules football', *International Journal of the History of Sport*, vol. 6, pp. 172–92

William F. Mandle 1973, 'Games people played: cricket & football in England & Victoria in the late nineteenth century', *Historical Studies*, vol. 15, pp. 511–35

Geoffrey Serle 1977, *The golden age: a history of the colony of Victoria 1851–1861*, Melbourne University Press, Melbourne

Ian Turner 1972, 'Harrison, Henry Colden Antill', in Douglas Pike (ed.), *Australian Dictionary of Biography*, vol. 4, Melbourne University Press, Melbourne.

In 1997, Penguin Books, Sydney published R.E.N. Twopeny's *Town Life in Australia* (1883) as a facsimile edition, and Twopeny's life and work are examined in Graeme Davison 1974, 'R.E.N. Twopeny and town life in Australia', *Historical Studies*, vol. 63, October, pp. 292–305.

On the history of football in Adelaide, see Bernard Whimpress 1983, *The South Australian football story*, South Australian National Football League, Adelaide. The press quotations and reports on the foundation of the SAFA were taken from *South Australian Chronicle*.

See also:

Geoff Christian, Jack Lee & Bob Messenger 1988, *The footballers: from 1885 to the West Coast Eagles*, St George Books, Perth

Rodney Gillett 1988, 'Where the big men fly: an early history of Australian football in the Riverina', *Sporting Traditions*, vol. 4, pp. 162–75

Ken Pinchin & A. Leeson 1979, *A century of Tasmanian football 1879–1979*, Tasmanian Football League, Launceston

Martin P. Sharp 1987, 'Australian football in Sydney before 1914', *Sporting Traditions*, vol. 4, pp. 27–45.

Chapter 2 Albert Thurgood

For a brief but accurate account of Thurgood's life, see John H. Reeves, 1990, 'Thurgood, Albert John', in J. Ritchie (ed.), *Australian Dictionary of Biography*, vol. 12, Melbourne University Press, Melbourne.

Thurgood's family history was traced through the Registry of Births, Deaths and Marriages, the Public Record Office Victoria, the 1881 UK Census and the Public Record Office of the UK (now The National Archives). The press quotations were from *The Age*, *The Argus* and *Leader*. The other quotation was from Richard Stremski 1986, *Kill for Collingwood*, Allen & Unwin, Sydney.

The section of C.C. Mullen's 1958 *History of Australian Rules football* dealing with Thurgood's career was reprinted in Garrie Hutchinson (ed.) 1989, *Great Australian football stories*, Currey O'Neil, Melbourne.

See also:

Henry L. Hall, H. Zachariah & G.F. James 1983, *Meliora Sequamur: Brighton Grammar School 1882–1982*, Brighton Grammar School, Melbourne

Clement Macintyre 1990, 'The "bouncing game" in Fremantle: Australian football and community identity in Western Australia', *International Journal of the History of Sport*, vol. 7, pp. 131–9

Michael Maplestone 1994, *Flying higher: history of the Essendon Football Club 1872–1974*, Essendon Football Club, Melbourne
Simon Matthews (ed.) 2002, *Champions of Essendon: ranking the 60 greatest Bombers of all time*, Hardie Grant Books, Melbourne.

Chapter 3 Phil Matson

Information about the playing and coaching career of Phil Matson came from a collection of cuttings and correspondence kindly lent to me by John Lysikatos. Other details were supplied by the Registry of Births, Deaths and Marriages. Press quotations were drawn from *The Age*, *The Argus*, *Castlemaine Mail*, *Kalgoorlie Miner*, *Richmond Guardian* and *Sporting Globe*.

See also:

Les Everett 1996, *Gravel rash: 100 years of Goldfields football*, Goldfields Football League, Fremantle
Matthew E. Glossop 1976, *East Perth 1906–1976*, East Perth Football Club, Perth
Lyall Hunt 1986, 'Matson, Phillip Henry', in Bede Nairn & Geoffrey Serle (eds), *Australian Dictionary of Biography*, vol. 10, Melbourne University Press, Melbourne
Jack Lee (ed.) 1998, *East Fremantle Football Club: celebrating 100 years of tradition*, Bill Benbow and Associates, Perth
John Lysikatos 1995, *True blue: the history of the Sturt Football Club*, Sturt Football Club, Adelaide
Ken Spillman 1998, *Diehards: the story of the Subiaco Football Club 1896–1945*, Subiaco Football Club, Perth.

Part 2 Theme parks for football fans

For details of Maley Hayward's career, see Colin Tatz 1995, *Obstacle race: Aborigines in sport*, UNSW Press, Sydney.

The quotations in this section were from:

Kathryn M. Hunter 2001, 'The drover's wife and the drover's daughter: histories of single farming women and debates in Australian historiography', *Rural History*, vol. 12, pp. 179–94
Alan J. McIntyre & J.J. McIntyre 1944, *Country towns of Victoria: a social survey*, Melbourne University Press, Melbourne

Martin Flanagan 2004, 'The meaning of football', *The Age*, 20 February

Jack Lee (ed.) 1998, *East Fremantle Football Club: celebrating 100 years of tradition*, Bill Benbow and Associates, Perth.

Chapter 4 Harry and Albert Collier

The definitive history of the Collingwood Football Club, which I relied on extensively, is Richard Stremski's 1986, *Kill for Collingwood*, Allen & Unwin, Sydney. I am also indebted to Dr Stremski for allowing me to use the audio-tapes of his interviews with Albert and Harry Collier, drawn from his archive of interviews with a number of Collingwood players from the 1920s to the 1970s. Further information was provided by Len Fitzgerald, and through interviews by Michael Williamson with Bruce Andrew, Percy Bowyer, Jack Hale and Bob Rose.

Profiles of the Collier brothers are included in Geoff Slattery (ed.) 2003, *The Brownlow: a tribute to the greats of Australian football*, Lothian Books, Melbourne; another useful source was James Griffin 2004, *John Wren: a life reconsidered*, Scribe Publications, Melbourne.

The Collier's family history was traced through the Registry of Births, Deaths and Marriages and the City of Collingwood rate books. Norm Smith's remarks about Leeter Collier were from 'My life in football', *The Truth*, 24 March 1962.

The quotations from Ivor Warne-Smith and 'Old Boy' were from *The Argus*. Information about the suspensions of the Collier brothers was from the VFL's minute books, held at AFL House.

For an account of the development of the Collingwood area in general, see Bernard Barrett 1971, *The inner suburbs: the evolution of an industrial area*, Melbourne University Press, Melbourne. The quote from Robin Boyd was from the preface of Barrett's book.

Chapter 5 Brighton Diggins

Information for this chapter was obtained from conversations with the late Beth Brighton (nee Lindau), a scrapbook of undated press cuttings compiled by Diggins's daughter, Lynette Thornber, and interviews with Harry Collier by Richard Stremski, and with Bob Pratt by Mike Williamson. Other useful sources were:

Mark Branagan & Mike Lefebvre 1995, *Bloodstained angels: the rise & fall of the Foreign Legion 1932–1938*, Mark Branagan, Melbourne

Paul Depasquale 2002, *The Farmer files: Ken Farmer — South Australian football's greatest figure*, Pioneer Books, Adelaide
Lionel Frost 1998, *The old dark navy blues: a history of the Carlton Football Club*, Allen & Unwin, Sydney
Brian Hansen & Jack Dyer 1996, *Jack Dyer's the greatest: the most sensational players of the century*, Brian Hansen Publications, Sydney
Leonie Sandercock & Ian Turner 1981, *Up where, Cazaly? The great Australian game*, Granada, London
Ken Spillman 1998, *Diehards: the story of the Subiaco Football Club 1896–1945*, Subiaco Football Club, Perth
Norm Smith 1962, 'My life in football', *The Truth*, 24 March.

Chapter 6 Bob Quinn

Much of the information in this chapter was drawn from conversations with Bob Quinn. Further information was supplied by his daughter, Pam Paull, and the Registry of Births, Deaths and Marriages, and in Quinn's defence service record, housed in the National Archives of Australia. Len Fitzgerald, Robert Oatey and Geof Motley provided insights into Bob's career. The accounts of the military action that Quinn saw were based on:

Chester Wilmot 1944, *Tobruk 1941*, Penguin Books, Melbourne
Joan Beaumont 1996, 'Australia's war: Europe and the Middle East', in Joan Beaumont (ed.), *Australia's war, 1939–45*, Allen & Unwin, Sydney.

Other useful sources were:

Jeff Pash & Paul Depasquale (ed.) 1999, *The Pash papers: Australian Rules football in South Australia 1950–1964*, Pioneer Books, Adelaide
Brian Kay 2003, *The master: the Bob Hank story*, Peacock Publications, Adelaide
Allen R. McLean 1971, *100 years with the Magpies: the story of the Port Adelaide Football Club*, Peacock Publications, Adelaide
John Wood 1988, *SA greats: the history of the Magarey Medal*, John and Wendy Wood, Adelaide
John Wood 1991, *Bound for glory: the story of the Port Adelaide Football Club Inc. 1939–1990*, John and Wendy Wood, Adelaide
John Wood 1995, *Simply the best: the story of the Port Adelaide Football Club part 1: 1870–1901*, John and Wendy Wood, Adelaide.

The press quotations were from *The Adelaide Chronicle, The Argus,* and *The Advertiser.*

Part 3 Modern football

This period in the evolution of Australian Rules football is covered well by Bob Stewart 1998, 'Boom-time football, 1946–1975', in Rob Hess & Bob Stewart (eds), *More than a game: an unauthorised history of Australian Rules football*, Melbourne University Press, Melbourne.

Chapter 7 Len and Norm Smith

The major sources for this chapter were conversations with Ron Barassi, Kevin Bartlett, Barry Bourke, Len Fitzgerald, Tommy Hafey, Norma Harmes, Allan Jeans, Bob Skilton and Peter Smith, and interviews by Mike Williamson with Graham Huggins and Hassa Mann.

Information about Len Smith's coaching career came from a scrapbook of mostly undated cuttings from the *Sporting Globe*, *Sun* and *Truth*, compiled by Norma Harmes, and from correspondence involving Len Smith, kindly lent to me by Norma Harmes and Allan Jeans. Other useful sources were:

Ron Barassi & Peter McFarline 1995, *Barassi: the life behind the legend*, Simon & Schuster, Sydney

Lynda Carroll 1999, *The grand old flag: a history of the Melbourne Football Club*, Hardie Grant Books, Melbourne

Mike Coward 1992, *Men of Norwood: the red and blue blooded*, Norwood Football Club, Adelaide

Jules Feldmann & Russell Holmesby 1992, *The point of it all: the story of the St Kilda Football Club*, Playright Publishing, Melbourne

Brian Hansen & Jack Dyer 1996, *Jack Dyer's the greatest: the most sensational players of the century*, Brian Hansen Publications, Sydney

Russell Holmesby 1995, *Heroes with haloes: St Kilda's one hundred greatest*, Playright Publishing, Sydney

Geoff Kingston 2001, 'Long-lasting legacy of the Jeans' pool', *The Advertiser*, 5 September

Robert Pascoe 1995, *The winter game: the complete history of Australian football*, Text Publishing, Melbourne

Tom Prior 1995, *Sheeds: a touch of cunning*, Wilkinson Books, Melbourne.

Chapter 8 John Kennedy

Much of the information in this chapter was derived from conversations with John Kennedy. Further information was obtained from interviews with John Longmire, and from interviews by Michael Williamson with Graham Arthur, Sandy Ferguson, Jack Hale, Peter Hudson, John Kennedy, Peter Knights, Leigh Matthews, David Parkin and Don Scott.

An outstanding club history that contains much useful material is Harry Gordon 1990, *The hard way: the story of the Hawthorn Football Club*, Lester Townsend Publishing, Sydney.

Bob Davis's observations about Hawthorn are recorded in Bob Davis with Jim Main 1996, *Woofa: football legend*, ABC Books, Sydney.

For an interesting perspective on the Hawthorn–North Melbourne rivalry of the 1970s, see John Powers 1978, *The coach: a season with Ron Barassi*, Thomas Nelson Australia, Melbourne.

Chapter 9 Jack Oatey

Information about Jack Oatey was provided through interviews with Paul Bagshaw, Tony Burgan, Keith Chessell, Dave Edwards, Len Fitzgerald, Malcolm Greenslade, John Halbert, Daryl Hicks, Wayne Jackson, Bruce Jarratt, 'Sandy' Nelson, John Nicholls, Robert Oatey, Brian Phillips and Bob Skilton.

The closest thing to a biography of Oatey is Sturt Football Club's 1982, *Jack Oatey: coach of a lifetime*, Sturt Football Club, Adelaide; in this book, Merv Agars and others collected tributes to mark Oatey's retirement as a coach. Details of Oatey's early life and career were taken from Mike Coward 1992, *Men of Norwood: the red and blue blooded*, Norwood Football Club, Norwood, pp. 179–93.

Needless to say, Oatey's Sturt career features prominently in John Lysikatos 1995, *True blue: the history of the Sturt Football Club*, Sturt Football Club, Adelaide.

The cited press reports were from *The Advertiser*, including Merv Agars & Gordon Schwartz 1990, 'Man who made footy an art form', *The Advertiser*, 10 February.

The quotations by Jeff Pash were from his 1999 book with Paul Despasquale (ed.), *The Pash papers: Australian Rules football in South Australia 1950–1964*, Pioneer Books, Adelaide.

The definitive account of Fos Williams's career, and of the Port Adelaide Football Club since World War II, is Fos Williams & Michelangelo Rucci 1999, *Dynasty: a legend, a family and the Port Adelaide Football Club*, Peacock Publications, Adelaide.

Useful information on the life and personality of Sir Donald Bradman was found in:

Roland Perry 1995, *The Don*, MacMillan, Sydney

Charles Williams 1996, *Bradman: an Australian hero*, Little, Brown, London.

Part 4 Nationwide

Information in this section was drawn from:

Ian Andrews 2000, 'From a club to a corporate game: the changing face of Australian football, 1960–1999', *International Journal of the History of Sport*, vol. 17, pp. 225–54

Ross Booth 2004, 'Labor market intervention, revenue sharing, and competitive balance in the Australian Football League', in R. Fort & J. Fizel (eds), *International sports: economic comparisons*, Praeger, Westport

Garry Linnell 1995, *Football Ltd: the inside story of the AFL*, Ironbark, Sydney.

The quotation was from John Harms 2002, *Loose men everywhere*, Text Publishing, Melbourne.

For an account of the current state of country football, see Paul Daffey 2001, *Local rites: a year in grass roots football in Victoria and beyond*, Black Duck Publications, Melbourne.

Chapter 10 Barry Round

Apart from conversations with Barry Round, information for this chapter was derived from:

Marc Fiddian 1987, *The roar of the crowd: a history of VFA grand finals*, Victorian Football Association, Melbourne

Sally Freud & Mark Cutler 1999, *Flying north for the winter: the story of the Sydney Swans*, Random House, Sydney

Trevor Grant 2001, 'Birth of a footy club', *Herald Sun*, 24–26 April

John Lack, C. McConville, M. Small & D. Wright 1996, *Unleashed: a history of the Footscray Football Club*, Aus-Sport Enterprises, Melbourne

Garry Linnell 1995, *Football Ltd: the inside story of the AFL*, Ironbark, Sydney.

Warragul Football Club is discussed in Paul Daffey 2001, *Local rites: a year in grass roots football in Victoria and beyond*, Black Duck Publications, Melbourne.

Chapter 11 Tim Watson

Much of the material in this chapter was obtained from interviews with Tim Watson, and from Watson's written work, especially:

Tim Watson 2002, 'Dick Reynolds: a tribute', *The Bomber*, no. 29, December
Tim Watson 2003, 'An Essendon era is coming to an end, even if Sheeds isn't', *The Age*, 18 June
Tim Watson 2003, 'Criticism the footballer's best motivation', *The Age*, 2 July
Tim Watson 2003, 'Captain Blood: a real-life hero', *The Age*, 27 August.

Further relevant information came from:

Bob Davis with Jim Main 1996, *Woofa: football legend*, ABC Books, Sydney
Simon Matthews (ed.) 2002, *Champions of Essendon: ranking the 60 greatest Bombers of all time*, Hardie Grant Books, Melbourne
Tom Prior 1995, *Sheeds: a touch of cunning*, Wilkinson Books, Melbourne
Michael Maplestone 1994, *Flying higher: history of the Essendon Football Club 1872–1974*, Essendon Football Club, Melbourne
Robert Pascoe 1995, *The winter game: the complete history of Australian football*, Text Publishing, Melbourne
Greg Gardiner 1997, 'Racial abuse and football: the Australian Football League's racial vilification rule in review', *Sporting Traditions*, vol. 14, pp. 3–25.

The quotations by Flanagan were from *The Age*.

Chapter 12 Jason Akermanis

Apart from conversations with Jason Akermanis, the major sources for this chapter were press reports from *The Age* and *The Australian*, and Akermanis's own column in *The Courier-Mail*.

Excellent profiles are provided in:

John Harms 2003, 'Lone wolf runs with the Lions', *The Age*, 20 September
Cameron Stewart 2003, 'The lion king — the lethal touch', *The Australian Magazine*, 29–30 March.

Further insights into the early years of the Brisbane Football Club were found in:

Rohan Connolly 1992, 'Breaking down barriers', *The Age*, 3 May
Ross Fitzgerald 1996, *The footy club: inside the Brisbane Bears*, University of Queensland Press, Brisbane
Garry Linnell 1995, *Football Ltd: the inside story of the AFL*, Ironbark, Sydney.

Other useful sources were the Brisbane Lions' yearbooks and premiership souvenir booklets.

I highly recommend Jason Akermanis's 2004 autobiography, *Aka: the battle within*, Pan Macmillan, Melbourne, written with Gary Smart.

Index

Abley, John 208
Adams, William 'Bull' 207
Adcock, Brenton 215, 219, 221
Adelaide Football Club (Adelaide Crows) 171, 225, 232, 268
Adelaide Football Club 20
AFL Auskick 274
Agars, Merv 205, 220
Akermanis, Jason 234, 271–94
Albiston, Alec 179, 180
Allan, Graeme 'Gubby' 282, 283
Amateur Athletics Club 17
Andrew, Bruce 70, 75, 76
Arthur, Graham 174, 181, 182, 184, 185
Ashcroft, Marcus 278, 279, 286
Austen, Col 179
Australasian Football Council 6, 23, 56, 65, 118, 231
Aylett, Allen 231
Ayres, Gary 171
Bagshaw, Hartley 208
Bagshaw, Paul 206, 216, 218, 219, 221, 222
Baker, Leon 261, 262
Baldock, Darrel 128, 155, 157–8
Balme, Neil 167, 236
Bant, Chris 54
Bant, Horrie 49, 57
Barassi, Carlo 55
Barassi, Ron 62, 128, 136–40, 143, 144, 150, 164, 169, 171, 183, 192, 193, 254, 257, 279, 280
Barassi, Ron Sr 55, 138
Barker, Trevor 258
Barrot, Bill 162, 163
Bartlett, Kevin 162, 164, 165, 166
Bateman, Vic 123
Baxter, Ken 104, 105
Beard, Bert 'Bluey' 93, 95
Beatson, Kinnear 282
Beckwith, John 168
Bedford, Peter 169, 241
Beitzel, Harry 165
Bendigo Football Club 49, 176
Bendigo Football League 54, 176
Bertram, Ossie 94
Bissett, Jack 93, 94, 99
Black, Simon 285, 292
Blackburn, Bill 83
Blight, Malcolm 172
Boulder City Football Club 5, 44–6
Boulder Stars Football Club 45
Bourke, Barry 134–5
Bourke, Francis 163
Bowe, Johnny 94
Bowyer, Percy 78
Boyd, Dave 208
Bradbury, Peter 266
Bradshaw, Daniel 290, 293
Brain, Terry 93
Breen, Barry 158
Brentnall, Reg 'Nashy' 53
Brereton, Dermott 263
Brisbane Bears Football Club 232, 234, 271–2, 277–9, 281
Brisbane Lions Football Club 232, 271–2, 274, 281–93
Broadstock, Jack 123
Broken Hill Football Club 46
Bromage, Keith 251
Brown, Colin 211
Brown, Gavin 267
Brown, Jonathon 286, 288, 289, 293
Buckley, Nathan 258
Bunton, Haydn 78, 113
Burgan, John 219
Burnie Football Club 55
Cahill, John 123, 208, 222, 225
Cahill, Laurie, 123
Cain, Tom 49, 54
Camberwell Football Club 87
Campbell, Hugh 'Bonny' 53
Cananore Football Club 81–2

Capper, Warwick 244
Cardwell, Jim 132, 134, 137, 139, 140, 162
Carey, Stephen 266
Carey, Wayne 291
Carlon, Ken 132
Carlton Football Club 16, 18, 19, 65, 69, 76, 81, 85, 86, 89, 95, 100–8, 128–30, 138, 143, 152, 154, 159, 162, 166, 168, 171, 172, 177, 181, 189, 192, 195, 223, 225, 230, 241, 257, 260, 269, 279, 287
Case, Geoff 183
Castlemaine Football Club 54–5
Cazaly, Roy 99
Central District Football Club 225
Charman, Jamie 286, 290
Chessell, Keith 216, 218, 219, 221, 222, 223
Chitty, Bob 104
Claremont Football Club 43, 61, 91
Clarke, Jack 145, 159, 256, 257
Clarke, Neil 257
Clarkson, Tony 'Doc' 219, 221
Clay, Dick 160, 163
Clayden, George 75
Cleary, Phil 246–7
Clift, Roger 208
Coburg Football Club 159, 174, 246
Cockburn, Jack 123
Coleman, John 31, 107, 143, 144, 256
Collier, Albert 61, 63, 64, 67–88, 105–7, 147
Collier, Harry 61, 63, 67–88, 98–9
Collingwood Football Club 35–9, 49, 64–88, 91, 96–9, 105, 106, 117, 128–33, 136, 137, 140–4, 147, 153, 156–9, 162, 175, 176, 183, 189, 190, 195, 203, 225, 230, 240, 241, 250, 251, 257, 266, 267, 279, 282, 283, 286, 289–92
Connor, George 74–5
Conway, Jack 16
Cook, Ron 178, 185
Copeland, Ern 71
Copeland, Robert 290
Coulter law 64, 81, 93, 128–9, 132, 153, 181, 230
Coventry, Gordon 65, 70, 84
Coventry, Syd 70, 79, 81
Crimmins, Peter 191, 192–3
Crisp, Micky 103, 104
Crofts, Archie 92–3, 101
Cronin, Paul 277–8
Crouch, Jared 291
Crowe, Neville 238
Cumberland, Harold 'Vic' 46
Cunningham, Brian 200
Curran, Kevin 179, 180
Daniher, Neale 258, 260, 264
Daniher, Terry 258, 264
Darcy, David 135
Darcy, Luke 273
Davey, Charlie 100
Davies, Rick 219, 222, 223
Davis, Barry 253, 255, 256, 258, 259
Davis, Bob 188–9, 249, 254
Dean, Roger 162
Deane, Jim 121
Dempsey, Gary 239, 240
Dempsey, John 45
depression of the 1890s 33, 37, 90
Dick, Alick 26, 35
Dickson, 'Delicate' Des 185
Diggins, Brighton 57, 89–108
Dimboola Football Club 252–3
DiPierdomenico, Robert 262
Ditterich, Carl 155, 157, 158, 236
Dixson, Hugh 22
Doig, George 65
Drake, Ian 153, 155
Duckworth, Bill 261, 262
Dunn, Ray 139, 159, 161
Dunn, Roger 219
Dunne, Francis 'Diver' 46
Dyer, Jack 97, 107, 160, 250

East Fremantle Football Club 44, 49, 51–4, 65
East Perth Football Club 52, 53, 56, 129
Edelston, Geoffrey 236
Edmonds, Horace 'Tubby' 70, 183
Edwards, Brendan 184, 190, 191
Edwards, Dave 215–16
Ellinbank Football League 238
Endersbee, Peter 219, 222
Essendon Football Club 25–40, 44, 49, 63, 87, 133, 141, 145, 152, 157, 159, 170, 181, 225, 234, 245, 250, 253–69, 287–8, 292–3
Exeter Football Club 116
Fanning, Fred 143
Farmer, 'Polly' 128, 188
Farmer, Ken 65
Faul, Billy 93
Fenn, Alan 'Fountain' 213
Ferguson, Dr 'Sandy' 177, 178, 180–2, 188, 189, 193
Fields, Neville 258
Fitcher, Alan 151–2
Fitzgerald, Len 70, 73, 87, 121, 124, 144, 199, 208
Fitzgerald, Ross 279, 280
Fitzroy Football Club 37, 38, 63, 68, 75, 79, 87, 102, 129, 140, 142–5, 149, 150–2, 159, 160, 230, 242, 257, 260, 271, 279, 281, 283, 286
Flanagan, Fred 147
Footscray Football Club 79, 83, 135, 148, 154, 166, 186, 238–41, 243, 245, 247, 265, 276
'Foreign Legion' 96–103
Fothergill, Des 87
Foulds, Garry 257
Francis, Jim 104, 154
Frankston Football Club 107
Fremantle Dockers Football Club 281
Fremantle Football Club 27, 34, 35
Gale, Allan 'Butch' 63, 149, 150, 158, 163
Gavin, Hugh 44, 45
Geelong Football Club 15, 16, 38, 69, 91, 94, 95, 104, 113, 116, 117, 128–30, 144, 147, 166, 175, 179, 188–9, 209, 240, 248–9, 279, 293
Gleeson, Brian 154
Glenelg Football Club 116, 212, 222, 223, 225
Goggin, Bill 240
gold rush, Australian 3, 7–10, 61, 67, 90, 252
gold rush, Californian 8
Goldfields Football Association 44, 49
Golding, Frank 46
Goninon, George 147
Gordon, Harry 174, 186
Graham, Jack 207
Graham, Michael 216, 222
Great Depression 63–5, 80–1, 91, 100, 117, 176, 185, 202, 204
Greenslade, Malcolm 214, 215, 217, 219
Griffiths, Daryl 158
Groom, Hector 53
Guy, Eric 155
Hadley, Richard 290
Hafey, Tommy 164–7, 172, 250, 257
Halbert, John 215, 218, 219, 221, 223, 225
Hale, Jack 76, 104, 106, 177, 180–5
Hammersley, William 11, 13, 14, 16
Hando, Arthur 55
Hands, Ken 143, 144
Hank, Bob 119, 120, 121, 123
Hanneberry, Tony 245, 246
Harms, John 229, 277
Harris, Dick 163
Harris, Wilbur 94
Harrison, Barry 'Hooker' 136
Harrison, Henry 'Colden' 3, 7–24, 39
Hart, Ben 225

Hart, Royce 160, 251
Hart, Shaun 279, 286, 288, 290, 292, 293
Harvey, Mark 258, 261, 268
Harvey, Mark 261
Hawker, Glenn 252, 257, 258, 262
Hawkins, Doug 265
Hawthorn Football Club 81, 129, 130, 144, 158, 170–95, 207, 208, 223, 230, 257, 261–3, 282, 287
Hayes, Neville 'Chic' 208
Hayward, Bill 61
Hayward, Eric 61
Hayward, Maley 61
Heard, Shane 257, 262
Hickey, Reg 104, 117, 129, 144, 147, 189
Hicks, Daryl 205, 217, 219, 220, 221, 225
Hird, James 264, 265, 273, 288
Holllingworth, Albie 117
Hopkins, Harold 83, 84
Hosking, Sampson 'Shine' 46, 115, 117
Hudson, Peter 130, 190, 191
Huggins, Graham 153, 154
Hughes, Dr Wilfred Kent 39
Hughes, Frank 'Checker' 56, 63, 131–3, 135, 142
Hutchison, Bill 63, 256
Industrial Revolution 9
Jarratt, Bruce 214, 216
Jauncey, Phil 283
Jeans, Allan 147, 152, 154–9, 164, 170–1, 191, 194, 259
Jennings, Geoff 240
Jesaulenko, Alex 130
Johnson, Bob 182
Johnson, Chris 186, 190
Jones, 'Percy' 236
Jones, Malcolm 'Emmy' 219
Jordan, Ray 160
Joyce, Alan 194
Judkins, Noel 261
Judkins, Stan 83, 84
Kadina Football Club 121
Kalgoorlie Football Club 93–4
Keating, Clark 286, 292
Keenan, 'Crackers' 236
Kennedy, Des 157
Kennedy, John 124, 173–96, 200, 257, 282
Kensington Rules 20
Keogh, John 243
Kerley, Neil 209, 225
Kickett, Derek 266
Killigrew, Alan 153–4
Kimberley, Craig 241
Kingston, Geoff 170–1
Klomp, Robbert 222, 223
Knight, Jack 'Cracker' 153
Knights, Peter 190, 191, 257, 278
Kutcher, Ray 213, 215
Kyne, Phonse 80, 144, 147
Kyneton Football Club 87
Lappin, Nigel 279, 285, 288, 290, 292
Latrobe Valley Football League 238
Leckie, Jack 52
Leonard, John 57, 93, 94
Leppitsch, Justin 279, 284, 286, 290
Limb, Herbert 46, 49, 50
Lloyd, Matthew 264
Long, Michael 233, 266, 268, 269
Longmire, John 195
Lucas, Scott 288
Luke, Kenneth 102–3, 104, 106, 129
Lynch, Alastair 279, 285–6, 288, 289, 293
Madden, Simon 245, 257, 262, 263, 264
Maitland Football Club 202
Malthouse, Mick 172
Mann, Hassa 134, 136–7, 140
Marshall, Denis 128
Marshall, Theodore 16–17
Matson, Phil 5, 6, 41–58
Matthew, Herbie 93, 96
Matthews, Leigh 187, 190, 191–2, 258, 282–90, 292, 294

Mayne Football Club 276–7
McCallum, Bill 123
McCarthy, Jack 121
McCaskill, Bob 176–83, 188, 189, 193
McCracken, Robert 30
McDonal, Beau 286, 289, 290
McDonald, Harold 208
McGhie, Robbie 166
McGregor, Ken 211
McHale, James 'Jock' 70, 74–6, 78, 79, 86, 87, 101, 105, 207
McKay, Andrew 225
McKenna, Peter 130
McLean, Bob 113, 118, 120, 122
McLean, Ricky 167
McLean, Rod 104
McRae, Craig 286
Melbourne Football Club 3, 6, 12–19, 25–6, 32, 35, 69, 77, 81, 99, 128, 131–45, 151–2, 157, 162, 165, 168, 175, 182–4, 186, 207, 241, 256, 287
Melbourne Rules 3, 14
Menzies, R.G. 40
Merrett, Roger 257, 278
Metherall, Len 91
Michael, Mal 286
Michael, Stephen 233
Miels, Brenton 215
Minogue, Dan 55
Moloney, George 91
Moorabbin Football Club 156, 158
Moore, Kelvin 190, 191
Mornington Peninsula Football League 107
Morris, Mel 55, 56
Morrison, Bruce 147
Morrow, Alan 158
Mort, Ian 185
Morton, 'Bo' 213
Morwood, Paul 244
Morwood, Tony 244
Moss, Graham 257
Motley, Geof 199, 200, 209, 211
Motley, Peter 224
Mueller, Jack 133, 152
Mundy, Max 123
Murdoch, Joe 96
Murphy, Frank 147
Murphy, John 169, 218, 219
Murphy, Len 98
Murray, Bob 155
Murray, Kevin 144, 152
Mynott, Brian 158
Nash, Laurie 94, 96, 97, 99, 101
Neagle, Merv 257, 258, 262
Neil Sachse 240
Nelson, 'Sandy' 205, 219
Nelson, Ernie 49
Nicholls, John 259
Nilma Football Club 235, 238
Nix, John 160
Nolan, Mick 236
North Adelaide Football Club 81, 84, 160, 169, 172, 177, 179, 192–6, 207, 230, 254–5
Northcote Football Club 93, 142
Northern Tasmanian Football Association 22
Northey, John 281, 283
Norwood Football Club 118, 123, 154, 197, 198, 200, 203, 204, 208, 209, 212, 216, 217, 222, 223
Notting, Tim 288
Nunan, Michael 219, 225
O'Mahoney, John 182
O'Meara, James 94
O'Mullane, George 16
Oakley, Ross 157, 232
Oatey, Jack 121, 123, 129, 178, 179, 197–226
Oatey, Peter 203
Oatey, Robert 203, 206, 207, 222
Oatey, Ted 202
Oliver, Harold 115
Orr, Billy 49, 50
Owens, George 'Staunch' 53
Pagan, Denis 172
Page, Percy 55, 56, 131, 132, 142
Pannam, Alby 76

Parkin, David 184, 185, 192, 194, 282
Parkin, Roy 54
Pash, Jeff 113, 123, 208, 209
Peck, John 186–7
Pelerman, Reuben 278
Perth Football Club 21, 49, 50, 55, 56, 102
Phillips, Ron 123
Pike, Martin 288, 289
Port Adelaide Football Club (Port Power) 199, 232, 226, 293, 294
Port Adelaide Magpies Football Club 46, 64, 113, 115, 116, 118, 120, 122, 124, 197–203, 208–11, 220–5
Port Victoria Football Club 202–3
Potter, Jeff 209
Power, Luke 286, 288
Pratt, Bob 65, 93–8, 100, 101, 191
Pritchard, Bob 237
Quade, Ricky 242–4
Quinlan, Bernie 240, 242
Quinn, Bob 61, 63, 64, 109–24, 198, 199
Quinn, George 110, 116
Quinn, Jack Jr 116
Quinn, Jack Sr 115, 116
Quinn, Tom 113, 115–17
Raines, Geoff 266
Rantall, John 169
Regan, Jack 70, 105
Reid, Jim 80
Reid, Morris 143, 146
Renfrey, Bert 46
Reval, Allan 'Bull' 117
Reville, Peter 93, 94
Reynolds, Dick 63, 78, 113, 239, 254–6, 263, 264
Rhys-Jones, David 244
Richards, Lou 250
Richardson, Barry 163, 259
Richardson, Mike 266
Richardson, Vic 47
Richmond Cricket Club 15
Richmond Football Club 15, 33, 42, 54–6, 83–5, 93, 95–8, 104, 128–9, 131, 138–40, 159–67, 175, 176, 179, 188, 230, 238, 239, 250–1, 253, 257, 259, 262, 279
Richmond, Graeme 140, 159–63, 166, 175, 238
Rickman, Ian 247
Rigney, Roger 216, 219, 222
Roberts, Brian 241
Roberts, Kevin 157
Roberts, Lew 117, 121
Roberts, Lou 85, 86
Roberts, Neil 155
Robertson, Austin 93, 102
Robertson, Colin 261
Robinson, Alec 44
Robran, Barrie 233
Rohan, Jack 93
Rose, Bob 70, 88, 159, 240
Round, Barry 235–48
Rowe, Percy 142
Rowland, Ian 158
Royal Park Football Club 16
Russell, Dick 'The Rock' 208
Ryan, Phil 178, 182
Sandhurst Football Club 154, 176, 177, 181
Sandringham Football Club 245
Scaddan, Joe 49
Scaddan, John 49
Schmidt, Paul 104
Schoff, Rick 219, 221
Schultz, John 239
Scobie, Jack 51
Scott, Brad 186, 188, 190, 194
Scott, Chris 179, 186
Scott, Don 175, 187, 191, 193, 236
Sea Lake Football Club 87
Sheedy, Jack 129, 207
Sheedy, Kevin 165, 172, 251, 259–62, 264, 266–9
Simmonds, Roy 180–1, 182
Skase, Christopher 278–9
Skilton, Bob 135, 169, 170, 200
Smith, Bernie 148, 209

Smith, Len 131–72, 187, 218, 224, 257
Smith, Norm 69, 77, 97, 131–72, 183–5, 187, 200, 207, 256, 262, 263, 269, 280, 292
Smith, Ross 158
Smith, Sir Edwin T. 64
Snow, Sid 49
South Adelaide Football Club 116, 121, 198, 212, 220
South Australian Football Association 22, 23
South Australian National Football League 4, 56, 115, 122, 124, 130, 197–9, 203, 213, 229, 234
South Bendigo Football Club 54–5
South Bunbury Football Club 44
South Fremantle Football Club 35, 52, 53
South Melbourne Football Club 38, 51, 55, 65, 92, 93, 96, 98, 100, 101, 103, 107, 108, 169, 177, 180, 203, 207, 230, 231, 234, 235, 241–6, 258
South Mildura Football Club 276
South Yarra Football Club 16
Southern Rugby Football Union 21–2
Springvale Football Club 247
St Kilda Football Club 30, 32, 33, 36, 46, 49, 128–9, 139, 152–9, 164, 169, 188, 191, 230, 241, 267, 270, 293
Steele, Wally 52
Stephen, Bill 257
Stewart, Ian 128, 155, 158, 241, 242
Stuchbury, Ward 142, 150, 151, 159
Sturt Football Club 5, 45–9, 123–4, 129, 169, 178, 181, 197–8, 200, 201, 203, 206–8, 212–26
Subiaco Football Club 48–54, 90–4
Swain, Arthur, 113
Swan, Bill 247
Sydney Football Association 21
Sydney Swans Football Club 235–7, 243–5, 277, 290–1
Tasmanian Football Association 22
Tasmanian Football League 82
Taylor, Johnny 120
Templeton, Kelvin 240
Thomas, Hugh 82
Thomas, William 'Digger' 49, 52, 53
Thompson, Clayton 'Candles' 181
Thompson, James 14, 16
Thompson, Mark 'Bomber' 261, 264, 268
Thorogood, Ian 183
Thorp, Vic 63
Thurgood, Albert 5, 25–40, 41, 254
Tilbrook, John 220, 222
Titus, Jack 139, 164
Todd, Ron 87
Torrens Football Club 123
Truscott, William 'Nipper' 44
Tuck, Michael 190
Tuddenham, Des 157, 158, 170, 257
Twopeny, Richard Ernest Nowell 19, 20, 21, 22
Union Football Club 52
Vallence, Harry 'Soapy' 104
Van der Haar 257, 266
Victorian Football Association 3–4, 6, 22, 25, 28, 30–3, 37, 46, 56, 65, 68, 69, 87, 92, 93, 102, 142, 156, 159, 174, 230, 234, 245–8, 260
Victorian Football League 4–6, 15, 23, 28, 35, 37–9, 42, 49, 54–7, 61, 64, 65, 68, 69, 72, 74, 77, 81, 83–5, 91–3, 96, 100, 101, 104, 106, 107, 113, 115–17, 128–30, 133–4, 138, 148, 153, 155, 158, 160, 162, 172, 174, 183–5, 188–90, 207, 225, 229–34, 235–6, 239, 243, 245, 250, 253, 254, 256, 268, 277–9
Victorian Rules 3, 19–22

Voss, Michael 279, 285, 286, 290, 292
Wade, Doug 130
Walker, Max 144
Wallis, Jim 155
Walls, Robert 172, 279–81, 283, 285, 287
Walsh, Kevin 262
Wangaratta Rovers Football Club 159, 246–7
Warragul Football Club 238, 248
Watson, Alan 250, 252
Watson, Bob 249, 250
Watson, Larry 253, 250
Watson, Mark 253, 250
Watson, Tim 249–70
Watson, William 'Poss' 34
Webb, W. 33–4
Weideman, Murray 136–7
Wellman, Sean 225
West Adelaide Football Club 120, 121, 123, 197, 198, 209, 211, 212, 225
West Coast Eagles Football Club 232, 266, 267, 277
West Perth Football Club 43, 49, 52
West Torrens Football Club 94, 119, 120, 202, 212
Western Australian Football Association 23, 34, 35, 52
Western Australian Football League 45, 49, 53, 56, 57, 61, 65, 234
Weston, H. 49
Weston, Paul 261, 262
Wheeler, Terry 245, 246, 247
Whelan, Ken 219, 222
Whelan, Marcus 70
Whelan, Ted 208
White Feather Football Club 115
White, Daryl 279, 286
Whitten, Ted 76, 148, 158, 239, 240
Williams, Darren 'Daisy' 261, 262, 266
Williams, Fos 121, 122, 197–200, 203, 208–12, 220, 221, 224–6
Williams, Glynn 212, 213
Williams, Jack 'Basher' 207
Williams, Mark 199, 226, 291
Williams, Stephen 199
Williamstown Football Club 245–8
Wills, Thomas 12–16, 23
Wilson, Mat 34
World War I 6, 27–8, 48, 63, 68–9, 71, 115, 174
World War II 51, 63, 68, 86–7, 122, 127, 129–30, 153, 174, 230, 254–5
Wraith, Frank 71, 81, 82–3, 85, 87
Wren, John 71, 82, 85, 86
Wright, Steven 244
Wrout, Jack 104
Wundersitz, Alby 123
Yorke Peninsula Football League 203
Young, Garry 186–7
Zucker, Lloyd 208